Law and Government in Israel

While most current studies on law and politics in Israel focus on the legal aspects of public policymaking within the courts, this book explores the relationship between law and government from a positive perspective. That is to say that the question asked is: how the political relationships between the three branches of government affect public policy and hence social outcomes.

The eleven contributors to this volume concentrate on Israel from theoretical, comparative and critical approaches, and hence the analysis presented could as well be applied to other polities.

This book was published as a special issue of *Israel Affairs*.

Professor Gideon Doron teaches Political Science and Public Policy in Tel Aviv University and is the president of the Israeli Political Science Association. He is the author of 17 books and dozens of articles on political economy, public policy and administration, electoral systems and political communication. He served as a chairman of the board of the Second Authority for Television and Radio, and headed several state commissions. He initiated the "President Commission for the Examination of the Structure of Government in Israel". He is the chairman of the "Total Representation" association for electoral reform.

Arye Naor is Professor Emeritus at the Department of Public Policy and Administration, Ben-Gurion University, Israel. Between 1977 and 1982, he served as secretary to the cabinet in the Menachem Begin government. The author of eight books and dozens of articles on politics, ideology, government and policy in Israel, currently he is the chairperson of the Academic Committee of the Jabotinsky Institute in Israel, and vice president of the Israeli Association of Political Science.

Assaf Meydani is a Senior Lecturer in Public Policy, Politics and Law in the School of Government and Society at the Academic College of Tel Aviv-Yaffo, Israel. A lawyer, he has served as a member of several public policy delegations including the Committee for the Nomination of Judges of the Zionist Supreme Court. The author of four books and several articles, Dr. Meydani was also a member of the Information Delegation during the Camp David negotiations in the year 2000.

Law and Government in Israel

Edited by Gideon Doron,
Arye Naor and Assaf Meydani

LONDON AND NEW YORK

First published 2010 by Routledge

2 Park Square, Milton Park, Abingdon, Oxon OX14 4RN
711 Third Avenue, New York, NY 10017, USA

Routledge is an imprint of the Taylor & Francis Group, an informa business

First issued in paperback 2016

This book is a reproduction of *Israel Affairs*, vol. 14.4. The Publisher requests to those authors who may be citing this book to state, also, the bibliographical details of the special issue on which the book was based

Typeset in Sabon by Value Chain, India

British Library Cataloguing in Publication Data
A catalogue record for this book is available from the British Library

ISBN13: 978-0-415-57652-9 (hbk)
ISBN13: 978-1-138-97949-9 (pbk)

Contents

Notes on Contributors

Professor Gideon Doron teaches in the Political Science Department, Tel Aviv University.

Ori Arbel-Ganz teaches in the Department of Political Science, Bar-Ilan University. David Nachmias teaches at The Lauder School of Government, Diplomacy and Strategy, Interdisciplinary Centre, Herzliya, Israel.

Ilan Saban is an Assistant Professor of Law at Haifa University. The author would like to express thanks to Gordon Anthony, Robert Chapman, Moshe Cohen-Eilya, Tammy Harel-Ben-Shahar, Hassan Jabareen, Yousef T. Jabareen, Barak Medina, Liav Orgad and Revital Sella for valuable comments.

Guy I. Seidman is a Senior Lecturer, the Interdisciplinary Centre, Herzliya, Israel.

Daphne Barak-Erez is a Professor of Law and the Stewart and Judy Colton Chair of Law and Security in the Faculty of Law, Tel Aviv University. The article draws on previous writings, especially: Daphne Barak-Erez, 'Distributive Justice In Israel Lands: Following the Agricultural Lands Case', *Hamishpat*, vol.10.

Yoram Rabin is a senior lecturer in the School of Law, the College of Management, Academic Studies Division. Yuval Shany is the Hersch Lauterpacht Chair in Public International Law, Law Faculty, Hebrew University of Jerusalem.The authors thank Prof. Barak Medina and Prof. David Enoch for their insightful comments on an earlier draft of this article.

Assaf Meydani teaches at the Academic College of Tel Aviv Yaffo, Israel.

Abstracts

Judges in a Borderless State: Politics versus the Law in the State of Israel

Gideon Doron

This article argues that because of the Israeli political system's failure to supply publicly desired goods and services, the court assumed upon itself a role as an active political player thus ensuring not only the supply of public goods and services but also affecting the particular distribution of welfare across society. It emphasizes the court's position as an interpreter and argues that in the context of Israel this institution became, over the years, politically very powerful. This is because it does not limit itself to the interpretation of laws, but rather it directly and indirectly becomes a law maker and an enforcer of public policies. By inviting everyone to appeal to the Supreme Court this institution becomes all-encompassing, dealing with all types of issues and getting involved in practical matters, as well as questions of principle. It concludes by wondering if it is not possible that the 'Keepers of the Law', who benefit from preserving a problematic legal situation, have an interest in continuing the flux and normative ambivalence of the status quo.

Public Responsibility of Elected Officials in Israel: Crossing the Bounds of Reasonableness

Ori Arbel-Ganz and David Nachmias

This article draws attention to a deep social problem: the rapid deterioration of public responsibility in Israel. It attempts to reach a better understanding of public responsibility in theory and practice. The article explores the different dimensions of responsibility and argues that public responsibility is not, and cannot be, just a judicial matter but also a social, cultural and subjective one as well. It concludes by arguing that attention should focus on strengthening the moral and ethical framework of public responsibility in education for moral values and public ethics and in their diffusion and internalization via socialization throughout the educational systems. Simultaneously, efforts must be directed towards the assimilation of moral values and public responsibility within the political system. Thus, an ethical contract for public officials could be drawn up that would obligate them to discharge their duties within the context of their public service in general, and within the framework of their positions as elected officials in particular.

After the Storm? The Israeli Supreme Court and the Arab-Palestinian Minority in the Aftermath of October 2000
Ilan Saban

The purpose of the article is to analyze major aspects of the performance of the Israeli Supreme Court vis-à-vis the Arab-Palestinian minority since October 2000. The article advances three arguments. First, the Supreme Court has truly held the post of guardian of democratic tenets with respect to the civil and political rights of Arab-Palestinian citizens. Second, the court serves (sometimes unintentionally) as a guide or a mediator demarcating an intermediate path for Israeli society, one which might cross the middle ground between two almost polar options for society: the bi-national state (an idea which is gaining popularity with the minority but is rejected outright by the Jewish majority), and the existing status quo (strongly resented by the minority). This intermediate path, or bridging vision, may prove a defence against the violent breakdown of inter-communal relations in Israel proper. The third argument goes in the other direction and criticizes the Supreme Court. The court often evades providing remedies in the direction it has signalled, and is reluctant to act in some instances. Taken together this two-steps-forward-one-step-back performance paints a somewhat ambiguous picture. The article does not solve the enigma, but by unfolding its traits it hopefully opens the way for further discussion.

Judicial Administrative Review in Times of Discontent: The Israeli Supreme Court and the Second Palestinian Uprising
Guy I. Seidman

This article describes the complexity and diversity inherent in the judicial review of the military in Israel. Using leading cases it emphasizes the significant achievements of the court from 1948 to 2000. It also provides a representative sample of the issues that arose during the Second Intifada of 2000 that came before the Supreme Court. It argues that the court attempts to balance non-interference in warfare with maintaining the effective review of the legality (essentially the reasonableness and proportionality) of IDF actions in the territories. It concludes that the court is perhaps more likely to broker an agreement than issue an order instructing the military on combat activity, but the court does have this option in its arsenal, and uses it judiciously.

Law and Politics in Israel Lands: Toward Distributive Justice
Daphne Barak-Erez

This article analyzes the development of the principles applying to the administration of Israel Lands, by distinguishing between three stages:

(a) the first three decades of the Israel Land Administration (until the beginning of the 1990s), characterized by broad administrative autonomy without any substantial judicial review of the Administration's actions; (b) the decade from the beginning of the 1990s, during which specific cases of discrimination were reviewed, but without reference to issues of land policy in general; and (c) the stage initiated by the new and ground-breaking decision of the Supreme Court in the matter of agricultural lands, which applied the principle of distributive justice to the administration of Israel Lands. The article elaborates on the meaning of applying the principle of distributive justice with regard to Israel Lands—addressing both substance and procedure. First, it points to initial guiding principles which should direct the substance of the decision-making, such as refraining from consistently disregarding the needs of any segment or group in Israeli society and considering the needs of future generations. In this respect the article calls for inspiration from the literature dealing with questions of just planning. Second, the article elaborates on the procedural aspects of the decision-making process, and points to procedures which would maximize the chances that proper consideration is given to the largest possible spectrum of relevant interests (such as public access to information about the administrative procedures while they are taking place, and opening up the process for the active participation of various groups). It concludes by examining future possible reforms regarding the administration of Israel Lands.

The Case for Judicial Review over Social Rights: Israeli Perspectives

Yoram Rabin and Yuval Shany

This article seeks to introduce an Israeli perspective into the debate over the appropriate constitutional status of social rights. Specifically, it addresses the question of the desirability and feasibility of judicial review on the basis of constitutionally protected social rights, which is a major source of contention in contemporary Israeli constitutional discourse. It seems that contemporary political and intellectual trends lean towards supporting the inclusion of social rights in any future constitutional instrument, albeit in a weak form, without substantive judicial review. It describes the main contours of the Israeli debate over constitutional judicial review, as applied to social rights, and reviews both potential incorporation projects; it concludes by arguing that the difficulties associated with constitutionaliz-ing social rights should not lead to an abdication of the court's role in enforcing such rights, but rather to a policy of judicial restraint in exercising constitutional supervision.

Judicial Behaviour: A Socio-Cultural Strategic Approach—Conceptual Framework and Analysis of Case Studies in Israel
Assaf Meydani

By analyzing two controversial decisions made by the Israeli Supreme Court, the 'Torture decision, 1999' and the 'Land decision, 2002', this article develops a policy determination model highlighting the strategic calculations of various social groups turning to the court, as well as the role of socio-cultural explanations and the ways in which social players act as agents of political and institutional change. It concludes that Israeli society with its formal and non-formal rules create the situation whereby the political system is unable to deal with problems which require the shaping of public policy. In light of this inability, Israeli society has adopted alternative behaviour, by filing an ever-increasing number of petitions with the Supreme Court, with a twofold purpose: to cause policy decisions to be made, and to apply pressure on politicians to change the institutional structure, in one way or another.

Judges in a Borderless State: Politics versus the Law in the State of Israel

GIDEON DORON

Israeli politicians may be likened to dancers whose aerial pirouettes command cheers from breathless audiences fearing, or perhaps hoping, that the maestros in tights will miss a step, fall down, and break their elegant necks. And, as expected, these politicians often do. Since independence in 1948 and the first national elections that were held early in 1949, only twice has the Knesset (Israel's parliament, consisting of 120 members) been able to complete its legal term of four years. At the same time, more than 32 governments have ruled the political scene, averaging less than two years in power.[1] Political crisis has become the norm rather than the exception. Nonetheless, despite this continuing situation of flux, the democratic essence of the state has been preserved.

This has not been an easy accomplishment for a polity governed without a written constitution or a constitutional tradition to compensate for its absence. Israel has also had to struggle with having no agreed upon international borders with all of its neighbouring states. The country lacks a social consensus on the definition of civil identity, and there is no collective commitment to preserve individual rights, be they related to property or other civil rights. Israel has had to grapple with unplanned and thus unexpected waves of immigration coming mostly from non-democratic countries and with almost constant protracted cycles of all-out wars against both internationally recognized states and illegal and unrecognized terrorist groups. Hence, the occurrence of frequent situations of instability in the economy, the political institutions and the public policy-making apparatuses should surprise no one. Yet this multi-party, coalition-governed political system, reflecting a social mosaic of sectors and divisions defined along ethnic and religious lines (e.g. Jews, Moslems and Christians; Ultra Orthodox, Orthodox, Secular) has shown a remarkable ability to sustain the democratic nature of its system of government.

This ability to hold things together without the support of firm, legal and institutional supports could partly be explained by the effective intervention of the court. The Israeli court, in particular the Supreme Court in its capacity as the High Court of Justice, instead of acting as a neutral referee between various competing groups, has decided to adopt an effective strategy of intervention. Whenever the political system fails to deliver the goods and services demanded by the public, as is commonly the case in a consensual political system,[2] the court intervenes by making sure that the services are provided in accordance with the law.[3]

The main argument advanced here is that because of the Israeli political system's failure to supply publicly desired goods and services, the court has taken upon itself the role of an active political player. By doing so, it has not only ensured the supply of public goods and services but has also affected the distribution of these goods and services among the society's constituent groups.

The various parts of this article are designed to demonstrate this point. The first part presents a simple model for public affairs in a political system, called the Problem Solver Model (PSM). The second part identifies several legally undefined areas in the Israeli public space where the state 'muddles through' its obligations with the aid of the court. These areas include relationships between majorities and minorities: Arabs and Jews, religious and secular Jews, etc. It also includes questions of property rights, the definition (or lack of one) of the internationally recognized boundaries of the country, and the issue of a written constitution. Part three shows how the court has provided temporary legal solutions to overcome problems or nip them in the bud before they arise. This article concludes with a discussion about the vested interests of the court in the prevailing status quo.

THE COURT AS A PROBLEM SOLVER IN A PARLIAMENTARY SYSTEM

From a political point of view, a state's law may be perceived as an equilibrium point arrived at by people with opposing interests who are in actual or potential conflict.[4] People sharing identical or similar interests and values need no laws. They need only, as Thomas Paine following David Hume phrased it, good 'common sense'.[5] They need to agree on procedures that would enable a fair division of desired items and values amongst themselves.[6] Laws, as a type of political institution, regulate behaviour to manage current or potential conflicts. Accordingly, one may view laws as if they were snapshots, frozen moments in time, when people with conflicting desires decided to compromise and formulate their agreements in the form of an explicit statement. Note that when the groups' power equation changes, one should expect that laws will be altered too.

Seeing laws from this political perspective—as power and time dependent—makes it easy to understand why constitutions, a set of rigid, hard-to-change laws, are so important for the enhancement of stability and order in a given polity. Constitutions provide anchors upon which the institutions of the regimes are grounded, where the ranges of publicly and privately accepted and expected behaviour are defined, and areas where frictions and interactions amongst government agents and individuals are permitted. In liberal polities, constitutions are drafted from the point of view of the individual's long-term interests.[7] In non-liberal polities, such as Israel, the unit of reference is the group, the community or society-at-large.[8] The Israeli legalist Barzilai, following the new multi-cultural tradition established by North American scholars like Kymlicka, suggested awarding special and distinct group rights to these 'legal communities'.[9] Not surprisingly, for the last several years a proposal to adopt a special bill on group rights or social rights as a Basic Law has been considered by the Knesset Committee on Constitution, Law and Jurisdiction (KCCLJ). First proposed in March 1996 and rejected, the bill was resubmitted in March 2001 by MK Anat Maor and fared no better.

Constitutional anchors enhance stability because they are based on tradition, cultural screening mechanisms and selective norms that are considered essential by the body of citizens in a given polity. As institutions, constitutions promote stability because they limit the scope of available alternative solutions to problems and reduce the uncertainty associated with future-oriented decisions.[10] People protect constitutions because they understand that they are engaged in repetitive sets of interactions, a process where the long-term costs of violation far exceed the immediate benefits gained by it.[11]

Montesquieu's idea of the separation of powers[12] is said to produce equilibrium—a balance of power of sorts, because each of the three branches of government (Legislative, Executive and Judiciary) checks the other two. This principle of power diffusion, producing the 'checks and balance' outcome, prevails in both presidential and, to some degree, in parliamentary political arrangements. In both, the Judiciary is assigned the role of interpreter of the spirit and meaning of the law. Thus, the court becomes an essential political institution because of its location above and beside the basic democratic power structure.[13] Hence, in theory if not in practice, the court should not be involved in the distributive function of politics, which is generally regarded as the task of the executive.[14] When such is the case, no one can criticize the Judiciary for favouring one political side over another. Furthermore, given that, at least in principle if not in practice, courts do not make the laws, their neutrality with regard to distributive politics may be preserved, a situation that benefits all of society's members.[15]

However, when the distribution of power in a given polity is not fully and formally institutionalized, public choices and the rules that regulate them may become vulnerable to a constant process of political bargaining and manipulation.[16] In such cases, the ability of the court to sustain its position as a neutral referee may become somewhat problematic. The court's rulings may become precedents and serve as points of reference for future decisions. Hence, judges may find themselves in a position of having to favour one or another side when it comes to distributing goods and services. Consequently, the personality of the judges, their preferences and their understanding of the relative position of the court in the political arrangement may significantly affect the nature of their decisions.

The story of Israel, to be presented in the next section, is one of a dynamic process whereby over the years the Supreme Court has been moving from a position of neutral interpreter to a position of major power broker and policy maker.[17] It has attained this powerful position in part because of the dysfunctional nature of other institutions of Israeli democracy. In such an environment of uncertainty, the Israeli court system became an island of stability and rationality. Yet because the court entered politically sensitive waters, it too became an object of political criticism.[18] Two possible models describe the politicization of the court.

The First Possibility

Suppose that in a situation resembling a two-person, zero-sum game, where players have diametrically opposed interests and where trust between the players is hard to obtain, a stable equilibrium has to be reached. The equilibrium that can be reached under such circumstances is known as the Nash Equilibrium.[19] According to this concept, for each player there exists at least one better and one worse solution. His/her desire to avoid the less desirable outcome keeps him/her loyal to the status quo. Suppose further that the executive branch of government and the legislature are two such players, each vying for control over the other. Given this dynamic, a satisfying, long-term compromise and hence durable outcome is difficult to achieve because, over time, one of the players may decide that he or she could do better relative to his/her potential or relative to the power of the others. As Douglas North has pointed out, in Great Britain the process of searching for parliamentary political equilibrium has taken several hundred years.[20] This situation of a conflict of interests over the accumulation of political power resembles a game called Prisoners' Dilemma.[21]

In such games, a third player, an agreed upon outsider, can impose an outcome on both antagonists that, while not favoured by either player, is still better than the current situation. While historically the exact position of the third player—the court—in the distribution of power in a given political system may differ from one system to another, its ability to intervene in the political game by interpreting the law is essential for the maintenance of structural stability.[22] When the legal structures are well defined by a constitution, as is the case in the United States, the role of this third player is well defined too. In Great Britain, on the other hand, the rules of the game are defined by history and tradition.

The Second Possibility

Suppose there is a constantly changing situation in which no rules of the game have been established either by a constitution or by tradition. Under such conditions, how can conflicts be resolved? Here, too, a third player is necessary. However, unlike cases in which there are established game rules, here a third party may play an active role in proposing and designing laws and regulations.

To put it more clearly, when the rules are not established or are unclear, the judiciary—the third player—may become an active lawmaker. In this new capacity, the court does not just interpret existing laws, it proposes the design and adaptation of new laws and regulations.

Since the establishment of the State of Israel in 1948, generations of politicians have left key social issues unresolved. Perhaps, in their minds, such ambiguity was preferable to clear-cut solutions that might have led to violence and social unrest. Indeed, in Israel, as in other countries like India and Ireland that have constitutions, sensitive issues are not addressed.[23] Essential civic values and social problems were thus left to be resolved by the judicial branch rather than by the other two branches of government. This tradition has endowed the Israeli court system with significantly more political power relative to courts in other democracies.[24] The following section traces some of the reasons that have led Israeli courts to accumulate excessive political power. It also assesses the probable political consequences of courts having too much power in democratic societies.

CONSTITUTING PRINCIPLES FOR GUIDING THE POLITY

On one cold winter evening in Jerusalem in 1999, about a quarter of a million religious and ultra-religious Jews gathered, for the first time in the state's history, to protest against a ruling by the Supreme Court.[25] They were protesting against proposed changes in the so-called 1947 Status Quo Agreement.[26] This formal agreement was signed by representatives of both the religious and the secular Jewish communities in pre-state Israel and assured the former the exclusive right of handling all private and collective religiously related affairs.

Since then, life cycle events for the Jews of Israel such as the issuing of birth and death certificates and the performance of marriages and divorces have been performed solely by the religious authorities. Furthermore, the state recognizes Saturday as an obligatory day of rest. The religious authorities also grant kosher certification to food products and restaurants and oversee conversions.[27] Representatives of the Orthodox branch of Judaism thus became the sole Jewish movement recognized by the state for all religious matters, especially those involving education.

Several months after that momentous gathering in Jerusalem, utilizing the same logic, two members of the Knesset (one from a religious party and the other from a right-wing party) initiated a bill to create a special High Court for Constitutional Affairs that would curb the flexibility and the scope of the Israeli Supreme Court's responsibility.[28]

These two demonstrations were the culmination of a long process of communal friction among various segments of the Israeli public. Ultra-religious Jews complained about the violation of the Sabbath in their neighbourhoods by secular Jews. Israeli Arabs complained about the state's consistent discrimination against them with regard to their funding. The Israeli Supreme Court judges were perceived as meddling in areas where they did not belong. Indeed, under the doctrine expressed by Professor Aharon Barak, the legendary president of the Supreme Court, that 'HaKol Bagizt' ('everything could be judged by the Supreme Court'), the Supreme Court seemed 'trigger happy'. On too many occasions it had involved itself in attempts to resolve communal problems and put out fires before they could spread. Given the lack of a formal set of difficult-to-change laws (like a constitution) or normative traditions by which to govern the social services apparatus, the court became very involved and very busy.[29] Thus, mounting social frictions and actual political crises were managed without having the protective shield of a formal constitution for guidance.

THE STATE'S BORDERS IN FLUX

Israel is an interesting example of a sovereign political entity not all of whose borders are internationally recognized. There are still some areas (in the Upper and Lower Galilee and in the Negev) that are bound by 'armistice lines' (the so-called 'Green Line'), the points where the participants in the 1948 War of Independence agreed to a ceasefire. Other areas such as the West Bank or the Golan Heights were captured during the 1967 Six Day War from Jordan and Syria respectively. Indeed, from one war to another the country's geographic area has expanded and contracted considerably. Since 1948, Israel has been involved in seven all-out wars or almost all-out wars with some or all of its Arab neighbours—not counting two Intifadas, one violent encounter with Iraq in 1991, and a protracted state of violence and terror.

For example, during the 1956 Sinai War, the desert peninsula, three times the size of Israel, was added to the Jewish state, to be returned shortly after to the Egyptians. During the 1982 war with Lebanon, Israel held on to a portion of the southern region of that country for security reasons until 2000.

However, over the years some borders have been legally determined and internationally recognized. In 1979, for example, Israel signed a peace treaty with Egypt fixing its borders in the south. In 1994, Jordan became the second Arab country to agree upon durable borders with Israel in the east.[30] During the IDF pull-out from Lebanon in 2000, the UN agreed that Israel had no more territorial holdings in that country. Syria, and of course the Palestinian Authority, have not yet come forward to sign an agreement with Israel over what they consider to be their respective legal international borders.

Dominating this issue of physical borders is the status of the city of Jerusalem—the capital of Israel. The entire area of 'Jerusalem and its environs' was designated by the United Nations in 1947 (in Resolution 181 of 29 November, which authorized the establishment of the State of Israel) as a 'Corpus Separatum' to be managed by international administration. The principal task of this international body was to make sure that the city would be kept open to the three monotheist religions and that their holy places would be protected. While Jerusalem has not been recognized as Israel's capital by members of the international community, over the years several embassies have been located there. Costa Rica and El Salvador were the last two embassies to leave Jerusalem on 29 August 2006.

The absence of defined borders is just one area of vacuum in which the court has a huge space for creative interpretations and solutions. The following section describes some approaches the court has taken to define Basic Laws in a variety of areas, property rights over land, and the relationship between the state and its people.

Basic Laws

The newly-established United Nations in 1945 demanded a democratic constitution from every new state wishing to have the organization's seal of approval.[31] Following World War II and the Holocaust, the Zionists accelerated their plans to declare their national sovereignty and political independence in Palestine. They therefore committed themselves to take the necessary steps for adopting a democratic constitution. Indeed, because of the commitment made by the Jewish leaders to the UN demand, the name of that organization (United Nations or in Hebrew *Umot Meuchadot*) was mentioned several times in the one-page Declaration of Independence of the State of Israel.[32] However, almost 60 years later, Israel still does not have a written constitution. The reason for the absence of this basic legal blueprint is political, as will be explained below.

When the results of the elections for the 120-member Constitutional Assembly held early in January 1949 were tabulated, most representatives supported a civil constitution. We know that from the mere fact that the elections were held so that people would elect their representatives to perform the sole task of drafting a constitution. However, when the members assembled and began arguing over the contents of the proposed document, David Ben Gurion, leader of Mapai, the Assembly's largest party, apparently changed his mind and argued against adopting a written constitution.[33] Politically, so it seems, the old collectivist leader was more comfortable ruling without the boundaries of the law. His rationale for opposing a constitution was simple, if spurious: because the rest of the Jewish people were still outside the country, it was not fair to draft a constitution without their participation.[34]

The proposed notion to adopt a constitution was rejected by the Assembly although Ben Gurion could have easily mobilized a majority in the house for its adoption.[35] The members decided to rename the Assembly the Knesset (parliament) and to begin the process of governing without a formal constitution or a constitutional tradition.

Given the need to fulfil its promise to the UN and until the Jewish people came to Israel from the Diaspora, the Knesset decided to pass a series of Basic Laws. These are special laws with constitutional status, which could form the basis of a future constitution. However, once the 'grand opportunity' in Braybrook and Lindblom's terms[36] for adopting a constitution—that is, the time of national independence or of another major breakdown in the social routine—has passed and been replaced by 'normal times', it becomes very difficult to adopt such a document. As it turned out, it became extremely hard and politically costly to adopt even these Basic Laws. Indeed, almost six decades after Independence, only 11 Basic Laws have been adopted: Knesset (1958); Lands of Israel (1960); President of the State (1964); Government (1968, 1992, 2001); State Economy (1975); the Army (1976); Jerusalem, the Capital of Israel (1980); Judgment (1984); State Comptroller (1988); Freedom of Occupation (1992); Dignity of Man and his Freedom (1992). Four other Basic Laws are awaiting legislation by the Knesset. They are Basic Law: Legislation; Basic Law: Rights in Court; Basic Law: Freedom of Expression and of Association; and Basic Law: Social Rights.

In February 2006, MK Michael Eitan, the tireless chairperson of the permanent KCCLJ, introduced to the public a draft of a constitution his committee had been labouring over for quite a long time. However, the heart of the document was missing. The document had no politically related material such as sections dealing with the nature of the government and the distribution of power amongst its various branches.

While constitutions are usually hard to change, it is relatively easy to alter a paragraph in a given Basic Law or omit it altogether because these laws are protected by merely absolute majorities of Knesset members. Hence, while Basic Laws are perceived as more important than regular laws—those adopted by simple majorities—they do not contribute to the stability of the political system in the same way that constitutions usually do.

Given that there are few safeguards on these laws, they are often subject to change. The Supreme Court is then asked to intervene in the ensuing disputes between 'reformers' and 'conservers' of the law. The dynamics of the conflict between the two groups is explained below.

Who Owns the Land?

The central motif of the Zionist Movement—the national movement of world Jewry that was established in Europe at the end of the nineteenth century—was to 'Establish a Jewish homeland in the Land of Israel'.[37] Indeed, when commenting on the territory in which the future state would be founded, Theodore Herzl, the founder of the movement, declared, 'We are bringing a people without land to a land without a people'.[38] However, because most newcomers to Palestine were supporters of socialism, the political system that they developed reflected their norms and was based on the approach that property rights over the land should be defined as essentially collective.[39]

Accordingly, the land belongs to the collective of the Jewish people, even to those who live outside the state's international borders, not to individual citizens.[40] Thus, for many members of the Labour Movement that dominated the Israeli political arena for over 70 years since the early twentieth century, public control over the land was an ideological dictum. For others, including religious and non-Labour, secular Jews, control over the land was a way of preserving the community's resources from the machinations of ill-meaning outsiders.

Therefore, it is not surprising that the legal mechanism used by the state reflects this need to have control over the land.[41] Consequently, in accordance with Basic Law: The Lands of Israel (1960), all of the lands in Israel belong to the state. In fact, about 95 percent of Israel's territory is owned by, or belongs to, the state.[42] Land in Israel cannot be owned by individuals. Land can only be rented by the individual for a specific period of time. Even the small percentage of property that is described as 'private land' actually belongs to the state but has been rented for an extended period of time.

There may be several explanations for this excessive state control over the land. Lustick believes that the Jewish 'state' wishes to deny non-Jews access to the land.[43] Indeed, every land transaction in Israel must go through some form of approval by one of the state's branches. However, while one may argue that the denial of ownership rights applies to all citizens regardless of their religion and ethnic affiliation, one may find it difficult to defend communal opposition to the presence of non-Jewish neighbours. Indeed, in Israel, Jews and Arabs (Moslems and Christians) live in close proximity. The Arabs maintain sizeable communities in 'mixed' cities such as Nazareth, Lod, Ramle and Jaffa. As individuals, however, Arabs live in every part of Israel.

What if an Arab family (or for that matter, even a Jewish one) would like to live in a community whose members want it to maintain a certain character? Such was the subject of a case brought to the Supreme Court. It involved the Jewish members of the Kazir community in the north of

Israel who denied an Arab family the right to dwell amongst them. The court was asked to intervene in order to resolve the problems non-Jews encounter in their attempt to utilize 'state' lands. The court position was that the Arab family should not be denied access to the land even if the land legally belongs to the Jewish people (Bagatz, 6689\95). Implementation of the court's ruling was a different matter. The Arab family has not utilized the right it was awarded by the court.

Definition of State and Nationality

Israel is the only state in the world that defines Arabs politically. Everywhere else, an Arab is generally regarded as a person with a distinct cultural identity, not as a member of a particular political entity. In Egypt, that person is defined as an Egyptian; in Syria, as a Syrian, and so on. In addition, in Israel, the term 'Jew' is ambiguous. It simultaneously signifies a particular form of culture and religion, as well as a distinct nationality. This confusion was at the heart of one of the most significant court rulings known as the 'who is a Jew' case.[44] In this case, a Polish-born Carmelite priest, Brother Daniel, who used to be a Zionist Jew named David Oswald Rufeisen, asked the Ministry of Interior to grant him citizenship in accordance with the 'Law of Return'.

This law assures Israeli citizenship to every Jew. Indeed, according to the traditional religious definition of a Jew, Brother Daniel qualified as a Jew because his mother was Jewish. Common sense dictates that if a person formally converted, he should lose his status as a Jew. On the other hand, according to Halacha (Jewish Laws): '[even] Israel that sinned—is [forever] Israel'. Not surprisingly, the full nine-member Supreme Court split their decision. The majority ruled that even if Brother Daniel were born a Jew, by practising his commitment to a different faith he had explicitly abandoned his ties to the Jewish community. Indeed, in addition to the traditional religious definition of a Jew and the nationalist definition created by the Zionist movement, in 1962, the Supreme Court added a cultural dimension to the definition. As noted earlier, conversion in Israel is controlled by the Orthodox branch of Judaism. This monopoly leads to the phenomenon whereby non-practising, secular Jews born to Orthodox families are favoured in the process of naturalization over practising Jews who happen to believe in the Reform approach to Judaism.

Moreover, because of the Law of Return at least two types of national Jews have developed:[45] people who qualify as Jews according to Halacha and people who qualify as Jews according to secular law. In accordance with the revised Law of Return, an individual must have just one Jewish grandparent to qualify as a Jew. Accordingly, many Christian Russians who immigrated to Israel during the 1990s are national Jews but do not meet the more general definition of a Jew as one who is born of a Jewish mother.

THE POLITICAL IMPERATIVE OF THE PRESENT

There are several advantages associated with a state lacking both external and internal fixed borders. In such a state of flux, public decision-making processes can be accelerated, politicians can take short cuts and be creative with regard to daily routines, and improvise ingenious solutions to mounting problems.[46] Indeed, it is not clear in the context of Israel if a lack of both fixed rules and explicit boundaries bred a specific political culture, or if the particular political culture bred the kind of relaxed attitude towards processes and laws. Still, one may argue that there are several advantages to such an approach for a young nation building itself at a fast pace. Such an approach maximizes flexibility and allows for the use of trial and error to solve small crises before they develop into major ones.

The disadvantages associated with this state of flux are clear. It is almost impossible to plan for the long term, to include a vision of society in the decision-making process, and to maintain stability in government and society. For stability, long-term planning, and a vision of how the state should ideally be needs not only a consensus on basic societal values but also a majority of society's members who are willing to commit themselves to the preservation of these values. Using the three cases mentioned above as examples, Israelis should adopt a definition of a Jew that includes all branches of Judaism. It should formulate property rights that ensure that every citizen and his/her property are regarded as an independent entity. Finally, Israel should accept the idea that Basic Laws are special and should be amended only under very specific and well-defined circumstances.

While many people agree in principle with the need for such steps, they still value the maintenance of the status quo as more important because for them the present, not the future, is politically relevant. Using the three cases discussed above, one can demonstrate how politicians, motivated by myopic self-interest, act in ways that favour their self-preservation over the long-term good of society.[47]

Case Number 1: Basic Laws

Given that to amend a Basic Law one needs no more than an absolute majority and because to rule comfortably one needs to form what Riker calls a MWC (minimal wining coalition),[48] it follows that each government coalition can change any Basic Law, any time it wishes. And they do. For example, in 1999 when Prime Minister Ehud Barak did not honour his campaign promises to nominate women to his cabinet, he changed the paragraph in Basic Law: Government 1992 limiting the size of the government to only 18 ministers.[49] Likewise, in early 2007 when Shimon Peres planned to run for the post of president, Prime Minister Ehud Olmert initiated moves to alter Basic Law: President and change the paragraph that calls for a secret ballot in this election. The assumption was that the 'unelectable' Peres would improve his chances in the electoral body (that is, the 120 Knesset members) if the voting process were publicly transparent.[50]

Case Number 2: Land Ownership

Control over the land is part of the Zionist dictum. It serves as a control mechanism over the Arab minority in Israel and preserves Jewish holding rights over the land.[51] Israel's illiberal approach to public affairs reflects itself in Basic Law: Lands of Israel's position that the land belongs to the people, not to individuals.[52]

In the Kazir case,[53] the Supreme Court ruled that the public cannot discriminate against people on the basis of their religion. Turning this ruling into reality, however, is more difficult. Even within the Jewish community, there are small communities that exercise control over who can live amongst them. Kibbutzim, for example, in the name of maintaining 'ideological purity', have a membership selection process that has often excluded Jews who come from a country of origin different from that of the kibbutz majority. The law can pave a legal entry road, but overcoming social prejudice is much more difficult.

Case Number 3: Who is a Jew?

The question of who is a Jew really includes another question, namely who decides who is the rabbi who decides who is a Jew. This question involves the definition of the relationship between state and religion or, better, between religion and nationality,[54] and has been addressed and readdressed. The solutions have not always been unconcerned with the interests of the state. For example, an estimated one-third out of one million new immigrants who have arrived in Israel from the former Soviet Union since the early 1990s (one-sixth of Israel's population) could be considered non-Jews. They have been welcomed because they have filled the 'brain drain' created by emigrants who have left the country. Political representation in the Knesset in the form of two immigrant parties (Israel Bealiyah and Israel Beitenu) and various government positions (e.g. Minister of the Interior) have helped integrate these newcomers into the Israeli power structure and into wider society. On the other hand, while the Jewish sources of the Falasha Mora immigrants from Ethiopia are questionable, they are no doubt 'more' practising Jews than the practicing Christians arriving from Russia, the Ukraine and the other regions of the former Soviet Union. Nonetheless, because the Africans' contribution to the welfare of Israeli society is less central (compared to the contribution of the ex-Russians), state policies to deal with their problems seem to be less than enthusiastic.

CONCLUSIONS

Montesquieu's formulation of the separation of powers into three branches of government is more relevant to presidential than to parliamentary regimes. The democratic game in parliamentary regimes could be compared to a two-person, zero-sum (or perhaps constant-sum) game.[55] On one side we have the executive branch, which could be considered a non-random sample of the parliament (i.e. the legislative branch), and on the other side we find the court system, which assumes the role of interpreter of the other branches' decisions.

The position of interpreter may become politically very powerful, as Meydani and Mizrahi have demonstrated.[56] The court not only provides a specific interpretation of the laws, but it also directly and indirectly becomes a lawmaker and an enforcer of public policies. By inviting everyone to appeal to the Supreme Court, this institution becomes all-encompassing in dealing with all types of issues and involves itself in practical problems, as well as matters of principle.

The democratic power equilibrium that exists between the various groups in Israeli society is tilted in favour of the court. The court members are not elected, they are the highest paid public officials, and they stay in office until their retirement. Hence, the court's personnel are the constant and the members of the other branches are the variable. Members of the court develop traditions and share common interests and a protective attitude towards the preservation of their highly exclusive network.

In that context, having a polity in a permanent state of flux and ambivalence is conducive to the accumulation of the extra political powers and prestige that the role of interpreters provides. If so, is it not possible that the important interests of the 'Keepers of the Law' are to preserve the legal situation, the flux, the normative ambivalence as it is—borderless and problematic?

NOTES

1. Gideon Doron, *The Power of the Citizen*, Tel Aviv, 2006.
2. Arend Lijphart, *Democracies*, New Haven, CT, 1984.
3. Menachem Mautner, *The Fall of Formalism and the Rise of Values in the Israeli Legal System*, Tel Aviv, 1993.
4. Robert North, 'Conflict: Political Aspects', in David Shills (ed.), *International Encyclopedia of Social Sciences*, New York, 1968.
5. David Hume, *Essays on Moral Political and Liberty*, Part II, London, 1752; Thomas Paine, *Common Sense*, Philadelphia, 1776.
6. Steven Brams and Alan Taylor, *Fair Division: From Cake-Cutting to Dispute Resolution*, New York, 1996.
7. Joseph Agassi, *Between Nationality and Religion: Toward an Israeli National Identity*, Tel Aviv, 1995.
8. Uri Ben Eliezer, 'The Meaning of Political Participation in Nonliberal Democracy: The Israeli Experience', *Comparative Politics*, Vol. 25 (1993) pp. 397–412.

9. Gad Barzilai, *Communities and Law: Politics and Cultures of Legal Identities*, Ann Arbor, 2003; Will Kymlicka, *Multicultural Citizenship*, Oxford, 1995.
10. Kenneth Shepsle and Mark Bonchek, *Analyzing Politics*, New York, 1997; Gideon Doron and Itai Sened, *Political Bargaining*, London, 2001.
11. Robert Aumann and Michael Maschler, *Repeated Games with Incomplete Information*, Cambridge, 1995.
12. Charles Louis De Secondant Montesquieu, *The Spirit of Law*, New York, 1949 (first published, 1748).
13. Assaf Meydani and Shlomo Mizrahi, *Public Policy: Between Society and the Law*, Jerusalem, 2006.
14. David Easton, *The Political System*, New York, 1953.
15. Theodore Lowi, *The End of Liberalism*, New York, 1979.
16. William Riker, *The Art of Political Manipulation*, New Haven, CT, 1986; Doron and Sened, *Political Bargaining*.
17. Menachem Mautner, *The Fall of Formalism and the Rise of Values in the Israeli Legal System*, Tel Aviv, 1993; Assaf Meydani and Shlomo Mizrahi, *Public Policy: Between Society and the Law*, Jerusalem, 2006.
18. Assaf Meydani, 'The Supreme Court as a Political Agenda Setter', Master's Thesis, Ben Gurion University, 1999.
19. John Nash, 'Equilibrum Points in N-Person Games', *Proceedings of the National Academy of Science*, Vol. 36, No. 1 (1950), pp. 48–29.
20. Douglas North, *Structure and Change in Economic History*, New York, 1981.
21. William Poundstone, *Prisoners' Dilemma*, New York, 1992.
22. Norman Schofield (ed.), *Collective Decision Making*, Boston, 1999.
23. Hanna Lerner, 'Constitution Making in Deeply Divided Societies: The Incrementalist Option (Israel, Ireland, India)', PhD Dissertation, Columbia University, 2006.
24. Amnon Rubinstein, *The Constitutional Law of the State of Israel*, Tel Aviv, 1996.
25. Gideon Doron and Michael Harris, *Public Policy and Electoral Reform: The Case of Israel*, Lanham, MD, 2000.
26. Don Peretz and Gideon Doron, *The Government and Politics of Israel*, Boulder, CO, 1997.
27. Rubinstein, *The Constitutional Law of the State of Israel*.
28. Gideon Doron and Assaf Meydani, 'Constitutional Court: A Structural Solution to the Ruling Problems of the Political System?', *Iyunim Betkumat Israel*, 17 (2007), pp. 319–343. [In Hebrew].
29. Ruth Gavison, Yoav Dotan and Mordechai Kremnitzer, *Judicial Activism: Pros and Cons*, Tel Aviv, 2000.
30. Don Peretz and Gideon Doron, *The Government and Politics of Israel*, Boulder, CO, 1997.
31. Gideon Doron, *Presidential Regime for Israel*, Jerusalem, 2006.
32. Ibid.; John Snetsinger, *Truman, the Jewish Vote, and the Creation of Israel*, Stanford, CA: Hoover Institution Press, 1974.
33. Giora Goldberg, *Ben Gurion against the Knesset*, London, 2003.
34. Joseph Agassi, *Between Nationality and Religion: Toward an Israeli National Identity*, Tel Aviv, 1995.
35. Gideon Doron, *Games in Israeli Politics*, Tel Aviv, 1988.
36. David Braybrook and Charles Lindblom, *A Strategy of Decision*, New York, 1963.
37. Don Peretz and Gideon Doron, *The Government and Politics of Israel*, Boulder, CO, 1997.
38. Ibid.
39. Zeev Shternhal, *Nation Building or Nation Fixing*, Tel Aviv, 1995.
40. Rebecca Kook, *The Logic of Democratic Exclusion*, Lanham, MD, 2002.
41. Ian Lustick, *Arabs in the Jewish State*, Austin, TX, 1980.
42. Kook, *The Logic of Democratic Exclusion*.
43. Lustick, *Arabs in the Jewish State*.
44. H.C. 72/62, *Rufeisen v. Minister of the Interior*, PD 16, 2428 (in Hebrew)
45. Kook, *The Logic of Democratic Exclusion*.
46. Benjamin Akzin and Yezhekel Dror, *Israel: High Pressure Planning*, Syracuse, NY, 1966.
47. David Mayew, *Congress: The Electoral Connection*, New Haven, CT, 1974; Bruce Bueno de Mesqita *et al.*, *The Logic of Political Survival*, Cambridge, MA, 2003.
48. William Riker, *The Theory of Political Coalitions*, New Haven, CT, 1962.

49. Doron, *The Power of the Citizen.*
50. Orli Azulai-Katz, *The Man Who Did Not Know How to Win: Shimon Peres in Sizipus Trap*, Tel Aviv, 1996.
51. Lustick, *Arabs in the Jewish State.*
52. Kook, *The Logic of Democratic Exclusion.*
53. H.C. 6698/95, *Kaadan v. Israel Lands Administration*, P.D. 54(1), 258 (in Hebrew)
54. Charles Liebman and Eliezer Don Yehiye, *Civil Religion in Israel*, Berkeley, CA, 1983; Agassi, *Between Nationality and Religion*; Kook, *The Logic of Democratic Exclusion.*
55. Doron, *Games in the Israeli Politics.*
56. Meydani and Mizrahi, *Public Policy: Between Society and the Law.*

Public Responsibility of Elected Officials in Israel: Crossing the Bounds of Reasonableness

ORI ARBEL-GANZ AND DAVID NACHMIAS

Public responsibility has served as a means of maintaining the allegiance of elected officials towards citizens. There is widespread agreement that a democracy whose norms of public responsibility are lax may be compared to a car that races downhill: as it accelerates with the steepness of the incline, the driver's ability to control the vehicle declines, whereas the braking distance necessary to stop the car increases. A society that lacks well-entrenched norms of public responsibility denies the very basic, moral principles of 'reward and punishment'.

The situation in Israel with regard to the norms of public responsibility has been rapidly deteriorating. Despite numerous instances of political corruption and abuse elected officials fail to regard themselves as responsible. On the contrary, they proclaim their innocence and afterwards publicly declare that 'Our hands have not spilled this blood, and our eyes have not witnessed it'.[1]

In this article we attempt to reach a better understanding of public responsibility in theory and practice. Several well-publicized instances will be discussed in which public responsibility should have been assumed by elected officials. The public's low level of expectation of public officials', as well as the weakness of the judicial and law enforcement systems, calls for a thorough re-examination of guidelines and the internalization of appropriate norms of public responsibility. The article explores the different levels of responsibility and argues that public responsibility is not, and cannot, be just a judicial matter only but also a social, cultural and subjective issue as well.

PUBLIC RESPONSIBILITY: A CONCEPTUAL FRAMEWORK

Responsibility may be defined as the system of duties borne by an occupant of a formal position or status in an organization. Formal positions are intended by design to fulfil particular purposes. Thus, the office of 'general manager of a company' is intended to serve the company's overall purpose: increasing profits.[2] The office of 'youth movement counsellor' is intended to fulfil the movement's purpose, which is that of socializing youth into certain values. Organizations can fulfil their functions via their office-holders, and in many ways their behaviours are, in fact, the actions of the organization itself.[3] Every position has its distinct authority, formally granted to enable the office-holder to achieve the position's objectives. Powers are delegated to office-holders only within the framework of their position. When they no longer occupy the position the powers are taken away.

An office is not forced on the person occupying it. However, once accepted, the office-holder is subject to the rules of the organization and he or she can use only those powers accorded within the context of the position.[4] Office-holders are to use their powers only to fulfil the purposes of the offices, and thus to attain organizational objectives. Accordingly, a company director is not authorized to use company funds to make acquisitions that do not benefit the company either directly or indirectly.

The democratic state may be regarded as a super-organization owned by the group of people who founded it.[5] Any of the state's authorities may be considered a sub-organ of the organization as a whole. Since the state was founded by people, with the principal objective 'to unite free citizens under the rule of law',[6] state authorities must carry out this purpose. Only the public interest has to guide state authorities and public officials:

> The individual domain is not the same as the public domain, since the former acts on the basis of its own resources, according or refusing them as it may see fit; whereas the latter was created entirely for the purpose of serving the public and has no resources of its own: all that it possesses has been given to it in trust, and it has no additional rights or duties beyond those, or different or separate from those, which stem from this trusteeship or which have been accorded or placed upon it by virtue of legal instructions.[7]

As an inseparable component of the obligation of loyalty[8] that civil servants owe to the public, they are required to safeguard the trust placed by the public in elected officials, in the system of governance, and in state institutions.

In the private sector, shareholders who lose their trust in office-holders will act to replace them; if they lose their trust in the company, they will attempt to reorganize it or, alternatively, they will seek other investments. Similarly, a public that has lost its faith in a particular public official will attempt to dismiss him or her. If it has lost its trust in the regime it may refuse to comply with its decrees, and may seek to replace the prevailing 'rules of the game', or, alternatively, may seek to settle in a state whose method and style of governance suit its own nature and aspirations.[9] The public's loss of trust in the regime and its representatives threatens the existence of the state. Democratic regimes cannot survive without being legitimate, trustworthy, and efficient in the eyes of the public:

> Trust in the fundamental purposes and design of the political system, in the representation and integrity of its decision-making structures and processes, and in the ability of government to produce policies that satisfy citizen needs is essential, in all these regards, to the maintenance of viable democratic order.[10]

The obligation of loyalty and the obligation to safeguard the public's trust are expressed in the obligations placed upon the civil service[11] by three sources: the organization, the office and society.[12] The first places obligations, that is, responsibility, on all public officials due to their membership of the 'public organization', that is, to the state with its various institutions. Thus, all civil servants must follow the general goals of the civil service, its regulations, its basic laws, administrative orders and rulings. For example, the instructions that 'there shall be no violation of the life, body or dignity of any person as such' or 'there shall be no violation of the property of a person' obligate all public authorities as such.[13]

The second source of obligation consists of the particular office's mandate. Every office comes with rules, procedures, laws and rulings specific to it. A bureau chief and a physician in the public health service are subject to the rules of the civil service in general (the first source of obligation), but each also places upon the office-holder particular duties, including professional obligations. The third source derives from society itself. As civil servants are considered to be public trustees, there are societal norms of conduct that they are expected to adhere to.

Furthermore, society may place an obligation of public responsibility on the office-holder in cases where the other sources of obligation do not do so. Whereas the first two sources—the organization and the office—place formal obligations on the civil servant (laws and regulations), and disciplinary obligations (within the framework of disciplinary rulings and civil service regulations),[14] society places only moral-behavioural obligations. The public, in its social and unofficial mechanisms, does not develop a binding, permanent code of ethics, nor does it have the means for doing so. The public's expectations of civil servants, which are derived from the entire array of values and norms in which it believes and to which it adheres also place obligations on public officials. Thus, public officials that comply with the dictates of the law and discharge their official duties in accordance with the obligations placed upon them by the organization and the office, may still find themselves subject to public criticism if they behave contrary to public expectations.

In sum, a civil servant's public responsibility obligates him or her to act only in the public interest, to safeguard the public's fundamental trust in the state and its system of governance. Civil servants must comply with the official and unofficial rules of behaviour that apply within the framework of their employment, in their particular position, and be subject to the public's ethical expectations. To these three sources of obligation an additional distinction that covers them must be made: objective responsibility and subjective responsibility, as they are described below:

> Two types of responsibility can be identified. They are sometimes referred to as objective and subjective responsibility. Objective responsibility has to do with expectations imposed from outside ourselves, whereas subjective responsibility concerns those things for which we feel a responsibility. . . . [T]his is not to be understood as a difference between real and unreal; subjective responsibility, as an expression for our beliefs, personal and professional values, and character traits, is just as real as the more tangible manifestations of objective responsibility.[15]

Objective public responsibility may be expected due to organizational arrangements, the nature of the office, or public protest. However, public officials may actually regard themselves responsible by virtue of their personal moral standards. The recognition of these two responsibility perspectives raises the very difficult question: in the event that the two contradict each other, which norms should the public servant adhere to? There is no simple answer to this difficult question. There are instances in which it may be determined that the obligation of responsibility is derived from the more demanding of the two normative systems. For example, a breakdown occurs in the main computer system of a government ministry, leading to a series of mishaps including problems with task performance, damage to programmes and an electrical blackout. The conduct of the ministry's computer division director was found to be appropriate with regard to all of the safeguards made to prevent such a breakdown. In fact, an exhaustive investigation revealed that the system was sabotaged. Accordingly, the director is not responsible according to the external objective perspective. However, the director's values may lead him to submit his resignation as an expression of his overall managerial responsibility. In such a case, the subjective normative dimension is more demanding than the objective, and the employee behaved in accordance with this. This will apply in the opposite situation as well: if the investigation (objective external responsibility) had concluded that the director was negligent, but the director himself was convinced (subjective responsibility) that he did everything possible to prevent the breakdown, there can be no doubt that the objective perspective would prevail.

Indeed, there are cases in which it is difficult to determine which of the two normative perspectives is more significant. An example is the refusal of soldiers to serve in the occupied territories. In such a case, the organizational (external) normative system—the military law—calls for a certain kind of conduct, whereas groups within society (external source), as well as one's conscience, dictates contradictory behaviour. There is no clear-cut normative solution to such situations.

Public responsibility can be divided into two main groups: responsibility for personal conduct and responsibility for professional functioning. Within the first group two separate dimensions may be distinguished. The first relates to situations in which elected officials are required to bear personal–public responsibility for their actions in the private domain. In theory, public officials are appointed or elected to fulfil their public duties according to their professional qualifications, and therefore whatever they do in private is of no interest to the public. However, the justification for public interest and intrusion in a public official's private life follows from the possible consequences of conduct in the private domain on the official's ability to fulfil his public duties, as well as from the expectation of exemplary behaviour.[16] According to this approach, the inability to distinguish in practice between the civil servant's private and public lives means that he does not and cannot lead two separate lives. The public official's conduct in private has implications for the public's perception of his public conduct. If an individual shows signs of aggressive behaviour, drunkenness or indifference to those around him in his private life, the public will view this as a personality flaw and will not want him in public service.

The second dimension on which a public official may be expected to be publicly responsible for his private behaviour has to do with his conduct within the context of the office held. This refers to the possible use of one authority to attain goals that are not related to the purpose of the office and/or that breach the principles of sound management. Beyond the criminal aspect of such transgressions, they are generally referred to as instances of 'political corruption':[17] acts in which the office-holder makes use of his power, status, authority and resources in order to advance matters that are completely unrelated to the public interest, or, alternatively, when he engages in such acts in order to promote the public interest—as he sees it—but by breaching the rules of sound management. In this context a distinction is usually made between personal motives, ones seeking to benefit the civil servant himself and/or persons related to him, and public, group or political party motives. The two kinds of motive translate into the same idea: abuse of the powers of the office.

The second type of professional responsibility includes four factors. The first is that in which responsibility derives from policy design and/or its consequences. In the business sector it is usual practice for a chief executive officer who has failed to promote the company's aims to bear responsibility for failure. Considering that elected officials are voted into office in order to fulfil a particular purpose, responsibility should be taken if the purpose is not attained. The second factor calls for public responsibility with respect to the decision-making procedure. The position-holder is required to use systematic decision-making procedures while maintaining a neutral and professionally impartial stance as much as possible.[18] Strict fulfilment of this obligation is vital in order to maintain the rule of law, to preserve the public trust, and to enable the purpose of the office to be fulfilled.

The third factor relates to discretion. The difficulty of setting detailed decision-making procedures capable of addressing all situations and all constraints necessitates using personal judgement before making a decision on any particular issue.[19] The allocation of resources for a transportation project, for example, is within the jurisdiction of the minister appointed to handle transportation issues, and thus it is his duty to examine, consider, assess and decide among alternative projects. Judgement in a matter that arises within the context of the public service means to act with fairness, in good faith, and without favouritism when a decision has to be made among different interests, among groups competing for resources, and among individuals in need of assistance. Moreover, judgement may also require the personal interpretation of the office-holder.[20] According to this approach, both judgement and interpretation have to reflect reasonableness on the part of the civil servant. Reasonableness is a criterion by which behaviour is evaluated. It reflects the social values in the context of which public authorities use their discretion in accordance with common sense and with due attention to the circumstances.[21]

The last factor concerns the ministerial base of the office-holder's public responsibility. That is, it is not based only on the office-holder's personal instructions or on acts that he himself carries out, but rather it has to do with acts carried out by his subordinates, without his knowledge and without any explicit instructions ordered by him—with no personal 'blame' attached to the position-holder himself.[22] The principle of ministerial responsibility was strengthened in particular during the nineteenth century, due to two processes that took place in parliamentary systems: the decline of parliamentary power and the emergence of the executive branch in leadership roles. Ministerial responsibility emerged in response to the principle that all government actions should be under the supervision and responsibility of public officials elected democratically,[23] and based on the approach that for every action or inaction someone must be accountable and must bear responsibility. Some scholars also view the importance of ministerial responsibility from the point of view of the supervisor's obligations towards the employee: the supervisor also has to bear ministerial responsibility in instances in which the employee bears personal responsibility for his negligence, his oversight or his decisions and, at the same time, in order to express the supervisory echelon's obligation towards the subordinate echelons, the employee's supervisor also bears public responsibility—not necessarily personal but ministerial.[24]

All in all, public officials bear public responsibility based on the complex considerations of various parameters and dimensions. First, the broader context views public officials as trustees and calls on them to safeguard the public trust. Second, three sources place official and unofficial obligations on public officials: the organization, the office and the socio-cultural environment. Third, objective (external) responsibility may be placed upon the public official, whereas the latter may use subjective (internal) responsibility. Fourth, responsibility may be required in two main sets of circumstances: where personal conduct is at issue (whether in the private or the public sphere), and where professional conduct is at issue—policy outcomes, decision-making procedures, judgement and interpretation, and ministerial responsibility.

PUBLIC RESPONSIBILITY IN ISRAEL: AN EMPIRICAL VIEW[25]

Israel has only partially succeeded in cultivating norms of public responsibility in general and professional conduct in particular. There have been over 90 cases in which elected officials have resigned or have been dismissed from office. In most of these cases political power struggles rather than public responsibility were at issue.[26]

Public responsibility for personal misconduct in the private domain led to Prime Minister Rabin's decision not to run for re-election in 1977, because of the disclosure that his wife had an illegal bank account in the United States. Although the suspicions were raised against his wife, Rabin chose to take personal responsibility.[27] Benjamin Netanyahu, the 1996 Likud Party candidate for prime minister, faced events that overlapped between his private and public lives. In confessing to having committed adultery he publicized matters that ordinarily should not have interested the public. Netanyahu recognized the legitimacy of the public's demand that its senior elected officials display ethical behaviour in their private lives.[28]

However, behaviour in the private domain is not usually of sufficient import to lead an elected official to make public disclosures. Former minister of the interior, Deri, and deputy minister Pinhasi refused to resign after serious charges were filed against them. Consequently, the Supreme Court asked Prime Minister Rabin to dismiss them. This ruling established the precedent for two later resignations—that of minister of justice Ne'eman after the attorney general decided to conduct an investigation of his activities, and that of transportation minister Mordechai, indicted for sexual harassment and assault. Had Ne'eman and Mordechai not resigned, they would have been dismissed by the prime minister, or by a court order. It should be pointed out that although Mordecai resigned from his ministerial position, he did not to resign from the Knesset. Other public officials ignored the norm set by the Deri–Pinhasi ruling and refused to resign. For example, former minister Lieberman decided to ignore his conviction in a case of assaulting a minor. He attributed no public importance to the conviction, remained in public office and refused to convey regret.

Upon examining public responsibility for improper personal conduct within the context of the public office itself, we also do not find norms for such responsibility. Former minister Hanegbi, who appointed dozens of his political loyalists to public offices during his brief tenure in the environment ministry, actually took pride in his behaviour. In his previous position as justice minister, against the background of his involvement in the controversial appointment of Bar-On as attorney general, Hanegbi refused to be held publicly responsible for his conduct, much less to recognize his public responsibility for the events that took place. Hanegbi was also involved in the 'Derech Tzalacha' affair, in which, in a conflict of interests, he abused his power as a Knesset member on behalf of an organization that he headed and which paid him a salary for his services.

Knesset member Zucker was found by the Knesset Ethics Committee to be responsible for the submission of a fraudulent financial statement detailing remuneration he received from the Camera Obscura photography school. The committee fined him three months' wages, the Knesset by-laws' maximum penalty. Zucker himself did not see fit to take public responsibility for his actions. Neither Prime Minister Netanyahu (in 1996) nor Prime Minister Barak (in 1999) regarded themselves publicly responsible for their apparent involvement in the creation of facade organizations during their election campaigns. In 2004 deputy minister Blumenthal refused to cooperate with police investigators and invoked her right to silence while being investigated for alleged bribery of Likud central committee members. Despite the public criticism levelled against her, she decided not to resign from her office and was eventually dismissed by Prime Minister Sharon. But Sharon himself refused to acknowledge any public impropriety in his attempt to influence public officials in the Israel Lands Authority Administration in order to promote a particular decision, despite the fact that he acted in a situation of conflict between interests, and in spite of the state comptroller's warning at the time to refrain from such behaviour. Nor did Likud Knesset members Gorolovsky and Ratzon, who voted in place of fellow members that were absent during a Knesset vote, take any responsibility for their improper behaviour.

With respect to public responsibility for professional conduct, the situation is similar. Whereas in many Western democracies norms exist for public responsibility in this area,[29] in Israel this is not the case. We have witnessed no instances in which a transportation minister who declared 'war on road accidents' in order to reduce the number of fatal accidents held himself responsible when statistics showed that the number of accidents had actually increased. Has an education minister ever held himself responsible for the dramatic decline in pupils' attainments? Has a health minister ever seen himself as responsible for the collapse of the healthcare system? Except for Prime Minister Meir and her defence minister Moshe Dayan who resigned, no Israeli government minister in the history of the state has ever taken public responsibility for a policy failure or any other administrative disaster.

Nor do elected officials bear public responsibility for their decision-making methods. Although the Supreme Court has addressed the issue of desirable normative decision-making procedures, and although government by-laws presume the existence of a system of structured and methodical decision-making procedures,[30] methods of decision-making are mainly incremental, carried out hastily and with little attention to the details of the proposed plans and their alternatives.[31] Such decision-making procedures have strong negative effects on long-term infrastructure projects and public policies. For example, the decision regarding the evacuation of the Pi-Glilot fuel and gas facility has been discussed, by the government officials for the last 12 years. The Tel Aviv and greater gush Dan light rail (subway) project has been subject to problematic decision-making processes. Other delayed projects include the privatization of El-Al (which took place in 2004 following deliberations over two decades); Bezeq, defence industries, the refineries and commercial banks. Despite the severe negative consequences not one single elected or appointed public official publicly took responsibility.

An example of poor decision-making procedures may be seen in a May 1997 cabinet meeting. At the meeting on the 'war against road accidents' a report was presented to cabinet ministers. The 49 inter-ministerial projects described in the report served as a platform for deliberations. The report was adopted by ministers with no discussion of the details of the projects, and without the presentation of alternative recommendations and of the budgetary resources for funding the projects. One recommendation that was approved stipulated that every five years, as a condition of driver's licence renewal, veteran drivers be required to pass a test and examinations of vision and hearing. The funding sources mentioned in the report were intra-ministerial. The decision would have entailed the examination of half a million drivers per year, at an estimated cost of 40 million NIS. The recommendations were not implemented.

Another example of faulty decision-making procedures can be seen in the government's decision to open the Wailing Wall Tunnel in Jerusalem in September 1996. Despite the warnings of the security forces about the danger involved in opening the tunnel, it eventually turned out that the cardinal decision to open it had been made in the office of Prime Minister Netanyahu, after discussions with a select group of ministers, Jerusalem's mayor, the head of the general security services and the cabinet secretary. Other key officials were not consulted. The operative decision was made and the opening date set later on during a telephone conversation between the prime minister, the minister of public security and the mayor of Jerusalem. Subsequently, the minister of defence stated that he was informed of the decision to open the tunnel about five minutes before the event took place.

Budget considerations are characterized by convoluted and inconsistent decision-making procedures. The decision-making process is secretive, the public remains uninformed about its content, and the major portion of the budget is actually set up by the ministry of finance's budget division, with no possibility of elected officials having meaningful influence over the budget's basic parameters, on the interpretations of the current economic situation, or even on the manner of allocations. No systematic alternatives are ever presented to cabinet ministers and Knesset members that would enable them to make intelligent comparisons. The thousands of items contained in the budget document are meant to provide extensive information, but this information overload actually makes it difficult to distinguish among individual items and to understand the overall budget structure.

The budget document is brought up every year between June and September for government approval, but very few serious deliberations are held. Cabinet ministers are concerned primarily with their particular interests and do not take a macro-view of all of the budget's economic, social and political ramifications. Evidence actually indicates that ministers do not go over the budget document, but approve it after they negotiate the budgeting of those areas for which they are responsible.[32] When the budget proposal reaches the Knesset the process repeats itself. Knesset members approve or reject the budget on first reading without scrutinizing the thousands of items and considering their implications. Even if they wish to they cannot because of the short time available for the task.[33]

In addition, the Economic Emergency Bill (*hok ha-asderim*) that since 1985 has been submitted alongside the Budget Law to counter the severe economic crisis at the time, changes legislation based on the budget. This constitutes a means of circumventing legislative principles, since the Knesset approves via one bill amendments to numerous laws. Knesset committees are not involved in the changes, nor is the public aware of the nature of the changes, their implications, and the degree to which they are necessary in the first place.[34] Over the years several proposals were made for improving government decision-making procedures.[35] They were adopted but not implemented.

The Supreme Court has noted the difficulty of formulating detailed decision-making procedures able to tackle every situation and most constraints. It is precisely due to this that the court reached the conclusion that civil servants—and, it goes without saying, elected officials—are obligated to use their judgement before deciding on an issue.[36] To display judgement regarding an issue that arises within the context of the public office means to conduct oneself with fairness, good faith, and without showing favouritism in the effort to strike a balance between differing interests, between groups competing for the same resources, and between individuals in need of assistance. The use of judgement, as mentioned earlier, generally involves personal interpretations. For example, the Commission of Inquiry into the Events at the Refugee Camps in Beirut (the Kahan Commission) found the defence minister at the time, Ariel Sharon, responsible for the failure to prevent the massacre since his decisions, which led to the entry of Phalangist forces into the Sabra and Shatilla refugee camps, were unreasonable.[37] In spite of this, Sharon refused to abide by the Commission's findings, and only after a compromise was reached between him and Prime Minister Begin did he resign.[38]

The attitude of elected officials towards their ministerial responsibility is even more troubling. In Israel 'it is not accepted practice for a minister to resign or to be dismissed from his post due to the disclosure of failures within his ministry, whatever they might be'.[39] The Knesset, in its constitutional role as a legislative authority, has determined that 'each minister is responsible to the prime minister for his areas of responsibility'.[40] This formulation is ambiguous with regard to ministerial responsibility: it remains unclear whether it refers only to acts performed by the minister himself and subordinates that he instructed to perform, or whether it also includes acts performed by subordinates without the minister's explicit authorization or direct involvement. In our opinion, the wording of the law is only superficially unclear; after all, there can be no doubt that, just as the government is incapable of addressing all of the issues that it faces and therefore divides up the various functions between the ministers, so each minister is unable to handle personally all the matters under his jurisdiction, and therefore responsibility is delegated to others.[41]

Moreover, in accordance with the rule that 'one messenger cannot appoint another messenger', ministerial responsibility for acts carried out by subordinates is always with the minister. Although 'from a legal point of view responsibility exists only when the failure to discharge a duty leads to sanctions',[42] nevertheless 'responsibility may exist on levels other than the legal one, such as the public or the moral'.[43] In all the cases examined not even a single elected official took ministerial responsibility for adverse occurrences in his ministry.

Within the context of discussing ministerial responsibility, the question of collective responsibility is paramount. In Israel, the Knesset confers upon the government the authority to manage the affairs of the state,[44] and thus 'the Government is collectively responsible to the Knesset'.[45] From a constitutional point of view, the legislature recognizes only one executive entity that is accountable to it—the government; a minister is 'responsible to the prime minister for his areas of responsibility'.[46] This approach views any public policy formulated by a minister or a ministry as that of the entire government. Collective responsibility obligates cabinet ministers to act in office according to governmental instructions as a collective body, and to comply with governmental decisions even when they disagree with them.[47]

Nevertheless, as has been observed many times, the relationship between governmental instructions and the behaviour of individual cabinet ministers is weak. For example, in breaking the government by-laws stating that 'by virtue of the principle of collective responsibility no minister or deputy minister shall, while appearing in the Knesset plenum or in one of its committees, express disagreement with, or criticize, government decisions',[48] prime ministers have ignored the absence or abstention of ministers from Knesset votes, or even instances in which they voted against government decisions. Furthermore, there has been an increase in critical expressions of individual ministers against government policy, even when in fact they have voted in favour of government decisions. Except for certain very specific cases, the principle of collective responsibility has not been enforced. In the Netanyahu administration of the late 1990s, for example, the National Religious Party ministers spoke out against the Hebron agreement and chose not to support it in the Knesset vote. The prime minister did not dismiss them, nor did they resign.[49] Similarly, the Shas party ministers criticized Prime Minister Barak's foreign policy, but he did not remove them from office.

This article has argued that there are three sources that place obligations on elected officials: the organization, the office and the public. These obligations can exist on a formal level (such as in legislation or other internal instructions—this in reference to the first two sources), or on an informal one (such as unwritten ethical norms). Although on the formal level the legislature created an appropriate normative framework for public responsibility, in reality elected officials do not comply. Within the informal dimension the situation is even worse. An elected official is 'expected to display behaviour that is appropriate and free of any hint of deviation from the correct path'.[50] He or she is also expected to behave according to 'principles and values that have not been determined by law or by court rulings. [And despite the fact that] these principles and values have no legal status that can compel legal sanctions if they are violated ... they nevertheless do exist ... and their violation should have ramifications'.[51] This expectation should not be viewed as exceptional; even among elected officials it is generally agreed that 'ultimately, in a modern society, ethics should have the same status as, or even be above the law; they should be ... no less binding than the law'.[52] However, public officials admit that 'there is an increasing tendency to define right and wrong in the conduct of public figures according to measures of legality/illegality; whatever is not explicitly prohibited by law is considered publicly to be sound conduct'.[53] The weakness of ethics in public affairs has led the Supreme Court to fill the void: 'When ethics themselves have no power to prevent improper conduct or deplorable consequences ... law must at times be called in to aid them'.[54]

One well-known case occurred when former minister of interior Deri and deputy minister Pinchasi opted to remain in office. The court formulated the norm according to which public officials at a high level must be free not only from blame but also from any suspicion of crimes involving dishonour. Although this norm may fall within the category of desirable moral behaviour, it is not anchored in law. Despite this, and perhaps because it never took root or was assimilated by virtue of any other normative, non-legal framework, the Supreme Court ruling became a binding norm. By contrast, in the Movement for Quality Government in Israel's petition against Prime Minister Sharon on the appointment of Hanegbi as minister of public security,[55] the court refrained from crossing the boundary between law and public ethics. The line has been crossed only in exceptional cases, whereas as a rule, even when

> the Court does not take a favourable view of the minister's conduct ... the administrative authority's ethical responsibility, like its responsibility to be efficient and to make wise administrative decisions, as opposed to its legal responsibility, is not in the hands of the Court ... the Court cannot, and need not, stand in the place of ethics, except in a partial manner, in specific instances, in a controlled and careful process ... in cases of exceptional severity, in which unethical conduct is liable to turn into illegal conduct.[56]

The attorney general also sets boundaries for public responsibility within the framework of the 'positive' or 'negative' instructions issued,[57] and within the framework of the public reports published on several issues in recent years. For example, with regard to the conduct of former minister of justice Hanegbi in his appointment of Bar-On as attorney general, it is stated that:

> Nothing in the history of State of Israel is similar to this affair in terms of its sensitivity, the ranks of those involved, or the heavy shadow of suspicion that there was a premeditated attempt to threaten the rule of law in a manner well-known in certain countries by appointing an attorney general, the chief of the prosecution system, someone who might be beholden to certain individuals who do not hold the public interest or the rule of law as matters of prime concern ... The interweaving of politics and law is a slippery and dangerous area. The use of political power to further personal interest is a slope with disastrous potential.[58]

Also with regard to the appointment of Hanegbi as minister of public security, the attorney general chose not to dispute the prime minister's decision, but nevertheless expressed his opinion, in a public report, that

'Although according to statute and judicial precedent there appears to be no legal impediment to the appointment, the appointment itself is *prima facie* problematic from a public perspective'.[59] The attorney general, like the Supreme Court, can also be involved in situations where the norms are definitely unacceptable but he lacks the legal authority to eradicate them. Therefore, he retreats from the legal discourse yet tries to leave his mark on the civic discourse by communicating the normative message that he regards appropriate.

The state comptroller has also contributed to defining public accountability and responsibility in the civic, non-legal dimension. In addition to the examination of the degree to which public officials act legally, efficiently and economically, the comptroller is also authorized to assess the integrity of civil servants, the quality of their judgements and the soundness of their interpretations.[60] The comptroller's investigations of non-criminal cases have actually enhanced the institution's prestige and the public's trust in it. Thus, for example, in *Annual Report No. 35* the audit examined the police norm that in the event of a terrorist attack, all Arabs in an area are rounded up, kept in custody, harshly interrogated and subjected to bodily and other searches. In *Annual Report No. 37* strong criticism was levelled at the measures taken for the provision of gas masks to the public prior to the Persian Gulf War of 1991, and the fact that the masks constituted the home front's primary means of defence. In *Annual Report No. 42* the comptroller presented the great discrepancies between the allocation of resources to education in the Jewish sector in comparison to the Arab sector. In *Annual Report No. 43* strong criticism was levelled against the activities of the Likud government, including the waste of tax-payers' money and unsound management that characterized several government ministries.

One case that drew widespread public attention was the Tze'elim disaster, in which the state comptroller was asked to examine the conduct of former army chief of staff Ehud Barak from a civic perspective. In an investigative report published in *Yedioth Aharonoth* several individuals claimed that Barak left the site of a serious accident without taking injured soldiers in his helicopter, thereby endangering their lives, in addition to failing to act in accordance with the norms required from a commander and leader in the field.[61] Two years later, on 24 June 1997, the Knesset's state audit committee asked the state comptroller to investigate the incident, and in the report published two weeks before the 1999 general elections the comptroller explicitly determined that

> there was no justification for stating that the chief of general staff had left the site of the disaster with undue haste; and even had he left after the landing of the evacuation helicopters and before the evacuation of all of the wounded, it still could not be said that by this action he had prevented the rescue of a wounded soldier.[62]

The most recent example of critical attention to compromised integrity and a violation of the rules of sound management may be found in *Annual Report No. 53B*. Here the comptroller determined that Prime Minister Sharon's involvement in Resolution 755 of the Israel Lands Authority, with regard to agricultural lands, was tainted by a conflict of interests. The comptroller warned Sharon of this as early as January 2002, yet the prime minister ignored the warning. This affair provides an illustration of the significance of the state comptroller's office and its contribution to the formulation of norms of proper behaviour. At the same time this event also demonstrates the comptroller's institutional weakness from an enforcement perspective.[63]

Brief mention should also be made of the roles of official commissions of inquiry in defining public responsibility in Israel. The Commissions of Inquiry Law 5729-1968 states that, should 'the government find that a matter of vital civic importance exists which requires clarification, it has the right to establish a commission of inquiry to investigate the matter and to submit its report to the government'.[64] A commission 'may accept any evidence which appears to it to be useful, and it may determine the order of witness interrogations ... [and] it is not subject to the laws of evidence'.[65] Precisely because the commission of inquiry is meant to serve as the government's investigative and clarifying mechanism for matters of the highest public importance, as a basis for making operative decisions,[66] and because its role is not to judge, it appears that the duty of the commission of inquiry is to consider 'not necessarily the legal aspects of the issue at hand, but also, and at times primarily, the civic and moral aspects'.[67] Research on Israeli commissions of inquiry shows that the commissions address issues of judgement and reasonableness.[68] The Kahan Commission, for example, in regard to the actions of foreign affairs minister Shamir, pointed out that 'in this situation the foreign affairs minister should have been expected to display sensitivity to, and awareness of, the things that he heard from another minister'.[69] However, despite their prestige the commissions of inquiry do not set time limits on their recommendations. Thus, many who were found to be responsible for failures by commissions of inquiry continued to occupy senior official public offices, and they were even promoted. Neeman, who as director-general of the ministry of finance was found personally responsible for many of the blunders that facilitated the commercial banks' 'shares scandal', served later as finance minister in the Netanyahu government, as chair of the Investigation Committee of the Temple Mount Affair in 1991, and as a member of the Bank of Israel Advisory Council. Sharon, who was found to be personally responsible as defence minister for oversights that resulted in the failure to prevent the massacre carried out by the Christian Phalangist forces in the Lebanese refugee camps, was later elected prime minister.

Finally—the public at large. In democracies the public has the right to criticize government actions, and the conduct and policies of public officials. It appears that in Israel criticism on the part of the general public—not counting articles and journalistic investigations published in the media—is scarcely heard, and if it is heard it has no influence on the norms of conduct applicable to those in public office. The latter continue to behave as they see fit. The public's weakness and its indifference actually enable elected officials to continue their behaviour. The accountability of public officials to the general public is seldom expressed, and consequently the public has lost its trust in state institutions and elected officials.[70]

CONCLUSIONS

Despite laws, rules, job definitions, Supreme Court intervention, the expressed opinions of the attorney general, state comptroller reports and comprehensive reports of official commissions of inquiry, a political culture which obligates elected officials to public responsibility has not emerged. Perhaps the public's great trust in the state's auditing and judicial bodies, and its expectation that these bodies will set the boundaries of public responsibility have, in fact, enabled public officials to use Supreme Court 'authorizations' as a cover, and have left the issue of their responsibility to the public outside of the public discourse.

Moreover, even when objective public responsibility has been precisely defined, elected officials evade their responsibility unless it is directly forced on them and they have no choice in the matter. When there is no authority to impose responsibility, elected officials flee their moral, not to say their legal, duty to take responsibility for their conduct, their policies, their decisions, the judgements that they have displayed, and the failures that have occurred under their authority. All of this represents a sharp deviation from the bounds of normative moral conduct. Except for certain specific cases, elected officials' subjective responsibility is lower than the objective standard, as the latter is determined by external sources—the organization, the office held, and the socio-cultural environment. Golda Meir and Moshe Dayan did not resign from their posts due to severe blunders leading up to the Yom Kippur War; they ultimately resigned only after the public took to the streets in mass demonstrations against them. Ariel Sharon did not choose to resign from his post as defence minister even after the public demanded that he do so due to the illegitimacy (in the eyes of many citizens) of the 'Peace for Galilee' War, just as he refused to resign after the Kahan Commission published its report.

Netanyahu and Hanegbi, together and separately, refused to provide an account regarding the appointment of Bar-On as attorney general, much less to be held publicly responsible for it. Deputy minister Blumenthal refused to cooperate with the investigation of her activities, and vigorously opposed the cancellation of her immunity by the Knesset committee. Prime Minister Sharon refused to recognize his public responsibility despite the fact that it had been explicitly concluded by the state comptroller, and he chose to act in contravention of the rules of sound management. Consequently, it can be concluded that individual norms that dictate to public officials the subjective range of their responsibility are flawed and far from being compatible with the objective normative framework that exists for public responsibility. Furthermore, the sense of shame, and the fear of public disgrace and condemnation, have ceased to influence the conduct of public officials. Behaviour that falls short of the highest moral standards not only does not raise eyebrows but actually impresses political functionaries.

In our opinion, attention should focus on strengthening the moral and ethical framework of public responsibility. Investments must be made in education for moral values and public ethics and in their diffusion and internalization via socialization throughout the educational systems. Simultaneously, efforts must be directed towards the assimilation of moral values and public responsibility within the political system. Thus, an ethical contract for public officials could be drawn up that would obligate them to discharge their duties within the context of their public service in general, and within the framework of their positions as elected officials in particular. The ethical contract, which would be formulated in a positive manner and would insist on the public official's recognition of his social and national mission, would have no legal force, but every official would be required, while being sworn in to the Knesset or upon assuming office, to commit him or herself to adhere to the ethical principles set forth in the contract.

A supreme ethics committee for public officials, whose authority would be declarative only, may also be established. The committee could be composed of former Knesset chairpersons, a former Supreme Court president, a retired Supreme Court justice, a former president of Israel, senior academics from the social sciences, humanities and law, a former state comptroller, a former attorney general, a former civil service commissioner, a former prime minister and/or cabinet minister, former heads of social organizations, and winners of the Israel Prize in relevant fields. Committee members could be appointed by the president of Israel for a period to be determined by law, and they would deliberate over ethical issues posed by the conduct of public officials, whether on the committee members' initiative or upon the request of an organization, a public authority, or a group of citizens. The committee would be authorized to publish its opinion, which would be based on the ethical principles set forth in the ethical contract for public officials.

The ultimate goal is to restore to Israeli public officialdom a sense of modesty, humility, shame and, above all, a sense of the dignity of public office and of the reality of public sovereignty. Contrary to the rule that one should not humiliate others, elected officials should be paraded shame-faced before the public with a black cloud of disgrace hovering over them—disgrace imposed not by the media or even by mass public demonstrations, but rather by the ethical arbiters of Israeli society. The latter will not be empowered to enact legal sanctions, but the re-introduction of shame as a factor in the world of public service may institutionalize proper behaviour in general and the obligation to bear public responsibility in particular. And perhaps, in time, public officials will themselves come to raise the standards of subjective responsibility.

NOTES

1. *Deuteronomy* 21:7.
2. See Article 11(a) of the Companies Law, 5759-1999.
3. See ibid., Clauses 46–47.
4. See, for example, in Raanan Har-Zahav, *Israeli Administrative Law*, Jerusalem, 1996, p. 27.
5. See in Haim H. Cohn, *The Law*, Jerusalem, 1999, p. 284.
6. Ibid, p. 286.
7. See HCJ 140/70 *Shapira v. District Committee of the Israel Bar Association*, Jerusalem, *P.D.* 25(1) 325, 331: compare with HCJ 7074/93 *Suissa v. The State Attorney General*, *P.D.* 48(2) 749, 774.
8. The obligation of trusteeship places additional obligations and duties on the civil servant, such as fairness, reasonableness, honesty, integrity and straightforwardness (see for example HCJ 840/79 *The Association of Contractors and Builders in Israel v. The State of Israel*, P.D. 34(3) 729, 746–745), the obligation to act with efficiency (see for example in Yitzhak Zamir, *The Administrative Authority*, Jerusalem, 1996, p. 675), the obligation to be truthful (see for example HCJ 6163/92 *Eizenberg et al. v. The Minister of Construction and Housing*, P.D. 30(1) 673, 676), the obligation not to be involved in a conflict of interests (see for example HCJ 3132/92 *Mushlav v. The District Committee on Planning and Construction*, Northern District, P.D. 47(3) 741, 747).
9. See, for example, Albert O. Hirschman, *Exit, Voice and Loyalty: Responses to Decline in Firms, Organizations, and States*, Cambridge, MA, 1990.
10. See Joseph Cooper, 'The Puzzle of Distrust', in Joseph Cooper (ed.) *Congress and the Decline of Public Trust*, Boulder, CO, 1999, p. 1. Compare also with HCJ 6163/92, *Eizenberg*, p. 266.
11. In this article we will be dealing with elected officials only. Nevertheless, see the legislature's broader definition of 'civil servant' in Article 34(24) of the Penal Code, 5737-1977. Compare with Article 1 of the Interpretation Ordinance [New Version], and also with Article 1 of the Administrative Procedure (Statement of Reasons) Law, 5719-1958.
12. See in Asa Kasher, 'Professional Ethics', in Gabi Shpeller, Yehudit Achmon and Gabriel Weil (eds.), *Ethical Issues in the Emotional Therapeutic and Counseling Professions*, Jerusalem, 2003, pp. 15–29.
13. See Articles 2–3 of the *Basic Law: Human Dignity and Liberty*, and, later, Articles 5–7.
14. See for example in the *Report on Systemic Disciplinary Measures in the Public Service* (Kremenitzer Committee), Jerusalem, 1998.
15. See Terry L. Cooper, *The Responsible Administrator: An Approach to Ethics for the Administrative Role*, San Francisco, 1998, p. 66.
16. See HCJ 4267/93 *Amitai v. Prime Minister Yitzhak Rabin* 47(5) 441, 467 on the issue of Deputy Minister Pinchasi. Compare with the attorney general's letter regarding Deputy Minister Pinchasi and Minister Deri (ibid.).
17. A distinction may also be made between political corruption and 'managerial corruption', which refers to public administration employees who are not politicians. See more in James Campbell Scott, *Comparative Political Corruption*, Englewood Cliffs, NJ, 1972. Also

compare with John G. Peters and Susan Welch, 'Political Corruption in America: A Search for a Definition and a Theory', in *America Political Science Review*, Vol. 72 (1978), pp. 974–984.

18. See HCJ 297/82 *Berger v. The Minister of the Interior*, P.D. 37(3) 29, 47. See also HCJ 4537/96 *Massoud Shoshan et al. v. the I.D.F. Chief of General Staff*, P.D. 50(4) 416, 419.
19. See HCJ 4537/96 *Massoud Shoshan*, p. 422. Also compare with HCJ 297/82 *Berger*, p. 29.
20. See Ahron Barak, *Interpretation in Law (Volume 2—Interpretation of Legislation)*, Jerusalem, 1993, p. 42.
21. See Ahron Barak, *Judicial Discretion*, New Haven, CT, 1989. It should be noted that precisely for this reason the obligation of reasonableness is the subject of vigorous debate both among scholars and among the judges themselves. For further discussion see HCJ 1635/90 *Jarjavsky v. the Prime Minister*, P.D. 45(1) 749, the contradictory approaches of Justice Barak (who supports the obligation of reasonableness) and Judge Alon (who is vigorously opposed to the obligation of reasonableness).
22. Many have sought to define ministerial responsibility over the years. See, for example Geoffrey Marshal, 'Introduction', in Geoffrey Marshal (ed.), *Ministerial Responsibility*, Oxford, 1989, p. 7.
23. In 1918 in Great Britain the Haldane Committee decided on the issue of the distribution of responsibility. See Diana Woodhouse, *Ministers and Parliament*, Oxford, 1994, p. 49.
24. This is because junior employees are always the ones to perform the tasks in question, and thus are much more likely to be accused of negligence, of having erred or of having made incorrect decisions. See Cooper, *The Responsible Administrator*, pp. 71–75.
25. It should be reiterated that the present discussion is meant to address elected officials only (Knesset members and government ministers), not appointed bureaucrats.
26. See the detailed discussion of the majority of these cases in Dan Korn and Boaz Shapira, *Koalitziot* (Coalitions), Tel Aviv, 1997, pp. 239–364.
27. It is a commonly-held and erroneous assumption that Rabin resigned due to the dollar account incident; this was not the case. Yet, Rabin resigned in December 1976, after National Religious Party faction ministers initiated a vote of no confidence in the government in protest of F-15 jet landings in violation of the Sabbath.
28. Although from a critical perspective Netanyahu's act may be regarded as having been based on electoral motives rather than on ethical and moral considerations, it may still be concluded that the candidate for prime minister had recognized the voter's interest in his personal conduct, and the connection that the voter could presumably draw between the candidate's private behaviour and his ability to recruit supporters and to win the election.
29. In Great Britain, for example, Lord Carrington resigned from his government post due to accusations of faulty judgement and wrong decisions regarding Britain's Falkland Islands conflict. In the US, Speaker of the House and Republican Party leader Newt Gingrich resigned after the 1998 Congressional elections and the party's subsequent decline in power (despite the fact that it maintained its electoral advantage over the Democratic Party). In Norway, Labour Party leader Tornjoren Jegland resigned in a highly unusual incident while the party won 165 seats, and despite the fact that this represented twice the number of seats won by the second-largest party it still fell short by two (!) of the number of seats won by the Labour Party in the previous elections (in which it had won 167 seats).
30. See, for example, Article 10, which determines that agenda proposals (submitted by a particular minister) should include a description of the nature of the issue. Article 5 of the code of regulations states that when a decision's practicable interpretation involves a budgetary expenditure, the minister must present a financial estimate and the proposed funding sources, whether from the budget or not.
31. For further discussion see Yehezkel Dror, *Tazkir LeRosh Hamemshala* (Memorandum to the Prime Minister), Jerusalem, 1989.
32. For further discussion see David Deri and Emanuel Sharon, *Kalkala VePolitika BeTaktziv Hamedina* (Economics and Politics in the State Budget), Tel Aviv, 1994.
33. Budgetary procedures in other countries demonstrate that Israel's existing procedures are not carved in stone. See for example in Aaron Wildavsky and Naomy Caiden, *The New Politics of the Budgetary Process*, 4th edition, NJ, 2000. Compare with A. Schick, 'The Road to PPB: The Stages of Budget Reform', in F.J. Lyden and E.G. Miller (eds.), *Planning Programming Budgeting*, Chicago, 1996.

34. For further discussion of this topic see in David Nachmias and Eran Klein, *Hok Ha'Hesderim* (The Economic Arrangements Bill: Between Economics and Politics), Jerusalem, Israel Democracy Institute, 1999. In 1985 the Economic Arrangements Bill contained only 35 articles. On proposals to change the budgetary procedures see David Nachmias and Alona Nuri, *Tiktsuv Lefi Tfukot* (Output-Driven Management and Budgeting Principles in the Public Sector), Jerusalem, 1997.
35. On 28 January 1975 Aharon Yariv resigned his post in protest over the government's powerlessness while strongly criticizing the existing inefficient work methods. The Kobarsky Committee, appointed by the government in 1986 to conduct a comprehensive study of the civil service, also pointed out, in one of its recommendations, the need to change decision-making patterns. However, these recommendations, which were adopted by the government, were never implemented.
36. See Barak, *Interpretation in Law* (note 20 above and its accompanying text).
37. See the *Report of the Commission of Inquiry into the Events at the Refugee Camps in Beirut, 1983*, Jerusalem, the State of Israel, 1983, Section 91(b).
38. Sharon was appointed deputy prime minister on that day.
39. See Cohen, *Law*, p. 347.
40. See Article 4 of the *Basic Law: The Government* (5761-2001). In the *Basic Law: The Government* (5762-1992, containing the direct prime ministerial election procedure), it is stipulated that 'each Minister is responsible to the Prime Minister for his areas of responsibility, and he is accountable to the Knesset for the discharge of his duties' (Article 33(g) of the Law).
41. See, for example, Zamir, *Administrative Authority*, p. 351.
42. See Amnon Rubinstein, *Ha'Mishpat Ha'Konstitutsyini Shel Israel* (The Constitutional Law of the State of Israel), Tel Aviv, 1991, p. 731.
43. See Rubinstein, *The Constitutional Law*, p. 731.
44. This is the principle of parliamentary democracy, the essence of which is conveyed by Article 3 of the *Basic Law: The Government* (5761-2001): 'The Government holds office by virtue of the confidence of the Knesset'.
45. See Article 4 of the *Basic Law: The Government* (5761-2001).
46. See ibid.
47. See Article 11(g)(1,2) of the *Transition Law*, 5709-1949. In Article 11(g)(3) the principle of collective responsibility further obligates factions belonging to the government coalition. See also the Attorney General's opinion, 'The Obligation of Ministers to Government Decisions', of 19 Tammuz, 5757 (24 July 1997).
48. See Article 79(b) of the by-laws.
49. Incidents of this nature occurred during the period of the *Basic Law: The Government* (1992), which provided for direct prime ministerial elections, thereby moving the locus of responsibility to the prime minister while weakening even more the principle of collective responsibility. In Great Britain, for example, criticism of government policy by a minister in office is utterly inconceivable. See Amnon Rubinstein, 'Basic Law: The Government in its Original Form – in Practice', in *Mishpat Umimshal*, Vol. 3 (1996), p. 587.
50. See CA 281/82 *Abu Chatzeira v. M.Y.*, P.D. 37(3) 673, 704.
51. See *Report on Systemic Disciplinary Measures* (note 14 above), p. 8.
52. The words of Minister Tzipi Livni at a conference on 'Ethics for the Civil Service', held on 11 July 2001 (Ma'aleh Hachamisha Hotel), Jerusalem, the Prime Minister's Office, State and Internal Audit Department, February 2002, p. 9.
53. See ibid.
54. See *Report on Systemic Disciplinary Measures*, p. 9.
55. See HCJ 1993/03 *The Movement for Quality Government in Israel v. Prime Minister Ariel Sharon [et al.]*, P.D. 57(6) 817 (see the Judicial Authority website: www.court.gov.il).
56. See HCJ 2533/97 *The Movement for Quality Government in Israel v. the State of Israel*, P.D. 41(3) 46, 61–62.
57. See, for example, the attorney general's decision with regard to the prime minister's permitted manner of using military helicopters for political and party purposes (Instruction No. 1.1095); or his decision regarding appointments to public office during elections (Instruction No. 1.1501).

58. Elyakim Rubinstein, 'Decision of the Attorney General in the Matter of the Appointment of Roni Bar-On as Attorney General', quoted in Asher Arian, David Nachmias and Ruth Amir, *Executive Governance in Israel*, New York, 2002, pp. 70–71.
59. See HCJ 1993/03 *The Movement for Quality Government in Israel*, Section 3 of Justice Rivlin's ruling.
60. See Article 2b of the *Basic Law: The State Comptroller.*
61. For further discussion of the Tze'elim disaster as it relates to Ehud Barak, see Ben Caspit and Ilan Kfir, *Ehud Barak—Soldier Number 1*, Tel Aviv, 1998, pp. 255–268.
62. See the *Office of the State Comptroller (Special Report)—Report of the Comptroller's Findings Regarding the Tze'elim B Disaster*, Jerusalem, State Comptroller, 1999. See also the State Comptroller's Internet site: www.mevaker.gov.il.
63. See in Arian *et al.*, *Executive Governance in Israel*, pp. 80–84.
64. See the *Commissions of Inquiry Law 5729-1968*, Article 1. The legal authority to appoint a commission of inquiry is also given to the Knesset Committee for State Audit Affairs, according to Article 14(b) of the *State Comptroller Law.* Compare also with HCJ 390/85 *Bank Leumi LeIsrael, Ltd. v. the Commission of Inquiry on the Regulation of Bank Shares*, P.D. 39(4), with regard to the authority of a commission of inquiry established by decision of the Committee for State Audit Affairs, rather than by government decision.
65. See ibid., Article 8(a–b). Compare with Avigdor Kalgsblad, *Vaadot Hakira* (Official Commissions of Inquiry), Jerusalem, 2001, pp. 21–23, on the elements common to all official commissions of inquiry in the countries reviewed.
66. See Zeev Segel, 'Commission of Inquiry by Virtue of Commissions of Inquiry 1968', in *Mechkerei Mishpat* (Bar-Ilan Law Studies), Vol. 3 (1984), p. 220. Compare with M. Ben-Ze'ev, 'The Political Echelon and Commissions of Inquiry—Conflict, Tension, Fears', in Menahem Alon (ed.), *Sefer Yitzhak Cohen*, Tel Aviv, 1989, p. 236.
67. See *Report of the Commission of Inquiry into the Events at the Refugee Camps in Beirut*, pp. 76–77.
68. Up to now there were 15 official commissions of inquiry that have been appointed by virtue of the *Commissions of Inquiry Law 1968.*
69. See *Report of the Commission of Inquiry into the Events at the Refugee Camps in Beirut*, 86–88, Section 81(c).
70. See Asher Arian, David Nachmias, Doron Navot and Daniel Shani, *Madad Hademokratia* (The 2003 Israeli Democracy Index), Jerusalem, 2003.

After the Storm? The Israeli Supreme Court and the Arab-Palestinian Minority in the Aftermath of October 2000

ILAN SABAN

In late September 2000, the Oslo process collapsed and the second *Intifada* erupted. Soon after that (during the first two weeks of October) something momentous occurred in inter-communal relations in Israel. The Arab-Palestinian citizens of Israel engaged in violent demonstrations. The police reacted with excessive violence and 13 demonstrators were killed. The wave of violent demonstrations within Israel soon receded and ended, but Israeli society has not returned to the same point.[1] The purpose of the article is to analyze major aspects of the performance of the Israeli Supreme Court vis-à-vis the Arab-Palestinian minority since October 2000.

The article will advance three arguments. First, the Supreme Court has truly held the post of guardian of the democratic threshold. Second, the court serves (sometimes unintentionally) as a guide or a mediator demarcating an intermediate path for Israeli society; one which will thread the middle ground between two almost polar options for Israeli society: The bi-national state (an idea which gains popularity with the minority but is rejected outright by the Jewish majority), and the existing status quo (strongly resented by the minority). This intermediate path, or bridging vision, may prove a defence against a violent breakdown of inter-communal relations in Israel proper. The third argument goes in the other direction and criticizes the court. The Supreme Court often evades action corresponding with the direction it has itself signalled, and its reluctance to act in these instances cannot be explained by major legitimization difficulties in standing by the minority. Taken together this two-steps-forward-one-step-back performance paints a somewhat enigmatic picture.[2]

An assessment of the 'margin of appreciation' allowed to the court in recent years and an examination of its action within this margin is at the heart of the analysis offered in this article. The margin of appreciation is a term that in legal discourse has mainly served the Supreme Court (and other courts) in its review of other authorities. It refers to the scope of discretion enjoyed by domestic state institutions in the execution of the authority vested in them—the degree of deference the judiciary must exercise in reviewing their performance.[3] This article intends to redirect this 'scope of discretion issue' towards the court and use it as the basis of a review of *its* actions and evasions in regard to the Arab minority.

THE MARGIN OF APPRECIATION ENJOYED BY THE SUPREME COURT IN RECENT YEARS

The legal and socio-political environment in which the court exercises its authority defines the margin of appreciation under which it functions. This environment is dynamic and susceptible to many variables, and the court is not only an object of its fluctuations but also an agent in creating them. The following is a brief enumeration of seven of the major developments and processes that colour the legal and socio-political environment in recent years. Some of them leave the court at greater liberty to improve the lot of the Arab minority, should it so choose, and others limit this freedom.

(1) For a long time (especially from the second part of the 1970s onward), the court's jurisprudence has been marked by the theory of interpretation it has adopted—Purposive Interpretation. This theory provides a very significant interpretive weight to the basic values of Israel as a liberal-democratic 'Jewish and democratic state'.

(2) The court has exercised judicial activism in two main ways (a) widening access to it by redefining the thresholds for entry: liberalizing the right of standing and narrowing the doctrine of 'justiciability'; and (b) augmenting the basis for substantive judicial review by imposing important obligations upon every authority: especially the need for reasonableness and proportionality in the choice of means in the service of legitimate aims.

(3) In the early 1990s, important elements of constitutionalism became part of the Israeli regime. This included impressive constitutional developments, which came to be known as the 'constitutional revolution'. There were three such developments: the passing of Basic Law: Human Dignity and Liberty; the passing of Basic Law: Freedom of Occupation; and *Mizrachi Bank v. Migdal Co-operative Village*, perhaps the most important ruling ever in Israeli law, in which the Supreme Court determined the significance of the other two developments.[4] The net outcome has been that new legislation is now deemed valid only if it does not conflict with the Basic Laws. Crucial here are the conditions of the limitation clause, which states

that: 'There shall be no violation of rights under this Basic Law except by a law befitting the values of the State of Israel, enacted for a proper purpose, and to an extent no greater than is required.'[5]

(4) An escalating struggle against the Supreme Court is rolling on. The proponents of this move are mainly conservative, religious and right-wing Knesset members. Recently a disturbing occurrence has taken place. Minister of Justice, Professor Daniel Friedman, has been waging a campaign to deeply curtail the changes that followed the constitutional revolution, by proposing inter alia to change the judges' selection process, introducing restrictions on the basis upon which a judicial review of statutes is conducted, and adding a very broad 'overriding mechanism' (to allow the Knesset to revive statutes notwithstanding the finding of the court that they contradict one or more of the Basic Laws).

(5) However, as a (somewhat) balancing phenomenon, there is a parallel ascendance of an assertive civil society that often addresses the Supreme Court.[6]

(6) Outside factors are also at play. There is a global phenomenon that affects the environment in which the court operates. In the wake of horrific events of the past two decades in Africa and the Balkans, international civil society has become more vigilant. As it accumulates force this society is creating a 'human rights culture' bent upon closer scrutiny of state abuses of human rights. Monitoring Israel is more frequent nowadays, especially Israel's activities in the occupied territories, but also those within Israel's recognized borders.

(7) Probably the most important and critical events to our discussion of the court and the Arab-Palestinian minority were already mentioned: the violent shattering of the Oslo euphoria of 1993–1995 and the eruption of the second *Intifada*, in September 2000, and the October events within Israel proper.

These seven developments and processes are crucial to any socio-legal analysis of Israeli reality. However, an understanding of the margin of appreciation enjoyed by the Supreme Court in its dealing with the Arab minority is dependent upon a fuller picture of the fundamental characteristics of Israeli society.

The Margin of the Court's Freedom—Three Contributing Factors: Zionism's Tenets, the Israeli-Palestinian Conflict and Conceptions Concerning the Minority's Stand in the Conflict

This article will address only two of the basic facts that colour the socio-political status of the minority and that limit the court's ability to radically alter it (even should it wish to do so).

The first factor is the Jewish majority's fear of the Arab minority. In light of the relative strength of the two national communities this fear seems strange—like some commissioned emotion, the validity of which nobody cares to examine too closely. However unlikely it may seem, the fear is genuine. It is part of its inner discourse, as opposed to arguments which are directed solely to foreign observers. The fear is an outcome of several factors. One—the violent conflict between the nation of the minority and the state of the minority constitutes indeed a potentially inflammable triangle.[7] Two—there is considerable credibility to the common Jewish majority's fear that no sustainable resolution of the Israeli–Palestinian conflict is in sight.

It will probably not be resolved even should the two-state solution be finally adopted and implemented (not even if Israel withdraws fully to the Green Line and the question of Jerusalem is settled). The open issue of the right of return of the Palestinian refugees is likely to continue to fester and wreak havoc. Moreover, the future is clouded by the potential demands of the Arab-Palestinian minority for unification with their people in a bi-national Palestine/Israel. Alternatively, some Arab-Palestinian citizens of Israel will surely strive—even more forcefully than at present—for a bi-national Israel, alongside Palestine. In short, even should a two-state solution be concluded with the majority of the Palestinians some will still seriously challenge Israel's basic framework. What strengthens the (mutual) fear between Arabs and Jews is the presence of a non-constructive vagueness. The deep suspicion between the two peoples results in their tendency to 'fill the gaps', 'resolve' uncertainties, with the more apocalyptic scenarios.

The net outcome is that for many (on all sides) the conclusion is that a choice must be made with only two options to choose from—the bi-national state or the status quo. This dichotomy is dangerous because it produces an 'all or nothing' state of mind. Be that as it may, the majority community in Israel is continuously on guard in its dealings with the minority. This emotion is a disincentive to grant the minority rights to self-government and is partially the motive for ambitious national projects that have taken place such as Judaizing the Galilee.

The second basic fact that contributes to the marginalization of the Arab minority is the Jewish majority's perception of the Zionist project as an ongoing one, its requirements almost as vital today as ever. The Jewish state has defined its *raison d'être* as the ingathering of the Jews and creation of a safe haven for the Jewish people, so even if these goals had not been disputed, they have yet to be completed. This is the psychological mechanism that lends such potency to the Jewish law of return and to the conviction that land reserves must be held in wait for those still to come.

There are other basic factors of the Jewish community that play a role in the marginalization of the Arab-Palestinian minority, but lie outside the scope of this article. One such factor is the ethnocentricity of a large part of the Jewish community. To discuss this would involve the tough question of whether it is a hard-core, intractable trait or a reaction to the security threat that may fade away in brighter days. Thus, delineated by the perceived existential/security needs and by the perceived ongoing justifications and needs of Zionism, we find in Israeli society a set of strongly held axioms, which are almost impossible to change and are imposed (and self-imposed) on the court. They are the walls it cannot and will not break.

Another Factor Constructing the Court's Margin of Appreciation: The Need for Legitimacy, both Legal and Socio-political

The court cannot ignore the axioms of the Jewish state without losing its legitimacy in the eyes of a large portion of the majority community in Israel and will possibly cross, in the process, the lines of legal legitimacy.

From the standpoint of Israeli law this crossing of the lines may happen because the actions of the court are limited to the authority vested in it by Israeli law. The Israeli law's basic values include preserving Israel as a Jewish (and democratic) state—this is 'a constitutional basic fact'.[8] The court is not permitted then to approve petitions and provide remedies aimed at altering Israel's fundamental framework through interpretation or by any other means.

As regards the socio-political legitimacy—the past decade has been very trying for the Supreme Court. True, the constitutional revolution and other judicial processes mentioned above have empowered the court and enabled impressive achievements in the sphere of human rights (within Israel proper). At the same time, however, the court has become much more controversial. It became the object of intense and vociferous objection of the religious and ultra-orthodox parties and the political right.[9]

In the view of this author what dictates this caution is both the court's somewhat waning public legitimacy and its frail constitutional protection, and this frailty and its origins will be expanded on here. As a tool for social change the law is a double-edged sword. Though it may sometimes serve as a lever of change in the hands of the minority and its sympathizers, it is also a system mobilized by the majority to further its interests vis-à-vis the minority—to empower itself, gloss over its wrongdoings, etc. What we find is that whereas for the marginalized minority the court is an essential medium for translating the domestic law into social change, the majority community is much less dependent upon it. Moreover, when, and if, the majority comes to think of the court as a nuisance it can simply change the norms that the court interprets and enforces, or even use majority power to restrict the court's powers.

The question that arises is whether, after the constitutional revolution that introduced judicial review of legislation and set constitutional limits to majority rule, the majority can still exercise such overriding power. The answer is that the effect of the constitutional revolution should not be exaggerated. Majority rule has been circumscribed but not seriously enough. The Basic Laws are not entrenched. Change and annulment of the basic laws is an easy process under the current constitutional regime. For example, Basic Law: Freedom of Occupation has been changed three times since it was promulgated in the 1990s. With a few exceptions, all that it takes to change a basic law under the present conditions—even Basic Law: Human Dignity and Freedom and, indeed even Basic Law: The Judiciary—is an ordinary majority in the Knesset.[10] The easy formal procedure for amending the Israeli constitution is of course not equivalent to the practical possibility to do so; nevertheless the formal state of affairs marks the frailty of the constitutional safeguards on civil rights in Israel and on the Supreme Court itself. The court is apparently aware of its own vulnerability. A clarifying example may attests to that, it is the court decision regarding the painful issue of the displaced Arab citizens of the village of Ikrit.[11]

In the Ikrit case the court acknowledged that the government had made a promise to allow the displaced persons of Ikrit to return to their land, but freed it of the obligation on the basis of the Discharge Doctrine: the power of the authority to repudiate obligations it took when a vital public interest is at stake. So says the court:

> In the case under review, the Libai Committee has based its recommendations [to return the displaced persons to part of the Ikrit lands] among other things upon political changes that have occurred in the region, including the peace agreement with the Palestinian Authority (the Oslo Accord). However, as has been said, the political situation has since changed and the Prime Minister believes that in view of these changes, and at this time—when the demand for a Right of Return is again being voiced—the precedent of returning the villagers of Ikrit may be detrimental to the vital interests of the State. This position relates to a political matter in which the government has wide scope for discretion. Under such circumstances there is no legal basis for holding the State to the Governmental promise to resettle the displaced persons in Ikrit.[12]

The important point is that the compelling legal force of the displaced villagers' claim and the outcome of their petition cannot be reconciled from a legal point of view.

There is no real basis to the right-of-return precedent kind of argument, since the case of the displaced persons in Israel is markedly different from the Palestinian refugees' case. First, the displaced persons in Israel are its own citizens—allowing them to resettle has no bearing whatsoever on the demographic makeup of the Jewish state. Second, the displacement of the inhabitants of Ikrit and Biram (and a few other places) took place under a certain set of circumstances which bears a certain uniqueness. Indeed, when an Arab populace acted peacefully during war, left its hamlet when ordered and with the official promise of return after a short period, and when its return does not uproot others (who may have now lived there for decades), the obvious obligation is to respect the promise. In short, there is a strong case against linking the fate of the Ikrit villagers and their descendants to the demand for the right of return. The threat of precedence waved about by the government is simply false or at least utterly unsubstantiated. The governmental decision to break its promise falls then outside the bounds of reasonableness and should therefore not have been upheld by the court.

This is why this case is revealing. The court's choice to defer to the governmental decision illustrates its sense of vulnerability and its wariness of taking steps that could be construed as crossing axiomatic taboos (such as the Palestinian right of return). In other words, under the conditions of current Israeli political culture (and a weak constitutional safeguarding of its own status) the court probably found it hard to trust the public to follow such 'niceties' as the difference between displaced Arab-Palestinian citizens and the Palestinian refugees.

This example somewhat clarifies the margin of appreciation under which the court operates, or perceives itself to operate. To reiterate—this margin may somewhat widen but it is not unbounded nor is it determined by the court alone. It is not decided only on the basis of the legal legitimacy of a court decision but takes into account the socio-political legitimacy of it as well, i.e., we are led to consider what may erode the court's status to breaking point. Security and demography are the great popular fears which the court is wary of interfering with. On the other hand, and as a balance, the court's margin of appreciation should not be underestimated. After all Israel is a professed democratic as well as a Jewish state, and its democratic commitments also sketch its axioms and red lines and they too must not be crossed.

Moreover, Israel and its courts are monitored by the international community which helps recognize these red lines. If the Israeli Supreme Court is the local watchman, the international community is its bigger counterpart, there to back it up and bolster it.[13] Moreover, the court's margin of appreciation is deeply affected by the legal environment in which it operates, and to which it is also partially responsible. The court has consolidated some impressive tools: purposive interpretation, additional means of judicial activism and helping to bring about (moderate) judicial review of legislation. With this composite portrayal it is now possible to decide the central question of this article—how do we assess the court's activity vis-à-vis the Arab-Palestinian minority? This article will point to two real achievements and one major failure.

ANALYSIS OF THE COURT'S FUNCTION IN LIGHT OF ITS MARGIN OF APPRECIATION

Guard of the Democratic Threshold (within Israel Proper) and a Major Aid to the Establishment of an Arab-Palestinian Civil Society in Israel

The role of the Supreme Court as a guardian of the Arab-Palestinian minority's civil and political rights has come into sharp relief since the October 2000 events. View the following examples. The court reversed the decision of the Central Elections Committee to disqualify the candidacy of two Arab members of the Knesset running for re-election (MKs Bishara and Tibi) and the candidacy of a central Arab party (Balad) that advocates a radical agenda with regard to Israel.[14]

The court invalidated a decision of the chairperson of the Central Elections Committee who instructed against broadcasting an election campaign film which made use of the Palestinian flag. The court ruled that the use of the flag comes under the protection of freedom of expression.[15]

The Supreme Court revoked the decision of the Israeli Censorship Board to disallow the screening of the film *Jenin-Jenin*. Through the film the Israeli Arab director Muhammad Bakri gave voice to the narrative of the Jenin refugee camp population regarding the events that took place in the course of the Israeli army operation 'Defensive Shield' in March–April 2002.[16]

There is another, earlier, case, from March 2000, that is worthy of note—the *Kaadan* case. The direct result of the ruling was the limitation of the state's ability to discriminate against Arabs in the allocation of state-owned land, either directly or through a third party. A second result, to which this article will return below, is the highlighting, at least in the rhetoric of the court, of the need to regard public policy towards the Arab minority with due suspicion and strict scrutiny. 'Differential treatment due to religion or nationality is "suspect" and seemingly discriminatory.'[17]

Now, in addition to the provision of essential protection to the democratic threshold, the court has been instrumental in setting up extra-legal instruments for the benefit of the minority. I refer mainly to its contribution to the establishment and nurturing of Arab-Palestinian civil society. The court's contribution lies in the protection it vouchsafed over the years to the freedom of association, expression and information,[18] but even more so in the judicial developments enumerated above—purposive interpretation, judicial activism and the judicial review of legislation. These undertakings have empowered the legally oriented civil society associations. Once established within the minority, these organizations joined forces with Arab parties and other minority leadership bodies for a more systematic and thorough discussion of the aims of the minority and the methods by which they may be achieved. The result was that for the first time the minority presented the state with a developed, transformative agenda.[19] This agenda is expressed, among other means, by these civil society organizations constantly seeking recourse to the Supreme Court. They bring before the court matters never before discussed there and at an unprecedented rate.[20]

An Inter-Communal Bridge and Catalyst of the Public Debate in Israel

Besides its role as keeper of the red lines and in addition to its contribution to the evolution of an Arab-Palestinian civil society inside Israel, the court fulfils another less recognized role. As suggested above, one of the severe problems in the Israeli–Palestinian conflict and the relationship between Jews and Arabs in Israel is that most of those involved view it as a win all-lose-all type battle. All sides feel cornered.

These conceptions are based upon an assumption of a binary reality. It holds only two possible options for the adversaries—either a continuation of the current status quo abhorred by Palestinians in the occupied territories and in Israel, or the bi-national state solution that is rejected outright by Israeli Jews. The outstanding step that the court has been taking is to help break up this polar view of things. It is offering, albeit implicitly, a third way—a bridging vision: Israel will remain Jewish in a few important respects, but it will become much more democratic, by being genuinely committed to upholding the equality of the common citizenship rights (civil, political, social and economic rights), and expanding certain minority (group-differentiated) rights.[21]

The court decision discussed above, in which the Supreme Court ruled for Balad, Bishara and Tibi against the central elections committee, which wished to disqualify their candidacy for the Knesset, contains two bridging or anti-dichotomous aspects. First, as regards the relationship between the minority and its people—the court insisted on the right of the Arab minority to give a complex answer to the thorny question posed by a large portion of the Jewish public—are you for us or against us? The court rejected the yes–no ultimatum and sanctioned a fair middle road for the minority. It allowed the minority to voice clear and loud solidarity with its own and to object to the policy its state was executing against its brethren, while at the same time prohibiting it from joining forces with its people in the armed struggle against its state. Secondly, and importantly, in the Tibi decision the court sketched a 'thin version' of the Jewish state's taboos. See especially the following:

> What, then, are the 'core' characteristics that constitute the minimum definition of the State of Israel as a Jewish state? These characteristics have both a Zionist and a heritage aspect ... At their centre stands the right of every Jew to immigrate to the State of Israel, in which Jews will constitute a majority; Hebrew is the main official language of the state and most of its holidays and symbols reflect the national revival of the

> Jewish people; the Jewish heritage is a major element of its religious and cultural heritage.[22]

This is a 'thin' formulation of the axiomatic national characteristics of Israel, in the name of which the minority's right to attempt to change Israel's national character is restricted. The 'thinness' of the court's definition is twofold. First, while the synthesis 'Jewish and Democratic' guarantees the protection of the Jewish right of return as well as the dominance ('most') of the Jewish symbols in the symbolic order of Israel, it does not envision Jewish *exclusivity* in this realm of the cultural and national symbols. This may allow expansion of the presence of the minority in the images and symbols that represent 'Israeliness'.[23] Second, as regards all other public goods (apart from the symbolic ones and from immigration quotas) this understanding of the Jewish and Democratic synthesis led the court to assert that the state cannot discriminate against the minority in the allocation of any material public goods including in the sensitive sphere of land allocation.[24]

The second court case to be discussed has to do with the complicated and sensitive issue of group-differentiated rights (sometimes called, somewhat inaccurately, collective rights). It is usually assumed that the commitment to equality undertaken by the Jewish and democratic state relates only to the common citizenship rights (civil, political, social and economic rights, including the prohibition to discriminate on the basis of group affiliation), but that there is no obligation to equality in the realm of group-differentiated rights extended to the two national communities in Israel. This state of affairs has not changed. However, the court has clarified that the minority does enjoy various group-differentiated rights (linguistic rights, in this case) and Chief Justice Barak even found a way of extending the linguistic rights beyond what is granted in Article 82 of the Palestine Order in Council, 1922, that regulates this subject. I refer to the case of *Adalah and the Association for Civil Rights in Israel v. the Municipality of Tel-Aviv Jaffa et al.*[25] The court decision addressed the issue of the language(s) of the municipal signs in mixed towns—Tel Aviv Jaffa, Ramla, Lod and Nazareth Illit (in the mixed towns of Acre, Haifa and Jerusalem a previous arrangement regarding bilingual municipal signs was already in practice). The ruling is rather complex; I will only underline the development seen in the majority ruling of Chief Justice Barak. He seems there to take a step of real importance. He draws a distinction between the Arab minority and other minority groups in Israeli society, as a basis for the allocation of a group-differentiated right to the former and to no other minority. A central paragraph in the ruling states:

> Against this background the following question may arise: What distinguishes the Arabic language, and why is its status different from that of several other languages—in addition to Hebrew—that Israelis

> speak? Does our approach not imply that residents of different towns in which there are minority groups of speakers of various languages, will now be able to demand that the signs in their towns will be in their language as well? My response is negative, *since none of those languages are the same as Arabic*. The uniqueness of the Arabic language is twofold. First, Arabic is the language of the largest minority in Israel, *who has been living here for ages*. This is a language that is linked to cultural, historical, and religious attributes of the Arab minority group in Israel. This is the language of citizens who, notwithstanding the Arab–Israeli conflict, wish to live in Israel as loyal citizens with equal rights, amid respect for their language and culture. The desire to ensure dignified coexistence between the descendants of our forefather Abraham, in mutual tolerance and equality, justifies recognizing the use of the Arabic language in urban signs—in those cities in which there is a substantial Arab minority (6%–19% of the population)—alongside its senior sister, Hebrew.[26]

In short, the court is here expanding minority linguistic rights, based on a crucial distinction between homeland minorities and immigrant groups. For the first time, the Arab-Palestinian minority's distinctness as a 'homeland (national) minority' is recognized (albeit thus far only by the president of the court). In addition, the need for peaceful co-existence is not being used here to justify limitations on the minority (to safeguard public order, prevent incitement etc.) but rather as a source from which emanate duties of the state towards the minority.[27]

The third and last court decision the article will review is the ruling given in *The Association for Civil Rights in Israel v. The Government of Israel*.[28] It deals with the composition of the Council of the Israel Lands Administration, and the issue of nominating Arab members to it. The court ruled that an obligation of appropriate representation is in order in the context of the minority and the Council, and directed the government, giving basic guidelines, to realize this obligation. A significant point is that the decision was not based on existing legislation (the statutory obligations in the sphere of appropriate representation do not apply to the Council). It was a jurisprudential leap to fill a lacuna by drawing an analogy in light of Israel's basic values. However, this ruling in the present context is mentioned for another reason. The decision adds two distinctions to the one mentioned above (between a native minority and an immigrant group), and together they serve to counter a simplistic analogy present in the Israeli public discourse between the Arab minority and other marginalized groups. The first of these two additional distinctions is simply that the causes of discrimination of Arabs in Israeli society is a great deal more complex and harder to eradicate; the second is that the weight of communal needs of the Arab minority corresponds to a heavier claim for representation in various societal institutions. See, for example, the following extract from the court ruling:

> The question of what is appropriate representation in a particular body depends, among other things, on the nature of the body, and on its practical importance from the standpoint of the group that is entitled to appropriate representation. Accordingly, it appears that the importance of the representation and the extent of the representation in the Israel Lands Administration are greater for members of the Arab population than, for example, for people with disabilities.[29]

In short, in this series of rulings carrying significant remedies the court is fertilizing the Israeli discourse regarding Arab–Jewish relations in Israeli society. It argues convincingly against superficial symmetry; it outlines attributes that single out the Arab-Palestinian minority and its circumstances in Israeli society. On the basis of its singularity the court points out the fair claim of the Arab-Palestinian minority for group-differentiated rights (linguistic and participatory, in the concrete cases) and the need for more vigilance on behalf of the court with regard to the protection of the minority from discrimination (land allocation, in the concrete case of *Kaadan*).[30] By these moves the court might be seen as offering Israeli society a different pattern of inter-communal relations—the bridging vision mentioned above.

The Complementary Dimension: The Court is Not Doing Enough to Bring Israeli Society Closer to the Bridging Vision that it has Marked Out

A portrayal of the court's performance and function vis-à-vis the national minority in Israel would be incomplete without demarcating its shortcomings. To put things concisely but accurately, the court does not sufficiently practise what it preaches.

Most of the petitions brought before the court by human rights organizations on behalf of the Arab minority are not jurisprudentially innovative. They do not for the most part force the court to collide with the political branches, as would remedies of social rights (often linked to priorities in budgeting) or remedial historic justice (as was conceived to be involved in the Ikrit case). Most petitions led by the minority aim at civil and political rights or the allocation of material public goods. The latter kind of petition is founded on a quite simple legal claim—a demand that the state fulfil its most mundane obligation towards its citizens—that gives minority members the same as others. Moreover, there is no real argument regarding the facts—the persistent discrimination of the Arab-Palestinian minority, its scope and duration.[31]

Here one sees the gap between the rhetoric and practice of the court itself. In practice the court usually avoids strict scrutiny of governmental policy in petitions regarding discrimination of Arabs, whereas in other contexts such scrutiny has been implemented.[32] The following are a few examples.

First, in several cases, despite hard data presented by the litigants, the court has chosen not to shift the burden onto the government to explain away this data. See, for example, the following court rulings—the allocation of land for 'lonely farms' in undeveloped regions ('Hityashvut Bodedeem') only to Jews;[33] the Religious Affairs Ministry budget;[34] representation of Arab women in the directorate of government corporations;[35] kindergartens for the under-fives in unrecognized Bedouin villages in the Negev.[36] One may assert that as regards the burden of proof the Israeli Supreme Court is behaving very differently towards the Arab population than towards most other petitioners claiming group discrimination and differently too from other judicial systems bent upon eliminating discrimination. In the USA discrimination on the basis of race or national affiliation is perceived as particularly suspect and therefore requires the State to pass demanding tests of proof. The litigants in such cases have an initial relatively light burden of proof after which the burden of proof lies with the respondents (the authorities) and they have to prove the reverse is true.[37]

Secondly, a court that aspires to put an end to discrimination would be expected to provide suitable remedies. Among other things it is expected to instruct the discriminating authority to undo the wrong already committed in the disproportionate allocation of assets by allocation to the wronged party of at least part of its due to the past and longstanding discrimination. Failing to do so is tantamount to rewarding the culprit (all the discriminator has to fear is an injunction to cease discrimination from the time of judicial intervention). The court thus fails to adopt the appropriate remedy with regard to the Arab-Palestinian minority.[38]

Thirdly, a court that wishes to eradicate discrimination would be expected to intervene forthwith once such cases are brought to its knowledge. Such is not the case here. Petitions of this type often drag on for years and more often than not the court is satisfied with promises by the discriminating authority to 'make an effort' or to 'amend in the course of a few years'. So, for example, in the petition concerning the budgeting of a programme in aid of underperforming school children, the court issued its ruling three years after the petition was filed, and it deferred to the state's plan to eradicate the discrimination gradually over five more years.[39] Another case in point is the petition concerning discrimination against Arab municipalities in the allocation of equalizing budgets by the Interior Ministry that was filed in 2001 and was decided only in 2006.[40] This is a very partial list.[41]

All that can be said is that the 'bridging vision' that the court offers Israeli society through a few landmark cases is losing its credibility and its potential to become a real alternative, due to the court's own treatment of many of the petitions brought before it on behalf of the minority. As mentioned above, these petitions do not carry a heavy challenge—demanding only what seems to be indisputably the minority due, and in complete agreement with the moral rhetoric of the state. No judicial difficulty attends them and still they are dragged out over time and even if concluded in favour of the litigants they are often diluted in their remedies. Why should the Arab minority put its faith in the bridging vision that the court offers if the court itself behaves as if it is ambivalent about it?[42]

CONCLUSIONS

The three dimensions that make up the picture of the court's performance towards the Arab minority are all clearly defined but not so the resulting picture.

First, the Supreme Court has not tried, and is not likely to try, to urge Israel to replace the current paradigm ('a Jewish and democratic state') with a bi-national one. The minority may as well give up trying to challenge it into doing so. The reason is that the court would probably find such a transformation both legally insurmountable and not called for morally (or even morally improper).[43]

Second and inversely, the court is simultaneously aware of its own vulnerability and the frailty of Israeli society. It is therefore seeking a path for society that might alleviate the pressure upon its weak links a little. This quest has led it to guard seriously the democratic threshold of Israeli democracy within Israel proper (mainly in terms of the Arab citizens' civil and political rights), and occasionally it has led the court to mark out distinctions and take steps that break the dichotomy of status quo versus bi-nationalism without overriding the Zionist paradigm. It demarcated an option in which none of what the Israeli-Jewish community sanctifies is demolished but some of its sacred cows are slimmed down to allow more room for fairness in the inter-communal relationship vis-à-vis the Arab-Palestinian minority.

The last of the three dimensions that make up the picture throws shadows over the court's achievements. The court seems neither consistent nor determined enough. This is especially apparent in cases where the court rejects or offers inadequate remedies when petitions over discrimination in allocation of material public goods are brought before it, despite the fact that these claims are neither challenging from a legal point of view nor too sensitive politically.

There is no real explanation for this rather bewildering performance. Perhaps the court is tired of its role as the keeper of the moat. That would be understandable—it is a lonely and thankless mission, accompanied by censure more often than appreciation. However, neither the court nor anyone else may indulge in fatigue or in make-believe peace and quiet. This will only lead us to bad decisions at the fateful crossroad(s) that Israeli society has reached.

NOTES

1. Several points need to be stressed with respect to these grave incidents, known as the 'October events'. First, the Arab-Palestinian violence within Israel was limited to stone-throwing (in rare instances firebombs were also thrown). Second, to the discredit of some demonstrators, policemen were not the only target of their violence; occasionally stone-throwing was also directed at Jewish civilians, and in one incident a Jewish civilian was in fact killed. Third, in some cases, particularly in mixed cities, civil violence was perpetrated in the opposite direction, with Jewish demonstrators attacking Arabs and Arab property. Fourth, and most important, these violent events produced a deep distrust between the two communities within Israel. Israeli Palestinians, for their part, experienced a confluence of external repression (of their brethren in the occupied territories) and internal repression. The Jewish majority's experience, however, mirrored that of Israeli Palestinians: They were assaulted both externally (in the territories) and internally. Most of these points are lucidly set out in the report of the official Commission of Inquiry into the October 2000 events (*The Or Commission Report*, 2003) available [Hebrew] at: http://elyon1.court.gov.il/heb/veadot/or/inside_index.htm.
2. Another, fourth, role of the Supreme Court will not be dealt with here. It concerns the distinction between the performance of the court in a given context and its impact in that context. Addressing the latter would involve examination of what might be termed 'peripheral radiation'—the influence of the court upon the Arab minority emanating from the significance of general norms that the court defines in contexts other than the minority. This is too wide a question for the present analysis to accommodate. Suffice to say that due to the generic nature of legal norms, it is difficult to design or apply them in a selective fashion. Thus, the norms that were crystallized in cases involving individuals (or groups) versus the state in matters of religion and state, or political, economic, factional or gender-linked strife within the majority community, often have almost inevitable ramifications for individuals outside this community—i.e., Arab citizens. For a discussion of the court's impact via 'peripheral radiation', see Ilan Saban, 'The Impact of the Supreme Court on the Status of the Arabs in Israel', *Mishpat uMimshal*, Vol. 3 (1996), p. 541–569 (in Hebrew), especially pp. 551, 557–566. Only in one instance in the present article will I refer to the indirect impact of the court—its contribution to the ascendance of a civil society within the minority. Otherwise I will deal only with the court's performance.
3. The modern origin of the term 'margin of appreciation' is probably the jurisprudence of the European Court of Human Rights. The deference it implies varies according to the relevant institution function and status. So, for example, the Israeli Supreme Court has marked the parliament, the Knesset, in its legislative function, for special deference.
4. See C.A. 6821/93, *Mizrachi Bank v. Migdal Co-operative Village*, 49(4) P.D. 221.
5. Article 8 of Basic Law: Human Dignity and Liberty. A similar provision appears in Article 4 of Basic Law: Freedom of Occupation.
6. For an updated discussion see for example see Yoav Dotan and Menachem Hofnung, 'Interest Groups in the Israeli High Court of Justice: Measuring Success in Litigation and in Out-of-Court Settlements', *Law and Policy*, Vol. 23, No. 1 (2001), pp. 1–27.
7. Some familiar analogies would seem to validate the Jewish majority fear of this 'loaded triangle'-type situation. See, for example, the 1960s–70s violence between the Greek majority and Turkish minority in Cyprus that corresponded with the tension between Greece and Turkey; or the Albanian minorities in the Balkans and the Kosovo and Macedonia clashes of recent years. In many of these instances the problems arise from a situation of a 'double minority': the instability is engendered by some 'manic-depressive' factor in the make-up of each side, as they feel at the same time a minority and majority. The minority, by definition is such in its own state of citizenship, but the majority is often a minority on the regional level and feels besieged.
8. Chief Justice Agranat, E.A. 1/65 *Yardor v. Chairman of the Central Elections Committee*, P.D. 19(3) 367, p. 385; David Kretzmer, *The Legal Status of the Arabs in Israel*, Boulder, CO, 1990, pp. 22–31.
9. Gershon Shafir and Yoav Peled, *Being Israeli: The Dynamics of Multiple Citizenship*, Cambridge, 2002, pp. 276–277; Gad Barzilai, *Communities and Law: Politics and Cultures of Legal Identities*, Ann Arbor, MI, 2003, pp. 235–239, 243–245.

10. Compared to the long and arduous path to constitutional amendment in the US. Think for example of the poor chances of altering the Supreme Court decisions on abortions, freedom of expression, etc. So, in parenthesis I will comment on the problem of importing into the Israeli discourse the American constitutional debate around Judicial Review as if the two constitutional regimes are identical in this respect.
11. H.C. 840/97 *Sbeit v. Government of Israel*, P.D. 57(4) 803.
12. Ibid., pp. 814–815.
13. The distinct recent example, however, regards the occupied territories and not Israel proper—the case of the Fence/Wall. See the almost simultaneous opinions of the supreme judicial bodies of the international community and of Israel—the Israeli Supreme Court decision: H.C. 2056/04, *Village Council Beit Sureik v. Government of Israel*, P.D. 58(5) 807; and the International Court of Justice advisory opinion of 9 July 2004, www.icj-cij.org/docket/index.php?p1=3&p2=4&k=5a&case=131&code=mwp&p3=4. One can assume that the rather mild official reactions in Israel to the Supreme Court decision to order substantial relocation of the fence should be attributed to the pending and much harsher opinion of the ICJ.
14. Election Appeal 11280/02 *Central Elections Committee for the 16th Knesset v. MK Tibi and MK Bishara*, P.D. 57(4) 1 (hereafter, '*Tibi*').
15. H.C. 651/03 *Association for Civil Rights v. Chairman of the Central Elections Committee*, P.D. 57(2) 62.
16. H.C. 316/03 *Bakri v. Israeli Censorship Board*, P.D. 58(1) 249; F.H. 10480/03 *Bosidon v. Bakri*, P.D. 59(1) 625.
17. H.C. 6698/95 *Kaadan v. Israel Lands Administration and Katzir*, 54(1) P.D. 258, 276.
18. See for example C.A.4531/91 *Nasser v. Associations Registrar*, P.D. 48(3) 294, see too the rulings that shielded the Arab parties, inter alia—E.A. 2/84 *Naiman v. Chairman of the Central Elections Committee for the 11th Knesset*, P.D. 39(2) 225; E.A. 2/88 *Ben Shalom v. Chairman of the Central Elections Committee for the 12th Knesset*, P.D. 43(4) 221, 250; L.C.A. 2316/96 *Isaacson v. Parties Registrar*, P.D. 50(2) 529; and the *Tibi* ruling.
19. See mainly As'ad Ghanem, *The Palestinian-Arab Minority in Israel, 1948–2000*, Albany, NY, 2001, esp. pp. 170–174; Shafir and Peled, *Being Israeli*, especially chapters 4 and 10; Shany Payes, 'Palestinian NGOs in Israel: A Campaign for Civic Equality in a Non-Civic State', *Israel Studies*, Vol. 8 (2003), p. 60–90; Barzilai, *Communities and Law*, especially chapter 3.
20. I find here an interesting case of reciprocal empowerment: the court blazes a trail for the empowerment of organizations and they, in their turn, by bringing before it issues of great moment that had not come its way before, endow the court with greater socio-political significance.
21. For a seminal elaboration of the issue of minority rights (and the distinction between them and equal citizenship rights), see Will Kymlicka, *Multicultural Citizenship: A Liberal Theory of Minority Rights*, Oxford, 1995, esp. chapters 2 and 3.
22. *Tibi* ruling, p. 22.
23. This point was highlighted in the concluding paragraphs of the Or Commission Report: part 6, sections 40–43 and see a wider discussion of this point also in Ilan Saban, 'Minority Rights in Deeply Divided Societies: A Framework for Analysis and the Case of the Arab-Palestinian Minority in Israel', *New York University Journal of International Law and Politics*, Vol. 36 (2004), pp. 885–1003.
24. *Kaadan*.
25. H.C. 4112/99 *Adalah et al. v. Municipality of Tel-Aviv-Jaffa et al.* 56(5) P.D. 393.
26. Ibid., p. 418 (emphasis added).
27. For a further discussion of the status of Arabic in Israel, see inter alia, Ilan Saban and Muhammad Amara, 'The Status of Arabic in Israel: Reflections on the Power of Law to Produce Social Change', *Israel Law Review*, Vol. 36, No. 2 (2002), p. 5–39.
28. H.C. 6924/98 *Association for Civil Rights in Israel v. Government of Israel*, P.D. 55(5), 15.
29. Ibid., para. 31 of the ruling.
30. See the court's comment in *Kaadan* case.
31. See the Or Commission Report, part 1, chapter A, section 19 and part 6 section 12.
32. Compare with petition claiming gender discrimination: H.C. 4541/94 *Miller v. Minister of Defence*, P.D. 59(4) 94; H.C. 453/94 *Women's Network in Israel v. Government of Israel*, P.D. 48(5) 501; H.C.5325/01 *Society for the Promotion of Women's Basketball League v. Local Council of Ramat haSharon*, P.D. 58(5) 79. Compare too with petitions against irregular

funding of the ultra-orthodox, as in H.C. 7142/97 *The Israeli Youth Movement Council v. Minister for Education, Culture and Sport*, P.D. 52(3) 433.

33. H.C. 6532/94 *Abu-kaf v. Minister of Agriculture*, P.D. 50(4), 391.
34. H.C. 240/98 *Adalah v. Ministry for Religious Affairs*, P.D. 52(5) 167 but compare with H.C. 1113/99 *Adalah v. Ministry for Religious Affairs*, P.D. 54(2), 164.
35. H.C. 10026/01 *Adalah v. Government of Israel et al.*, P.D. 57(3) 31.
36. H.C. 5108/04 *Abu-Guda v. Minister of Education*, P.D. 59(2) 241.
37. Moshe Cohen (Elia), 'To Whom the Burden of Proof?', *Adalah Report*, Vol. 1 (1999) pp. 37–39 (Hebrew); Yousef Taiseer Jabareen, 'Constitutional Protection of Minorities in Comparative Perspective: Palestinians in Israel and African-Americans in the United States', PhD thesis, Georgetown University, 2003; Eyal Benvenisti and Dalia Shaham, 'Facially Neutral Discrimination and the Israeli Supreme Court', *New York University Journal of International Law and Politics*, Vol. 36 (2004), pp. 677–716.
38. Compare with H.C. 1438/98 *Conservative Movement v. Ministry for Religious Affairs*, P.D. 53(5) 337, where the court instructed that the petitioner be recompensed for funding it had not received in the fiscal year 1997 from the budgets of 1999 and 2000.
39. H.C. 2814/97 *Supreme Follow Up Committee v. Ministry of Education, Culture and Sport*, P.D. 54(3) 233.
40. H.C. 11163/03 *National Committee of Heads of Arab Authorities in Israel v. The Ministry of the Interior* (yet to be published).
41. There is another, important and very controversial, decision of the court (reached in May 2006) that deserves a separate analysis which I will not provide here. It concerns an attack against the constitutionality of a new statue: The Citizenship and Entrance to Israel Act (Temporary Order) 2003. The Act (with only very few exceptions) prevents Palestinians from the occupied territories married to Israeli citizens (i.e. Arab citizens of Israel) from uniting to live in Israel. The official reasons for the legislation were security reasons, but demographic overtones appeared as well (the court generally did not treat them). Six of the 11 judges in the case decided that the statute was not proportional, and therefore unconstitutional. However, the sixth judge sided with the other five judges in declining to provide a remedy against the statute. Thus, by a bare majority, this extremely problematic statute remained valid. It went through slight modifications and a new petition against it is pending. For analysis of the court decision, see, inter alia, Yoav Peled, 'Citizenship Betrayed: Israel's Emerging Immigration and Citizenship Regime', *Theo. Inq. L.*, Vol. 8 (2007), pp. 603–628; Daphne Barak-Erez, 'Israel: Citizenship and Immigration Law in the Vice of Security, Nationality, and Human Rights', *Int'l J. of Constitutional. L.*, Vol. 6 (2008), pp. 184–192.
42. One reader of a previous draft gently questioned my criticism, since the Israeli court's approach 'is certainly at one with the approach adopted in other jurisdictions; for instance, a time-honoured tradition in the UK is for courts to suffice themselves with declarations in difficult cases, for instance those concerning matters of resource allocation'. Let me lay out three points that 'drove my tone' here: First, there is a special need for the court to be the guardian of 'discrete and insular minorities' since these minorities 'may be [in] a special condition, which tends seriously to curtail the operation of those political processes ordinarily to be relied upon to protect minorities, and which may call for a correspondingly more searching judicial inquiry' (*US v. Carolene Products Co.*, 304 U.S. 144 (1938), n. 4). The call for an activist court is thus more persuasive in cases such as Israel, Northern Ireland, Sri Lanka, Macedonia and the like (as opposed to, say, Britain proper or Austria). Second, the argument for involving the court in budgetary considerations is less problematic when group X demands the allocation that was provided to group Y (when no substantive distinction appears), as opposed to asking the court to intervene in the standard of allocation to a social right of one kind or another. Many cases advanced by the Arab minority are of the first kind. Third, since, as explained above, 'the final word' is quite clearly in the hands of the Knesset (because most of the Basic Laws are not entrenched), should not the court have more of a 'margin of appreciation' than less? Let us compare the relative finality of the Supreme Court in Israel with say the US Supreme Court. The latter's decision is almost 'eternal' (unless changed by the court itself). Should we advance then the same pros and cons for judicial review in the case of the US Supreme Court as we do in the case of its Israeli counterpart?
43. See, inter alia, Aharon Barak, *Judge in a Democratic Society*, Haifa, 2004, especially pp. 157–161.

Judicial Administrative Review in Times of Discontent: The Israeli Supreme Court and the Second Palestinian Uprising

GUY I. SEIDMAN

Most democracies offer some form of judicial review of administrative action,[1] yet they differ greatly in the remedies available, and in judges' willingness to pass judgement on executive action and policy. One finds a much narrower range where it comes to judicial review of the military, especially in times of war. It seems that all Western court systems pursue highly deferential review policy, limiting themselves to extreme cases, and mostly deciding well after the winds of war have subsided.[2]

Until recently these dilemmas had little practical significance: since World War II, most Western nations have enjoyed long spells of peace and tranquillity. But things have changed in recent years, as a string of tragic events have shaken Western complacency. The horrors of the September 2001 attacks on the United States were followed by war in Afghanistan and Iraq and major terror attacks in Madrid, London and elsewhere, and Western nations have become painfully aware of the need to adopt stricter security policies. These, in turn, meant an increase in restrictions on human rights, and greater government oversight of private activity. Western nations have thus come to face the democratic dilemmas that Israel has known for too long, and have taken steps for which Israel has long been criticized.

The Israeli Supreme Court is often discussed in studies comparing court activism and judicial protection of human and civil rights.[3] One area where the Israeli court's experience is, in this author's opinion, of particular comparative interest is how it deals with crises. More specifically, the way the court strives to balance human and civil rights, on the one hand, and legitimate national security concerns on the other. It maintains the core values of democracy and the integrity of both the legal and the political system, even in times of war. The Israeli court has achieved unique results. While somewhat deferential to the military, especially in times of ongoing military activities, the court has coped well with the state of emergency continuous since 1948, and has, for the most part, been a clear and steady voice in curbing executive excess, especially when it infringed on individual liberties.

This article has four parts. The second explains the social and legal conditions that allowed the Israeli court to develop its public law jurisprudence. The third uses leading cases to illustrate the complexity and diversity inherent in judicial review of the military in Israel, and the significant achievements of the court from 1948 to the year 2000. Part four focuses on the Supreme Court's judicial response to petitions relating to the Palestinian uprising of 2000. The concluding section attempts to summarize the article and place all its parts in perspective, with an overall evaluation of the court's performance in tumultuous recent years.

THE SUPREME ARBITER: THE ISRAELI SUPREME COURT

The Israeli Supreme Court is the highest court of law in the State of Israel. It has the power to review all acts of lower courts, tribunals and administrative agencies and its decisions are legally binding precedents. The court can overrule its own precedents, and the Knesset, the Israeli Parliament, has the theoretical power to legislate around most court decisions, but both mechanisms are rarely employed.[4] Overruling Supreme Court decisions in constitutional matters may involve complex parliamentary procedures and require supermajorities.[5]

Yet the reason the Israeli Supreme Court has become one of the institutionally most powerful courts in the Western world is due to a unique blend of three elements: an unusually wide jurisdiction; an exceptionally hard-working group of judges; and public trust and esteem, allowing the court to face off the other branches of government, and triumph.

The first element is mostly a historical remnant. The Israeli Supreme Court's roots lie in the court system prescribed by the British during their League of Nations' mandate over Palestine. The Supreme Court was formed as the main instance of civil and criminal appeals, and sitting as a High Court of Justice—also as the main court of administrative appeals. The court became the busy centre for the entire judicial system, and an effective means for the authorities to keep the legal and administrative systems in check. It is noteworthy that the British kept control over judicial appointments in Palestine and that appeals could be brought before the Privy Council in London.[6] Israel gained independence in May 1948, yet the judicial system has remained essentially unchanged ever since. With appeal to London no longer available, the Israeli Supreme Court became just what the name implies—the highest court of the land—yet it functionally remained the main court of appeal, and a court of first instance for cases where it sits as a High Court of Justice.

In the final years of the Mandate, faced with an Arab uprising and the Jewish struggle for independence, the British authorities adopted extreme legal measures to ensure public safety. With emergency powers in place, the Supreme Court offered little remedy against harsh military measures carried out against the population.[7] Faced with similar difficulties, indeed faced with much the same emergency legislation, the Israeli Supreme Court acted very differently.[8]

The second element concerns the willingness of Israeli Justices, especially in recent decades and as a matter of judicial ideology, to undertake enormous workloads, and engage in activist review in all areas of the law, especially in public law.[9]

The Israeli Supreme Court is one of the hardest working tribunals in the Western world: it hears civil and criminal appeals and administrative appeals when sitting as a High Court of Justice.[10] The court increasingly removed jurisdictional and equitable bars—such as standing and justiciability—and opened its doors to ever growing numbers of private and public petitioners. Indeed, the Israeli Supreme Court admits almost any official decision—ranging from government procurement to the legality of military action—to be challenged before it. This allows the court, after its own views, to defend civil rights and liberties, uphold democratic values and place effective checks on all branches of government.

The final element concerns the massive public trust and support which the Israeli court enjoyed, at least until recent years,[11] and which allowed the court to become a political institution, a major player in all public policy decision-making in Israel. Over the years the court took on the public position of guardian of human rights, protector of citizens and bearer of the proper standards of public administration. Indeed, researchers have long suggested that the court is powerful enough to lead the way, educate the Israeli public and bring about a change in public opinion, even in the crucial issue of national security.[12] The court, of course, is well aware of its reputation, and holds public trust as one of its prime assets.

THE ISRAELI SUPREME COURT IN MILITARY AND NATIONAL SECURITY MATTERS

Background and Early History

Since 1948 the Israel Defence Forces (IDF) has played a dominant and complex role in Israeli society. The military employs more personnel than any other government agency, and through its massive budget it significantly affects the Israeli economy. Moreover, through the compulsory draft, military service is a concept literally brought into the homes of most Israeli families.[13] In the early years of Israeli history, the IDF was called upon to the carry out national policies ranging from frontier settlement to the education of underprivileged civilians. Many of these extra-military activities are still carried out by the IDF today. Finally, given Israel's national security constraints, the IDF is rightly seen as the nation's guardian and primary physical safeguard.

Given this background and the primacy of national security concerns above social and economic ones in Israeli politics, one could have expected the Israeli Supreme Court to be highly deferential to the military. This, however, has never been the case. Indeed, some of the most important precedents set by the Israeli Supreme Court in protecting human and civil rights came in the context of the military.

It is beyond the scope of this article to cover judicial review of the military from 1948 to the present. Thus, it will briefly present selected cases from 1948 to 2000 and, in the fourth part, it will examine how the Israeli Supreme Court dealt with the Palestinian uprising of 2000 through another set of selected cases.

At the Beginning—One 1948 Case

Several months after independence and while Israel was still fighting for survival, the Israeli Supreme Court received a petition requesting a writ of habeas corpus for the release of one Ahmed Abu Laban, arrested by the military under the mandatory emergency regulations of 1945.[14] Resisting intense pressure from the political and military establishment the court reached a classic common law outcome: defending civil rights by ensuring the fairness of criminal procedures, yet avoiding major constitutional upset. The court upheld the validity of the mandatory emergency regulations in the newly established democracy of Israel, yet took a very harsh view of the military's failure to perform the procedural requirement of establishing an advisory committee to the military commander, holding that the setting up of such a body is a precondition for the exercise of detention powers under the regulations. Abu Laban was to be released immediately. In a brave statement, demonstrating a firm commitment to the values of democracy and the rule of law, the court explained that this was not a question of mere formality:

> [T]he authorities are subject to the law like all citizens and the rule of law is one of the firmest foundations of the state ... True, national security, necessitating the arrest of a man is no less important than the need to maintain civil rights, but where one can attain both targets at once, one must not disregard the one or the other.[15]

The Six Day War: Handling the Territories after 1967

The 1967 Six Day War presented tough legal challenges to the Supreme Court. Israel took over the territories of Judea, Samaria and Gaza and their millions of Palestinian occupants. Israel neither annexed most of these territories nor did it apply Israeli law upon its Palestinian occupants.[16] The applicable norms were those of international law of belligerent occupation. Yet, as Israeli control over the territories lengthened, it became clear that these norms did not provide satisfactory legal solutions.[17]

The Israeli Supreme Court soon stepped in, reviewing petitions against military action in the territories. This review became a central feature of Israel's legal and political control over the territories, producing a unique body of jurisprudence on the international law of belligerent occupation.[18] Moreover, the availability of a petition to the Israeli Supreme Court for Palestinian inhabitants of the territories is quite remarkable in its own right, and far from obvious.[19]

Judicial review in the territories was made possible since the court found it imperative for maintaining the rule of law in the territories and the Israeli government was not willing to contest the court's jurisdiction. Since 1967, military commanders retained supreme power in the occupied territories, but they were subject to judicial review, as they are part of an Israeli administrative agency. This judicial review remains controversial in Israeli society. Some find the court too interventionist, others believe it rationalizes and legitimizes Israeli action in the territories. It seems to be clearly the case that the court speaks, at the same time, to Israelis, Palestinians, and the watchful international community, and that the court is fully aware of the audiences it addresses.

The Toughest Social Question: Drafting Yeshiva Students

Israeli Jewish men and women are drafted at 18 for military service. The most significant group exemption is that of ultra-orthodox Yeshiva Students. Since 1970, the Israeli Supreme Court has been petitioned to find this exemption discriminatory and hence illegal. The court repeatedly refused to hear the petition on its merits, hesitant to invalidate an entrenched and politically sensitive fixture of Israeli society.

In 1988, however, the court changed all the rules.[20] It announced broad rules recognizing the standing of public petitioners and the justiciability of essentially every act taken by a public officer. Thus, the court was willing to hear out petitioners—reservist soldiers of the IDF—but then, having examined the petition on its merits, the court narrowly avoided striking down the Yeshiva students' exemption.

Only a decade later, in the groundbreaking case of *Rubinstein and Ressler*,[21] the court invalidated the exemption as illegal. Yet that was on the relatively technical ground of the non-delegation doctrine: that the scheme was approved by the minister of defence, not the Knesset, and only the latter has the power to decide on such fundamental issues that divide society. The decision brought about a serious public debate, but not the drafting of the ultra-orthodox students, as the Knesset validated the exemption by statute.

Advancing Women's Rights through the Military

Advancing women's rights in Israel, as in other nations, required judicial activism. This has been especially the case regarding women in the IDF, and for two contrasting reasons. On the one hand, most Jewish women are drafted at 18, a very tender age, into a male-dominated hierarchical system, where most long term career prospects are reserved for men, who carry out most combat roles in the IDF. It is easy to see then why women often feel unnecessary in the IDF, and how they may fall prey to sexual misconduct. On the other hand, the Israeli Supreme Court found that its rulings on matters of equality and sexual harassment in the military find public acceptance and are quickly given effect throughout the military.

Two decisions stand out in this context. In the *Miller* case, the Supreme Court invalidated IDF policy prohibiting women's service as combat pilots. A majority of the court held that the IDF had to apply itself towards gender equality in deeds, not just in words, and that the military had to do its share—and bear the costs—in order to further equality in Israeli society.[22] The petitioner herself failed to become an air force pilot but the clear statement of the court had encouraging results: the IDF went on to open a significant number of combat and operational military positions to women. Thus, the decision became a source of empowerment for Israeli women, and the IDF's response enhanced both its image and the public perception of equality and fairness of the military service.

In the *Galili* case[23] the Supreme Court was asked by the petitioner, a former servicewoman, to prevent the IDF from promoting a brigadier general. The two had an affair several years previously while the woman served in the general's office. For the first time in Israeli history, the court halted a military promotion. Taking the high moral ground, the court made clear that abusing relations of subordination to obtain sexual favours 'is a flawed norm that should be condemned and uprooted'.[24] Coming shortly before a strong anti-sexual harassment statute went into force,[25] the decision was a clear statement by the court that sexual misconduct is simply unacceptable. As in the *Miller* case, the hierarchical IDF was able to quickly comprehend and apply down the ranks the societal norms of equality and non-harassment that the Supreme Court has set in the two cases.

Timing is Everything: Banning Torture, Forbidding Hijacking

In the eyes of the Israeli security services and probably most of the Israeli public the challenges of combating terrorism permits the use of extreme measures. Two such measures received official sanction, only to be banned by the court: firstly, the use of special measures of interrogation termed 'moderate physical pressure' were approved for use in extreme instances in a 1987 report of a National Commission of Inquiry headed by former Supreme Court president, Moshe Landau.[26] Second, in 1997, the Israeli Supreme Court examined the question of whether Israeli law allows for the administrative detention of Lebanese nationals for the singular purpose of maintaining 'bargaining chips' in the hands of the Israeli government in negotiating the release of Israelis held in Lebanon. In its 1997 decision, the court permitted the holding of such 'bargaining chips'.[27]

Yet in April 2000 the court reversed itself in a rare en banc rehearing, holding that Israel may not keep Lebanese citizens in administrative confinement as 'bargaining chips' towards a possible future exchange of prisoners with Lebanon.[28] Similarly, in September 1999 the Israeli Supreme Court ruled for an outright ban on the use of various special investigating techniques, holding them to be torturous, hence illegal.[29]

Both decisions, taken by an exceptional nine Justice panels, were not crowd pleasers in Israel although they won the Israeli court praise from the international community. In Israel, the decisions were viewed as severely curtailing the powers available to the security forces, and there was even statutory intervention in the matter of the 'bargaining chips'.[30] Yet as the court acknowledged, banning torture is mandated by both humanitarian and international law standards, to which Israeli democracy remains committed, even when faced with grave national security threats. Similarly, there is no legitimate power to detain individuals who pose no national security threat and who have completed their sentence or are not charged with any wrongdoing.

In hindsight, handed down just before the second Palestinian uprising began in September 2000 and before the events of 11 September 2001 in the United States, these decisions of the Israeli Supreme Court seem to come from a more carefree era. It is intriguing to wonder whether the outcome would have been the same had the cases been decided in more recent times. Clearly some of the extensive recent scholarship on these issues seems more amenable to consider serious limitations on civil and human rights in the face of credible terrorist threats.[31]

FACING THE HEAT: THE COURT AND THE PALESTINIANS

Millennium Troubles

On 27 September 2000, an Israeli serviceman was killed in a bombing in Gaza. The next day, then opposition leader Ariel Sharon visited the Temple

Mount in Jerusalem. These events marked the beginning of a renewed Palestinian–Israeli conflict, which came to be known as the Second Palestinian Intifada (or uprising). The conflict seems to have halted in late 2004. Unlike previous cycles of violence, the current conflict was not between Israel and an Arab nation, but between Israel and the Palestinian population of the territories, and unlike the first Palestinian uprising of 1987, the level of brutality escalated significantly: from mass demonstrations and stone throwing, the Palestinians moved on to use car bombs and suicide bombers. In retaliation, Israeli measures became increasingly harsh. In its five year course, some 3300 to 3600 Palestinians and over 1000 Israelis were killed, with many more injured.[32]

The violence of the Second Intifada was continuous, but there were several horrid peaks, when Palestinian suicide bombers inflicted terrible death tolls on Israelis eating pizza, standing in line for a night club, or celebrating Passover. In some instances, the IDF reacted with major operations aimed at the terrorist infrastructure and individual militants in the Palestinian territories, and later, in an effort to construct a wall of separation between Israel and the territories. These administrative actions brought a string of petitions to the Israeli Supreme Court, which will now be discussed.

Jenin, Spring 2002

By spring 2002, the Intifada had taken over 440 Israeli and 1500 Palestinian lives. A turning point was 27 March 2002. Palestinian terrorists attacked Israeli civilians celebrating Passover in a Netanya hotel killing 28 and injuring 140. Two days later the Israeli government approved 'Operation Defensive Shield' against the terrorist infrastructure. On that day, the IDF entered six of the largest Palestinian cities in the West Bank, occupying them and their surrounding areas.

Confrontations between the IDF and Palestinian militants were particularly intense in two cities: Bethlehem, where the IDF laid siege to the Church of the Nativity, where armed Palestinians had barricaded themselves in, and in Jenin and the refugee camp adjacent to it, where the toughest urban warfare occurred.[33]

The Jenin refugee camp was a hotbed of terrorism. On the eve of the Israeli operation it housed about 200 armed terrorists who operated from it. The Israeli government had charged that 28 suicide attacks were planned and launched from the camp, and would later point to arms caches and explosives laboratories found on site. The Israeli operation in Jenin led to (false) Palestinian charges of human right violations, even of massacre. Israel maintained that it took all possible measures not to hurt civilians, and charged Palestinian militants with adopting methods which breached international law.[34]

The events of Jenin, the most severe act of warfare in the second Intifada, came before the Israeli Supreme Court in several different contexts.

Starting on Monday 8 April 2002, while hostilities in Jenin were still ongoing, the court received numerous petitions, mostly from human rights groups, asking for its intervention. One petition claimed that Israeli soldiers shot at medical teams, stopped medical supplies from reaching the territories, and prevented the evacuation of the wounded, and the burial of the dead.[35] Another petition asked the court to require the IDF to give residents of Jenin a timely warning and the right to be heard before the army demolished their houses.[36] A third petition asked the court to instruct the IDF not to bomb any civilian targets or persons in Jenin, using jets, tanks or any other weapon.[37]

The petitions were denied, yet only in the third case did the court cite justiciability as a reason, and in all three cases the court first received what the Justices considered to be satisfactory statements from the government regarding its policy in Jenin: the IDF explained that it was operating in a complicated setting, where militants found refuge among civilians, even in hospitals, and had in the past used ambulances to transport munitions. The IDF stated that it was committed to the rules of humanitarian law as it is required under international law, morality and even for utilitarian reasons, and that instructions about this are given to fighting forces.[38]

Once the fighting in Jenin had ended on 11 April 2002 the court became less deferential. A petition filed on 12 April asked the court to order the IDF to avoid examining, moving or burying the bodies of Palestinians killed in Jenin, reserving the role of collecting the bodies to medical teams and representatives of the Red Cross, and allowing families of the deceased to bring them to a quick, proper and dignified burial.[39] Court president Barak, in person, issued that day an order preventing the removal of the Palestinian dead until the court made its final decision.

On 14 April, the court brokered a deal. Clearly only the Supreme Court—not any of the international mediators—enjoyed the trust and respect of both Israelis and Palestinians. The court handed down a short and highly dignified conciliatory decision. It stated that both sides agree that, under international law, it was for the Israeli authorities to find, identify, remove and bury the dead. Yet the Israeli government agreed to incorporate Red Cross teams, and possibly local teams in the process. 'These acts shall be conducted in all possible speed—all while respecting the dignity of the dead and maintaining the security of the operating forces.'[40]

The court then set the arrangements for the burial of Palestinians who died in Jenin. Breathing a sigh of relief the court added: 'Indeed, in humanitarian matters it is mostly possible to reach an understanding and an accord. The dignity of the dead is important for us all.'[41]

Finally, the court stated that petitioners failed to prove their claim of a massacre in Jenin. Indeed, the brokered agreement showed that Israel had nothing to hide. A tough battle did take place. Not a massacre.[42] Court president Barak summed up the case with the court's credo that

> even during times of battle the laws of war must be observed. Even in times of battle everything must be done to protect the civilian population. Surely this court will take no stand as to the way the fighting is conducted. As long as the lives of soldiers are at risk, the decisions shall be made by the commanders.[43]

The public controversy over what happened in Jenin erupted again when Israeli-Arab filmmaker Muhammad Bakri presented the Palestinian version in a documentary film. The Israeli Film Council denied the film a permit for commercial screening in Israel, considering it a fictional propaganda film. On 11 November 2003, the Israeli Supreme Court ruled for filmmaker Bakri, holding that the film deserved the protection of free speech: in a free society such as Israel, the public is exposed to a variety of statements, some true, some not; it is for the public to judge for themselves the veracity of the film. Release of the film would be a testament to the resilience of Israeli society to withstand war, terror and strife.[44]

Bethlehem, Spring 2002

On 1 April 2002, dozens of armed Palestinians broke into the Church of the Nativity in Bethlehem, one of the most sacred sites in Christianity, taking captive civilians and clergymen. This became a very complex hostage crisis. Israel was under intense international pressure not to enter the church compound. As the IDF laid siege to the Church, the matter came before the Israeli Supreme Court. First, came petitions of a humanitarian nature: the Church itself asked that supplies be provided to the clergymen inside the compound, that water and electricity supplies be reconnected and that bodies in the Church be brought to burial. As a formal matter, the petition was denied, as military action was still undergoing. But the court first had to be satisfied that the IDF was doing all it could do to treat the clergymen in a sensitive and humanitarian manner.[45] The court explained the delicate nature of the event and the fair treatment that the clergymen received from the IDF. Finally, the court also brokered an agreement during the hearing for food to be brought into the compound.[46]

Several days later, a petition contended that while the clergymen were receiving food, a number of Palestinian civilians in the compound were not. The petition argued that these Palestinians, who were neither armed nor suspected of any wrongdoing, were prevented by armed militants from leaving the compound, on the one hand, and denied food supplied by the Israeli authorities, on the other. Citing international law, petitioners asked to court to order the IDF to allow food to be brought in.[47]

The Israeli Supreme Court, per president Barak, rejected the petition, but not outright, nor without discussion and deliberation. President Barak stated that Israel had the right to defend itself against terror, but must do so according to international law. The reason was that Israel, a democratic nation, was fighting in the name of the law and for its sake, whereas the terrorists were fighting against the law and violated it. 'The war against terror', stated president Barak, 'is also the war of the law against those who rise against it.'[48]

The court, stated president Barak, was convinced that the Israeli siege did not infringe on international law in relation to the armed Palestinians barricading themselves in the compound, but what about the unarmed civilians in the compound? The court voiced its discomfort in this respect, and only after the Israeli authorities committed to arrangements to provide them with some food did the court hold that the duty of the Israeli government under international law had been fulfilled.[49]

The stand-off ended with an agreement brokered by international negotiators, under which the Palestinian gunmen left the compound unarmed, and were given free passage to Palestinian Authority-controlled Gaza or to foreign nations that agreed to permit them entry.[50] Then, on 5 May 2002, the court was petitioned by relatives of terrorism victims, contesting the legality of this agreement. Petitioners claimed that under the agreement Israel let the terrorists go free, including some known to have been involved in murderous acts and that this was an unreasonable action.[51] In a short per curiam decision, the three-Justice panel headed by president Barak showed sympathy to petitioners, yet denied their petition, because of its political nature.

A year later the court was petitioned by terrorism victims, who asked the court to instruct the state to seek extradition of wanted Palestinians who were let go in the Bethlehem deal.[52] 'No one denies', wrote court president Barak, rejecting the petition, 'that the reality that brought about the agreement … at the Church of Nativity was not simple, for humanitarian, religious, operational and international reasons.' The decision of the Israeli government, while uneasy and unpleasing, was held to be legally sound, leaving no basis for court intervention.[53]

Mass Detentions, Spring 2002

In operation 'Defensive Shield', the IDF detained about 7000 people. Most were released after an initial screening and investigation, but by 15 May 2002 about 1600 remained in custody. It soon became clear that the Israeli authorities would need more time to process the detainees than regulations permitted, and so the IDF commander in the West Bank promulgated a temporary order authorizing the military to hold detainees for up to 18 days before a judicial order be required for continued arrest. During these 18 days detainees must be given a chance to argue against the detention within eight days, but not before a judge; there is no judicial review of the detention order, and detainees are not allowed to meet a lawyer. Other orders followed, the final one allowing 12 days of detention, and requiring that detainees be heard within four days of detention, and be allowed to meet a lawyer within two days of being detained. The legality of all these orders was contested in a petition before the Supreme Court.[54]

Court president Barak addressed and answered four legal questions. The first question was whether the IDF has the power to detain for the purposes of investigation? This is answered in the cautious affirmative. There must be cause for detention. There must be suspicions that the detainee himself presents a danger to security. The orders examined here do just that.[55]

The second concerns the delay of judicial review. President Barak notes that such review is essential as a primary line of defence against arbitrariness. Indeed, both Israeli and international law demands prompt judicial review of detention orders. Yet these are special circumstances: it is carried out during warfare and anti-terrorism operations, and this must be taken into account.[56] But how long a delay is acceptable? The court holds that 18 or 12 days exceed appropriate limits, and the military orders unlawfully infringe 'upon the judge's authority ... [and] upon the detainee's liberty, which the international and Israeli legal frameworks are intended to protect'. [57] The court, however, left it to the military authorities to set the final—and shorter— timeframe for detention without judicial oversight.[58]

The third question concerned delay of detainee meetings with lawyers. The court found that both Israeli and international law requires such meetings to be generally permitted, and only significant security considerations justify the prevention of a meeting between detainee and counsel. The length of time that such a meeting may be delayed 'should be inferred from the specific circumstances, according to test as to reasonability and proportionality'.[59] Detainees should not be allowed to meet their lawyers while warfare continues, or if there is a suspicion that the meeting might be used to pass on messages, endangering the lives of forces, or if the meeting may disrupt the investigation. The court upheld the arrangement provided by the military orders.[60]

The fourth concerned the waiting period before the detainee must be heard. This first hearing is an initial investigation of the detainees' identity and his account of events. The military argued that the period cannot be shorter than four days, due to the large number of detainees and the limited number of professional investigators, but the court thought differently. The court agreed that investigations can be delayed during warfare or military operations, and also accepted that given the large number of detainees some time may pass from the moment a detainee had been brought to a detention facility until the initial investigation, but such interrogation must be done promptly. Lack of professional investigators is not an acceptable reason to delay the initial investigation. The court invalidated the provisions that set a four day period before the initial investigation, and once again required the military to make the necessary arrangements conforming to the rules.[61]

Rafah, Gaza Strip, Spring 2004

Perhaps the best example of the Israeli court's role in the conflict came in the spring of 2004, in a petition regarding Israeli action in Rafah.[62] Israel began military operations on 18 May 2004 in an effort to locate underground tunnels used to smuggle arms and people from Egypt.

Human rights groups active in Israel petitioned the Supreme Court, pointing to the harm inflicted on Rafah civilians by IDF operations, and asking the court to mandate the military to let medical teams operate freely, restore water and electricity provisions and allow the provision of food and medicine to residents. The military asked that the petition be denied as military operations were still ongoing, and stressed that the IDF had to take the needs of the local population into account.

The case is unique: the court heard the petition while military action was ongoing, so while it usually conducts judicial review *after the fact*, the court here offered judicial review *before* or *during* the fact. The court had no doubt it had jurisdiction over the case,[63] but was nonetheless very careful in its decision, stressing that the humanitarian concerns presented here 'have been resolved, without endangering the lives of soldiers or the military operation'.[64]

While the court did not interfere with the military operation, it did serve two important functions. First, that of mediator—a forum trusted by all parties, where Palestinians can get the attention of the Israeli military, receive accurate and timely information from the Israeli government, and win useful cooperation and possibly even concessions from the Israeli authorities—the IDF being well aware of the hard gaze of the court, fully expecting Israeli officials to 'do the right thing', and the Israeli and international press coverage of the Supreme Court's proceedings.

Second, the Supreme Court has a normative role, declaring what the law is, and an educative role. These roles are here directed towards the military in general, towards the individual citizen-soldier and towards the entire Israeli citizenry detailing proper military action in the territories.

The court heard the case on 21 May 2004, as the military operation was underway. The military left Rafah on 24 May, and the decision was handed down on 30 May. Reading it, one can see how the court was taking steps to alleviate the hardship of the local population until the crisis came to an end. On the Israeli front, the court does not interfere with military action but rather strives to educate the military for future reference, and to make a normative statement regarding Israel's duties under international humanitarian law.

The ruling begins with a clear statement: Israel is not an isolated island, but a member of an international system. Military operations are subject to legal norms—customary international law, treaties to which Israel is a party, and the fundamental principles of Israeli law which set out how military operations should be conducted.[65]

The court found IDF efforts to help restore services in the area satisfactory, given the circumstances, yet made it clear that it was the duty of the military to provide these services to the civilian population under its authority, and to anticipate such difficulties when planning a military operation. The court was also clear that the military must do everything possible, subject to the state of combat, to allow the evacuation of wounded local residents; the court seemed convinced that the IDF would proceed properly in this case.[66] The court was also keen on getting the dead properly buried and on allowing families to participate in funerals. The ruling described the daily negotiations between both sides on these issues, carried out under the auspices of the court, until the problem was resolved. 'Nevertheless, there are lessons to learn from the incident', and the court made them abundantly clear to the IDF.[67] The military was instructed to teach the rules of conduct under humanitarian principles of international law to 'all combat soldiers, from the Chief of Staff down to the new recruits', and to set up procedures to implement these rules during combat.[68]

The Separation Fence

A major issue to come before the court concerned the legality of the separation fence that Israel is building along the 'Green Line', the pre-1967 border, but within the Palestinian territories.

Between September 2000 and April 2004, the armed conflict took the lives of over 900 Israeli citizens with over 6000 injured. Over 9000 terrorist attacks had been carried out, 780 of them within Israel and the rest within the occupied territories. As noted, starting in April 2002, the Israeli government had undertaken a range of steps to reduce the threat of Palestinian terror. These included military action in the territories, some of which are discussed, and the building of a physical barrier preventing entry into Israel.[69]

This fence became the centre of enormous international interest. It raised profound philosophical, historic and social questions. In Europe, undergoing an integration process, memories of the Cold War's 'Iron Curtain' resurfaced. More generally, we are experiencing an era of growing international cooperation and globalization; the tearing down of physical barriers, the free movement of people, capital, goods and services. Is Israel going in the opposite direction? Is it physically barricading the tiny nation of Israel *in*, while fencing millions of Palestinians *out*? Is the peace process beyond salvation? Is the Israeli dream of integrating into a new Middle East gone? These are interesting questions. The more immediate concern of the international community was the legality of Israel's building of this physical barrier on Palestinian land. A full discussion of the separation fence is beyond the scope of this article, rather I will comment on the Israeli Supreme Court's involvement in the debate.

Israel decided to set up a physical barrier in the West Bank, in an effort to prevent terrorist attacks. Beyond the question of the efficacy of this measure, the international community has voiced criticism over other aspects of the decision. The fence stands on Palestinian lands, and some view this as an Israeli effort to establish final borders unilaterally while taking up a lot of land in a desperately overpopulated part of the world and bringing hardship to the daily lives of local Palestinians. That said, Israel does have legitimate security concerns, which the fence has alleviated significantly.

Beyond the debate in the press, diplomatic and NGO circles, two courts have been asked to state their opinion on the fence. In July 2004, the International Court of Justice in The Hague published an advisory opinion, requested by the United Nations General Assembly, on the 'legal consequences of the construction of a wall in the Occupied Palestinian Territory'. The court's opinion is quite clear: it accepts the Palestinian views and rejects Israel's. By a vote of 14 to 1 the court found the construction of the wall contrary to international law, finding Israel under an obligation to cease construction, to dismantle what had been built and make reparation for all damages caused by construction.[70] The Israeli government and public reacted to this ruling with anger,[71] seeing it as yet another manifestation of the international community's denial of Israel's legitimate security needs. Enter the Israeli Supreme Court.

A mere two months before the ICJ's decision, the Israeli court handed down its own decision in the matter of *Beit Sourik*, the longest and most detailed decision regarding the Second Intifada. The question before the court: was it legal for the IDF to take possession of lands in the village *Beit Sourik* for the purpose of erecting the separation fence?

Petitioners—landowners and town councils—asked the court to prevent the military from taking their land because that would cause severe and unbearable injury to the local Palestinian population. The erection of the fence would use up much of their lands and limit access to other parts of their land upon which the livelihood of many villagers depends.[72] The Israeli government argued that the military orders were legal and necessary to provide an effective barrier against terror attacks. It also claimed that in planning the route of the fence, great weight was given to residents' interests, in order to minimize, as much as possible, injury and loss to them.

The Israeli court heard extensive arguments, in an effort to bring about some compromise.[73] Then came decision time. The court raised no justiciability concerns. It simply had two questions before it: does the military have the power to construct the fence? If the answer was positive, the second questions was whether the route selected was within the military's power.[74]

President Barak agreed with petitioners that the military had no power to build a fence for political reasons, such as in an effort to annex lands. The military also had no power to make permanent arrangements in the territories.[75] Yet the court concluded that the building of the fence was motivated by security concerns, and the military command acted in good faith according to its best military understanding.[76]

The court then studied the legality of the route chosen for the construction of the fence. The military command—explained the court—must balance its authority to maintain security in the area and protect the security of the country and its citizens against the rights, needs, and interests of the local population. The test that the court employed is that of proportionality, well established in both international law and in domestic Israeli administrative law. The court proceeded to examine the route chosen by the military command for the fence, effectively changing all the contested parts of the route.[77] The court held various sections of the route to be disproportionately injurious to the local Palestinians, and therefore untenable, and the military was sent back to the drawing board to find such paths as would be significantly less damaging to the livelihood, life and private property of Palestinians in the West Bank. Court president Barak stressed that:

> We are aware of the killing and destruction wrought by the terror against the state and its citizens ... we ... recognize the need to defend the country and its citizens against the wounds inflicted by terror. [But] [t]here is no security without law. Satisfying the provisions of the law is an aspect of national security.[78]

CONCLUSIONS

As has been seen, the Israeli Supreme Court has ventured where few courts have gone before. While the Israeli–Palestinian conflict has unique features, the struggle of Western democracies with Islamic terror has unfortunately become quite familiar, and the Israeli judicial experience could be of practical as well as academic interest. I believe the Israeli Supreme Court is making its best effort to find fair and practical solutions to very troubling legal and humanitarian difficulties. The court attempts to balance non-interference in warfare and maintaining effective review of the legality (essentially of the reasonableness and proportionality) of IDF action in the territories. The court is perhaps more likely to broker an agreement than issue an order instructing the military on combat activity, but it does have this option in its arsenal, and uses it judiciously.

And Then There Is Much More Besides

This article provides a representative sample of the issues that arose during the Second Intifada and came before the Supreme Court. Caution and accuracy require that the following concluding remarks are added.

First, not all the humanitarian difficulties of the conflict come before the court, and not every case the court hears ends with a deal between petitioners and the Israeli government. Many petitions are denied without remedy. There is *Beit Sourik* but there is also the case of land sequestrations in *Bethlehem Municipality*;[79] there is review of mass detentions in *Marab*, but also the approval of 'regular' administrative detentions in *Salama*;[80] and human rights groups that see their petitions denied by the court may not be satisfied with repeated declarations of an IDF commitment to the rules of international humanitarian law.[81] Furthermore, Palestinians accuse Israel of a much wider range of abuses: land expropriations, the clearing of agricultural lands, mass arrests, the use of excessive force against Palestinians, extrajudicial killings and the imposition of closures and curfews on the general Palestinian civilian population.[82]

Second, there is a built-in asymmetry in the court's work, since the Israeli court only has power over Israeli officials. There is also no Palestinian forum providing Israelis with relief. Some Israelis believe the Supreme Court goes too far in its 'meddling' with military affairs and in applying pressure on the IDF to provide concessions to the Palestinians. Yet while the process may seem lopsided, there is a logic to it: the basic facts of the conflict have Israel as an independent, democratic, sovereign nation; the stronger side militarily and the belligerent occupier of some Palestinian territories. This state of affairs reflects the inner strength of Israeli democracy, the humanity of the Israeli people and their willingness to accept the review and arbitration of the Supreme Court in the conflict. As the court often explained, maintaining the rule of law in the territories strengthens the resilience of Israeli democracy and reinforces its national security; a ruling 'against' the military is a ruling 'for' democracy.

Third, it is worthwhile noting that petitions requesting review of IDF activities in the territories are but a small portion of the court's caseload. They do not even represent much of the court's docket in matters concerning the military or the territories. Thus, the court hears a varied caseload of petitions concerning the civil, economic and social rights of active, retired, disabled or deceased servicemen,[83] and cases concerning the military's criminal and disciplinary legal systems.[84]

NOTES

1. In common law systems, such review is typically pre-formed by a national court system of general jurisdiction; in civil law systems, by a system of specialized administrative law courts.
2. For further discussion see, for example, Rachel Vorspan, 'Law and War: Individual Rights, Executive Authority, and Judicial Power in England During World War I', *Vand. J. of Transnat'l L.*, Vol. 38 (2005), p. 261; Tracey E. George, 'Symposium: Other Disciplines, Methodologies, and Countries: Studying Courts and Crisis', *Mo. L. Rev.*, Vol. 69 (2004), p. 951; Diane H. Mazur, 'Rehnquist's Vietnam: Constitutional Separatism and the Stealth Advance of Martial Law', *Indiana L. J.*, Vol. 77, p. 701.
3. See Gary J. Jacobson, 'Judicial Activism in Israel', in Kenneth M. Holland (ed.), *Judicial Activism in Comparative Perspective*, London, 1991, p. 90; Martin Edelman, 'Israel', in C. Neal Tate and Torbjorn Vallinder, *The Global Expansion of Judicial Power*, New York, 1995, p. 403.
4. One such instance, concerning both a resetting of precedent and statutory intervention involved the question of the holding of human 'bargaining chips'.
5. While Israel famously does not have a Constitution, the Knesset has passed a string of 'Basic Laws', serving as chapters of a future constitution. For a useful introduction see Marcia Gelpe, 'Constraints on Supreme Court Authority in Israeli and the United States: Phenomenal Cosmic Powers; Itty Bitty Living Space', *Emory Int'l L. Rev.*, Vol. 13 (1999), p. 493; Menachem Hofnung, 'The Unintended Consequences of Unplanned Constitutional Reform: Constitutional Politics in Israel', *Am. J. Comp. L.*, Vol. 44 (1996), p. 585; Stephen Goldstein, 'Protection of Human Rights by Judges: The Israeli Experience', *St. Louis L. J.*, Vol. 38 (1994), p. 605.
6. On the background to the British mandate see www.mideastweb.org/mandate.htm; see the http://domino.un.org/UNISPAL.NSF/0/c7aae196f41aa055052565f50054e656?OpenDocument (on the formation of the mandatory court system; especially sections 43–44).
7. Of course the mandatory regime was non-democratic. For an overall evaluation see E. Malchi, *The History of the Law of Palestine*, 2nd edition, Tel Aviv, 1953, pp. 166–172 (Hebrew).
8. The Israeli court was more willing to hear appeals against administrative actions carried out by Israeli authorities under emergency powers—most often the very same emergency measures enacted by the British as the *Defence (Emergency) Regulations, 1945*.
9. The achievements are attributed in particular to court presidents Meir Shamgar (1983–1995) and Aharon Barak (1996–2006); on Barak's judicial vision see Aharon Barak, 'Foreword: A Judge on Judging: The Role of the Supreme Court in a Democracy', *Harv. L. Rev.*, Vol. 116 (2002), pp. 16, 97–110.
10. Data available at the Supreme Court's website suggests that during 2006 the number of undecided cases in the court's docket was about 6000 (!).
11. A poll of Israeli's trust of public institutions found that 81 percent of Israelis had trust in the IDF, 76 percent in the Supreme Court, 67 percent in the police, but only 44 percent trust the media, 40 percent trust government ministries and 17 percent trust 'the political system', *Ma'ariv*, 17 January 2003. A recent poll showed a deterioration in public trust: only 22 percent said they trusted political parties; one-third trust the Knesset, 44 percent trust the media, 68 percent trust the Supreme Court and 79 percent trust the IDF, *Jerusalem Post*, 5 October 2006. For rates of public trust in other countries see James L. Gibson, Gregory A. Caldeira and Vanessa A. Baird, 'On the Legitimacy of National High Courts', *Am. Pol. Sci. Rev.*, Vol. 92 (1998), p. 343, http://aja.ncsc.dni.us/courtrv/cr36-3/CR%2036-3.pdf.
12. See Gad Barzilai, Ephraim Yuchtman-Yaar and Zeev Segal, *The Israeli Supreme Court and the Israeli Public*, Tel Aviv, 1994; Yoav Dotan, 'Judicial Rhetoric, Government Lawyers, and Human Rights: The Case of the Israeli High Court of Justice During the Intifada', *Law and Society Rev.*, Vol. 33 (1999), pp. 319, 324–325; Ariel L. Bendor and Zeev Segal, 'Constitutionalism and Trust in Britain: An Ancient Constitutional Culture, A New Judicial Review Model', *Am. U. Int'l L. Rev.*, Vol. 17 (2002), p. 683.
13. Admittedly, not all eligible Israeli citizens are drafted. For details see Guy Seidman, Eyal Nun, 'Women, The Military and the Court: Israel at 2001', *S. Cal. Rev. L. & Women's Stud.*, Vol. 11 (2001), p. 91 (hereinafter, Seidman and Nun).

14. H.C.J. 7/48 *Ahmed Showky Al-Karbutli v. Minister of Defence*, 2 P.D. 5 (1949). The case was first brought before the court on 1 November 1948; the decision was given on 3 January 1949).
15. Ibid., at 15 (per Justice Olshan for the court).
16. There are two aspects to this statement: first, Israel has annexed some territories occupied in 1967—namely parts of Eastern Jerusalem and the Golan Heights—in a move that is yet to be recognized by the international community. Second, Israeli law applies personally to the Israeli settlers in the territories. As we shall see, the Supreme Court extends to them the full rights and privileges that Israeli citizens enjoy. See, for example, Asher Maoz, 'The Application of Israeli Law to the Golan Heights is Annexation', *Brook. J. Int'l L.*, Vol. 20 (1994), p. 355.
17. For discussion see Adam Roberts, 'Prolonged Military Occupation: The Israeli-Occupied Territories Since 1967', *Am. J. Int'l L.*, Vol. 83 (1990), p. 44.
18. The court applied international law—as interpreted by the court—and substantive principles of Israeli public law—primarily due process and governmental fairness—in addition to the law prevailing in the territories prior to the Israeli occupation. See David Kretzmer, *The Occupation of Justice: The Supreme Court of Israel and the Occupied Territories*, Albany, NY, 2002; Daphne Barak-Erez, 'The International Law of Human Rights and Constitutional Law: A Case Study of an Expanding Dialogue', *Int'l J. Const. L.*, Vol. 2 (2004), pp. 611, 615–616.
19. By comparison, it recently took the US Supreme Court over two years to hold that federal courts had the jurisdiction to hear challenges brought by an alien. See *Rasul v. Bush*, 542 U.S. 466 (2004). Also see *Hamdi v. Rumsfeld*, 542 U.S. 507 (2004); *Rumsfeld v. Padilla*, 542 U.S. 426 (2004).
20. H.C.J. 910/86, *Ressler v. Minister of Defence*, PD 42(2) 441; available in English on www.court.gov.il.
21. H.C.J. 3267/97, 715/98 *Rubinstein and Ressler v. Minister of Defence*, PD 52(5) 481; available on the Israeli Supreme Court website: www.court.gov.il
22. See H.C.J. 4541/94, *Miller v. Minister of Defence*, P.D. 49(4) 94 (8 November 1995).
23. H.C.J. 1284/99 *Doe v. Galili*, P.D. 53(2) 62 (28 March, 1999); translated in full: Seidman and Nun, pp. 135–151.
24. See Seidman and Nun, pp. 122, 143.
25. The Prevention of Sexual Harassment Law, 5758-1998; see in full www.justice.gov.il/NR/rdonlyres/53D06B83-FBC7-49C8-BA87-A452D4A07DB1/0/PrventionofSexualHarassmentLaw.doc.
26. See *Report of the Commission of Inquiry into the Methods of Investigation of the General Security Service (GSS) Regarding Hostile Terrorist Activity*, 1987, reprinted in *Isr. L. Rev.*, Vol. 23, 1989, p.146 (1989).
27. Administrative Detention Appeal [A.D.A.] 10/94 *Anonymous v. Minister of Defence*, 53(1) P.D. 97 (13 November 1997).
28. See Cr.F.H 7048/97, *Anonymous v. Minister of Defence*, 54(1) P.D. 721. See Emanuel Gross, 'Human Rights, Terrorism and the Problem of Administrative Detention in Israel: Does a Democracy Have the Right to Hold Terrorists as Bargaining Chips?', *Ariz. J. Int'l & Comp. L.*, Vol. 18 (2001), p. 721.
29. See H.C. 5100/94 *Public Committee against Torture in Israel v. Government of Israel*, P.D. 53(4) 817 (9 September 1999); available on the Israeli Supreme Court website.
30. The continued detention of some of the so-called 'bargaining chips' was authorized by the Knesset in the Statute for the Detention of Illegal Combatants, 5762-2002; an appeal by one of the Lebanese detainees was rejected by Supreme Court president, Barak, who refused to rule on the constitutionality of the new statute. See H.C. 2055/02 *Sheik Obeid v. Minister of Defence*. Obeid was released in January 2004 as part of an Israeli–Hezbollah swap. The Israeli government did not ask the Knesset to permit 'special interrogation methods' in the General Security Services Act, 5762-2002; human rights organizations maintain that the GSO have developed and implemented tortuous techniques replacing those banned by the Supreme Court.
31. See Melissa L. Clark, 'Israel's High Court of Justice Ruling on the General Security Service use of "Moderate Physical Pressure": and End to the Sanctioned use of the Torture?', *Ind. Int'l & Comp. L. Rev.*, Vol. 11 (2000), p. 145; Emanuel Gross, 'Human Rights, Terrorist and the Problem of Administrative Detention in Israel: Does A Democracy have the Right to Hold

Terrorists as Bargaining Chips?', *Ariz. J. Int'l & Comp. L.*, Vol. 18 (2001), p.721; John T. Parry and Welsh S. White, 'Interrogating Suspected Terrorists: Should Torture be an Option?', *U. Pitt. L. Rev.*, Vol. 63 (2002), p. 743; Emanuel Gross, 'Symposium Terrorism and the Law: Democracy in the War Against Terrorism—The Israeli Experience', *Loy. L.A.L. Rev.*, Vol. 35 (2002), pp. 1161, 1193; Stephen J. Schulhofer, 'Checks and Balances in Wartime: American, British and Israeli Experiences', *Mich. L. Rev.*, Vol. 102 (2004), p. 1906; Oren Gross, 'Are Torture Warrants Warranted? Pragmatic Absolutism and Official Disobedience', *Minn. L. Rev.*, Vol. 88, 2004, p.1481.

32. The precise number of Palestinian casualties is a matter of dispute. See, for example, http://en.wikipedia.org/wiki/Second_Intifada.
33. As the events have become highly contested, I rely here on the UN Report on the Incident in Jenin, available at www.jewishvirtuallibrary.org/jsource/UN/jenin.html. According to the UN report the effects of Israeli incursions from 1 March to 7 May 2002 were harsh: almost 500 Palestinians were killed and 1450 wounded; round-the-clock curfews affected an estimated 1 million persons; over 2800 refugee housing units were damaged and 878 homes were demolished or destroyed during that period, leaving more than 17,000 people homeless or in need of shelter rehabilitation.
34. Clearly there was no massacre, but there was great destruction. The UN report claims at least 52 Palestinians, up to half of whom may have been civilians, and 23 Israeli soldiers were dead; many more were injured; houses were destroyed and 450 families made homeless.
35. H.C.J. 2936/02 *Physicians for Human Rights v. Commander of IDF Forces in the West Bank*, 56 P.D.(3) 3 (8 April 2004), www.phr.org.il/phr/.
36. H.C.J. 2977/02 *Adalah—Legal Centre for Arab Minority Rights in Israel v. Commander of IDF Forces in Judea and Samaria*, 56 P.D.(3) 6 (10 April 2002) www.adalah.org/ara/index.php.
37. H.C.J. 3022/02 *Kanoun (Law)—Palestinian Organization for the Protection of Human Rights and the Environment v. Commander of IDF Forces in the West Bank*, 56 P.D.(3) 9 (10 April 2002) (per Justice Dorner for the court).
38. See *Physicians for Human Rights*, p. 4. Justice Dorner adds that this commitment of the IDF must be presented repeatedly before the troops to the level of the individual soldier in the field, together with the provision of concrete instructions that will prevent, to the extent possible even in tough situations, actions incompatible with the rules of humanitarian assistance. The IDF made similar statements in the other two petitions mentioned above.
39. H.C.J. 3114/02 *Knesset Member Mohammad Barakeh v. Minister of Defence*, 56 P.D.(3) 11 (14 April 2002)(additional petitioners were Knesset Member Ahmad Tibi, and Palestinian public interest groups; a group of Israeli reservist servicemen who fought in Jenin asked to join the cases as respondents; their request was denied).
40. Ibid., p. 15 (per court president Barak).
41. Ibid., p. 15 (per court president Barak).
42. Ibid., p. 16 (per court president Barak).
43. 'In the case before us it was not argued before us that the arrangement we have reached threatens our soldiers ... On the contrary, the arrangement we have reaches is one that all sides are interested in'. Ibid., p. 16 (per court president Barak).
44. For the entire decision see: H.C.J. 316/03 *Muhammad Bakri v. Israel Film Council*, 58 P.D. (1) 249; available on the Israeli Supreme Court website.
45. For instance, that medication should be supplied to the clergy by the IDF. H.C.J. 3436/02 *La Custodia Internazionale di Terra Santa v. Government of Israel*, 56 P.D. (3) 22, 24 (24 April 2002).
46. See Ibid., pp. 24–25 (per Justice Strassberg-Cohen, for the court).
47. The first petitioner was the Palestinian governor of Bethlehem, who was himself inside the compound then under siege. H.C.J. 3451/02 *Muhammad Almadani v. Minister of Defence*, 56 P.D. 30 (2 May 2002).
48. Ibid., p. 34 (per court president Barak).
49. Ibid., p. 35 (per court president Barak).
50. For details see Alan Cowell, 'Mideast Turmoil: The Overview; Exile Agreement Appears to Settle Bethlehem Siege', *New York Times*, 5 September 2002
51. H.C.J. 3900/02 *Terror Victim Headquarters v. Ariel Sharon* (8 May 2002).

52. H.C.J. 10223/02 *Fish-Lifschitz v. Attorney General*, 56 P.D.(6) 517; the two petitioners lost their husbands, whose car was ambushed. In December 2002, months after the siege in Bethlehem had ended, Israeli security forces concluded that several of the militants in the church were responsible for the attack on petitioners and their husbands. Hence this petition.
53. Ibid., pp. 519–520. Note that the court did not use justiciability of international agreements as a reason for the rejection of the petition.
54. H.C.J. 3239/02 *Iad Ashak Mahmud Marab v. IDF Commander in the West Bank*, 57 P.D. (2) 349. Available on the Israeli Supreme Court website.
55. See president Barak's opinion, sections 19–23.
56. President Barak, ibid. at section 31 (judicial review can be delayed until after the detainees have been removed from the battlefield and an initial investigation had been conducted).
57. President Barak, ibid. at section 34.
58. The court also held that this nullification would only go into force after six months, allowing the military to reorganize. See president Barak, ibid. at sections 35–36.
59. See president Barak, Ibid. at section 43.
60. The court notes that while detainees were not allowed to meet lawyers, they 'have the right to be visited by the Red Cross, and their families are informed of their whereabouts. At any time, they may appeal to the High Court of Justice in a petition against their detention'. See president Barak, ibid. at sections 44–46.
61. President Barak, ibid. at sections 47–49. Here too, the court suspends its declaration that parts of the Orders are void for six months, to allow the military to reorganize according to international and Israeli law.
62. See H.C.J. 4764/04 *Physicians for Human Rights v. Commander of the IDF Forces in the Gaza Strip*, 58 P.D. (5) 385 (30 May 2004) petition was submitted 20 May; available on the Israeli Supreme Court website.
63. President Barak explained that the court does not review the actual decision to take military action, but rather the legality of the military operations taken. See president Barak, ibid. at section 17.
64. See president Barak, ibid. at section 16.
65. Ibid. at section 13.
66. Ibid., at sections 40–45.
67. Ibid., at sections 52–53.
68. Ibid., at section 66.
69. See detailed description in H.C.J. 2056/04 *Beit Sourik Village Council v. Government of Israel*; president Barak's opinion, sections 1–8.
70. See: http://www.icj-cij.org/docket/index.php?p1=3&p2=4&code=mwp&case=131&k=5a.
71. See, www.mfa.gov.il/MFA/About + the + Ministry/MFA + Spokesman/2004/Amb. + Gillerman + - + Dark + day + for + ICJ + 9-July-2004.htm; www.mfa.gov.il/MFA/About + the + Ministry/MFA + Spokesman/2004/Statement + on + ICJ + Advisory + Opinion + 9-July-2004.htm.
72. Villagers will also lose access roads to urban centres required for work, medical attention, education and other services. See petition described in section 9 of president Barak's opinion in *Beit Sourik*.
73. The Israeli government did finally agree to some changes in the route of the fence. See, in greater detail, Ibid., sections 16–17.
74. See Ibid. sections 23-24.
75. See Ibid. section 27.
76. See Ibid. sections 28–31.
77. Only a small number of military orders were approved by the court. See Ibid., sections 50, 63–67.
78. See Ibid. section 86.
79. In H.C.J. 1890/03 *Bethlehem Municipality v. State of Israel—Ministry of Defence*, 2 June 2004.
80. In H.C.J. 5784/03 *Louie Salama v. IDF Commander in Judea and Samaria*, 11 August 2003.
81. See, for example, H.C.J. 2117/02 *Physicians for Human Rights v. IDF Commander in the West Bank*, 56 P.D.(3) 26 (28 April 2002; claims that the IDF shot at medical personnel); H.C.J. 727/02 02 *Physicians for Human Rights v. IDF Commander in the Gaza Strip*, 56 P.D. (3) 39, 2 May 2002.

82. Susan M. Akramm Terry Rempel, 'Temporary Protection as an Instrument for Implementing the Right of Return for Palestinian Refugees', *B. U. Int'l. L. J.*, Vol. 22 (2004), pp. 1, 49–52.
83. In two complicated recent cases the Supreme Court addressed delicate issues concerning the pensions to which the dependants of deceased soldiers are eligible. See H.C.J. 585/01 *Klachman v. Chief of Staff*, 58 P.D.(1) 694 (1 December 2003); H.C.J. 6758/01 *Lifschitz v. Minister of Defence* (21 January 2005).
84. In one such case the court reversed the IDF Judge Advocate General's decision to dismiss charges of sexual misconduct. See H.C.J. 4869/01 *Anonymous v. Judge Advocate General*, 56 P.D. (3) 944 (14 April 2002).

Law and Politics in Israel Lands: Toward Distributive Justice

DAPHNE BARAK-EREZ

In contrast to the tradition of other Western countries, the vast majority of land in Israel is publicly owned and administered by a government agency: the Israel Lands Administration ('the Administration' or 'the Lands Administration').[1] Private use of land is thus largely dependent upon the state's readiness (through the operation of the Lands Administration) to permit and facilitate such use. Therefore, the state has a direct influence on the distribution of wealth, power and life opportunities within Israeli society by its decisions regarding Israel's land resources.[2] The question of how to allocate rights and material benefits among individuals or groups is not a legal one; the answer to it should rather reflect principles of justice formulated in the realms of political theory and philosophy. Law, however, also plays an important role in this context. It must ensure that decisions with distributive implications are the product of an open, just, and fair process, primarily in view of the perennial danger that distribution will confer benefits exclusively to well-organized interest groups.

The developments in this area can be described by distinguishing between three stages: (a) the first three decades of the Lands Administration (until the beginning of the 1990s), characterized by broad administrative autonomy without any substantial judicial review of the Administration's actions; (b) the decade from the beginning of the 1990s, during which time specific cases of discrimination were reviewed, but without reference to land policy as such; and (c) the stage initiated by the new and ground-breaking decision of the Supreme Court in the matter of the agricultural lands, a decision that heralded the transition to a comprehensive review of administrative policy from the perspective of distributive justice in society as a whole. Of course, only time will tell whether this decision actually succeeded in bringing about the change it declared.

ADMINISTRATIVE AUTONOMY WITHIN AN OPEN-ENDED LEGISLATIVE FRAMEWORK

The disputes over decisions relating to Israel lands derive primarily from the fact that the law which applies to these lands—the Israel Lands Administration Law, 1960[3]—lacks the requisite legal tools for the challenges it is supposed to cope with. It does not state the objectives of the Administration's operation nor does it establish any priority scales to guide those charged with its implementation (in contrast with accepted legislative practice regarding administrative authorities). The only provision dealing with policy in this area is section 3 of the Law that provides: 'The Government shall appoint an Israel Lands Council which shall lay down the land policy in accordance with which the Administration shall act, shall supervise the activities of the Administration, and shall approve the draft of its budget, which shall be fixed by law.' Nonetheless, even with respect to the Israel Lands Council ('the Council'), there are no framework provisions or guiding principles within the Law. In effect it received a 'blank cheque'.[4] Furthermore, until recently the Law lacked any provisions for dealing with the Council's composition, and the appointment of its members was exclusively a matter of governmental discretion.[5]

In the absence of legislative guarantees that lands be administrated for the benefit of the public, judicial review becomes particularly important. Paradoxically, however, it is precisely where judicial review is needed most that it is confronted by the most formidable difficulties in discharging its role. For without guiding legislative directives, the objectives and purposes of such review are amorphous. Judicial review generally begins with an examination of the statutorily determined objectives, which should guide the relevant administrative agency. Sometimes, where the law refrains from specifically addressing the considerations that should define and guide the actions of an administrative agency, the court can infer them from the agency's composition. However, the vague references to the composition of the Israel Lands Council thwart any attempt to draw any decisive conclusions from this factor as well.

In practice, for many years, the selection of potential candidates for contracts with the Israel Lands Administration was not based on any clear, normative arrangement. Traditionally, Israeli administrative law did not recognize a general duty to offer contracts through tender,[6] unless there was legislation that explicitly mandated it, for example, in the case of local government.[7] Indeed, the Israel Lands Administration gradually adopted a system of internal directives which included provisions governing the duty to initiate public tenders.[8] However, these directives were not always complied with. Essentially, they reflected accepted procedures in the Israel Lands Administration, but their status as internal directives endowed them with a degree of flexibility that was vulnerable to abuse precisely in the sensitive cases, exposing them to improper preferences. Summing up this point, it is submitted that for many years the absence of an appropriate legislative framework meant that judicial review of the decisions of the Israel Lands Administration was minimal, and in the absence of a statutory duty to issue tenders, the allocation of public lands was conducted without due supervision.[9]

FROM ADMINISTRATIVE AUTONOMY TO INDIVIDUAL-BASED EQUALITY

From the beginning of the 1990s, the Supreme Court adopted a new policy, which deviated from the previous passivity that characterized its treatment of the Lands Administration's decisions. The judgment signifying the new direction in judicial policy was *Poraz v. Minister for Housing and Construction.*[10] In this case, the Israel Lands Council decided to lease lands to a number of politically affiliated religious associations, without conducting any preliminary competitive proceedings. Prima facie, the allocation had a commendable goal—to assist in increasing the supply of residential opportunities in the centre of the country. Yet the question remained as to why these associations were more deserving than other groups of families desiring to build their homes in that region? In a landmark judgment, Chief Justice Shamgar invalidated the decisions, ruling that fairness and equality dictated that any allocation of public lands be based on a mechanism that ensured equal opportunities, such as a tender or a lottery.[11] Just a short while later, a similar decision was given in *Elyakim 1986—Communal Agricultural Settlement Association Ltd v. Israel Land Administration.*[12] This decision dealt with a piece of land zoned for commercial initiatives. Again, there was no prior competitive proceeding for selecting the lessees. The intended lessees were a group of local *kibbutzim*, and their priority (over other potential lessees) was explained against the background of their previous losses, incurred in their agricultural activities. The court refused to accept this explanation as a justification for the total failure to conduct any form of competition, pointing at the possibility of initiating a competition restricted to residents of the region who had faced similar hardships.[13]

These precedents are significant because they constitute the normative basis for intervention in land allocation preferences based on protectionist considerations. While neither of the aforementioned judgments included a detailed presentation of the factual background of the rulings, it is difficult to ignore the fact that both cases concerned decisions which granted priority to organized sectors that were better equipped to operate as pressure groups in Israeli public life, and that benefited from cooperation with administrative agencies. Even so, the limitations of the precedents must also be acknowledged. In both cases, the court refrained from interfering with the determination of the Administration's policy priorities—whether to prefer young couples, new immigrants, or local residents—restricting its review to the aspect of individual-based equality in applying current policies. In the *Poraz* case, Justice Shamgar explicitly considered the possibility that allocation without competition might be justified by 'policy considerations' such as 'security needs, construction of a suburb in support of a development enterprise, an urgent extension of an existing enterprise, or the expansion of a settlement for the absorption of its second generation'.[14] While Justice Shamgar regarded these as being 'exceptional cases',[15] they exemplify the Administration's broad scope of discretion. In *Elyakim*, Justice Tal explicitly ruled, 'had the Administration issued a closed tender, intended exclusively for the settlements in the region of the local council, it would have been deemed reasonable. But granting an exemption from tender to one particular body in the council, and no other, even if the initiative originated with the two *kibbutzim*—is not reasonable'.[16] Here too, the court restricted its judicial review to an examination of whether the requirements of formal equality were satisfied, in the sense that all those included in the sector which the Administration had decided to prefer (in this case, farmers who had suffered financial losses), should merit the same treatment. In terms of the basic doctrines of administrative law, which charge policy making with the agency, this division of powers between the court and the Administration is understandable. However, in the absence of statutory guidelines, the meaning of these holdings was that the Administration and the Council had almost unlimited power in formulating their distributive decisions.

This consequence is of major importance when considering one of the exceptions to the general duty to conduct a tender open to all: the priority given to local residents. As mentioned in *Poraz*, the possibility of granting priority to members of the local 'second generation' was recognized as a legitimate exception to the general rule of open and equal competition, and this holding was also reaffirmed in later rulings. In *Rosenberg v. Ministry of Construction and Residence*[17] the court approved a decision to incorporate an element of preference for local residents within the framework of a 'Build Your Apartment' project in Ramat HaSharon. In another case, *Beerotaim, Workers Village for Cooperative Agricultural Settlement Ltd. v. Arad*,[18] the court affirmed a decision to allow a cooperative association for settlement (*moshav*) to select the candidates for receiving construction plots in the lands leased to it by the Israel Land Administration. The court ruled that this decision did not constitute unlawful delegation of administrative powers, because from a formal perspective, the cooperative association's position only served as a recommendation. This decision is also connected to the traditional preference given to local residents, because it is common knowledge that selection processes conducted by closed associations of this kind tend to prefer their own members. All things being equal, it was reasonable to presume that those recommended by the *moshav* would be approved as lessees and that they would be members of its second generation (provided that they were interested). This in fact was the factual background of the judgment itself, according to which the only candidates for the new plots were members of the cooperative association, as opposed to other residents of the *moshav*, who were not members of the cooperative. The legitimacy of preferring second-generation members was reaffirmed in another petition dealing with the expansion of the *moshavim*, in *Kefar Hittim Cooperative Agricultural Settlement Ltd v. Bein.*[19] In that case, specific emphasis was given to the legitimacy of granting priority to the children of the *moshav* members over the children of its other non-member residents. According to Justice Dorner,

> the continuing sons [children of members] have undertaken to become members of the *moshav*, bearing the burden of the Cooperative Association's debts; the *moshav* desires to maintain its existence, its continuity, and the number of members, a desire which receives expression in its decision to grant preferential conditions to continuing sons with respect to the purchasing of plots. This desire is a legitimate one.[20]

Apart from questions regarding a potential conflict of interests in such a situation, it is important to consider the distributive implications of these decisions. Maintaining the existing communal composition tends to preserve the status quo regarding the allocation of benefits deriving from public lands. Allocation to the second generation of the settlement reflects consideration of the communal aspect, but it also perpetrates existing preferences, the preservation of which is not always justified. Hence, someone whose parents missed out in the 'first round' of distribution becomes equally deprived once again in the 'second round'. These issues were not mentioned in any of the aforementioned judgments.

The enactment of Mandatory Tenders Law, 1992[21] did not substantially limit the scope of discretion exercised by the Israel Lands Administration. The general statutory duty to issue a tender[22] was applied to the Administration, like all other branches of central government. However, this law empowers the Minister of Finance to prescribe exceptions to this rule[23] and, in practice, this power was exercised generously also with respect to the contract initiatives of the Administration.[24] In some of these exceptions, the fingerprints of interest groups are clearly evident. The Administration's broad discretion in this area also derives from the fact that it is not even bound by the exemptions specified by the regulations. Even where lands can be leased without a tender, the Administration is at liberty to market them by issuing a tender open to all, and, in fact, is under duty to consider this possibility.[25] Indeed, issuing a tender even when the statutory duty to do so does not apply is usually desirable. At the same time, however, there are cases in which the tender procedure is inimical to the interests of weaker sectors, who have difficulty in competing for land leases with the wealthy under open market conditions (for example, the Bedouins, who are expressly mentioned in the exceptions stated in the regulations).[26]

When the Administration decides to utilize (or not to utilize) an exception to the statutory tender duty, it once again adopts a decision of distributive significance. In addition, decisions in these matters are not necessarily uniform. The lack of uniformity is exemplified by comparing two similar cases—the *Eilat Municipality v. Israel Lands Administration* case,[27] and the *Rosenberg* case already mentioned earlier. In the *Eilat Municipality* case, the court was requested to review a decision to lease plots within the framework of a 'Build Your House' project, by way of a lottery open to all. The Eilat Municipality opposed the decision, claiming that priority should have been given to the local residents. The court rejected this argument, holding that exemption from the duty to issue a tender in developing areas was voluntary and not obligatory. Accordingly, it ruled that the Administration was only required to ensure that the objective of the leasing would be realized by specifying conditions regarding a commitment to reside in Eilat for a few years.[28] Contrary to this decision, in the *Rosenberg* case, the decision petitioned against actually included an element of priority given to local residents in the framework of 'Build Your Apartment' in the municipality of Ramat HaSharon. The majority opinion dismissed the petition, conceding that considering one's connection with the community was indeed a reasonable consideration.[29] The judgment appears both logical and humane when read in isolation. However, considering it against the background of the court's decision in the *Eilat Municipality* case indicates that in the absence of legislative guidance, judicial review is liable to leave a wake of conflicting decisions, each of them intrinsically reasonable on its merits.

The tendency of judicial review to assess each case on its own merits and not within the broader context of decisions in other cases (as evidenced from the combined reading of the judgments in *Eilat Municipality* and in *Rosenberg*) is particularly problematic for claims of group discrimination in the administration of Israel Lands. Proving a claim of sectoral discrimination, i.e. discrimination concerning injustice caused to a particular sector in the allocation of land resources, requires a broad perspective, relating not only to the particular decision that constitutes grounds for the petition, but also to additional decisions that were adopted in the past. This broad perspective is required, for example, in order to assess the claims of discrimination against the Arab sector, whose engagements with the Administration over the years were quantitatively and qualitatively limited. It is difficult to prove claims of this kind in proceedings conducted in a judicial format, where the discussion is limited to the facts proven in court, and to the parties involved. This was the background for the rejection—due to insufficient factual substantiation—of a claim posed by Bedouin petitioners that they had been discriminated against in land allocations, in comparison to Jewish settlers.[30] Notably, the Bedouin claim was rejected on the basis of 'insufficient factual substantiation'.[31] However, when deliberating the question of the 'closing' of the Katzir settlement for Jews only, the court noted, in the background of its decision, that 'in fact the State of Israel allocates land only for Jewish communal settlements'.[32]

TOWARDS A THIRD STAGE: FROM INDIVIDUAL EQUALITY TO DISTRIBUTIVE JUSTICE

At the beginning of the twenty-first century, a ground-breaking judgment was given regarding decisions of the Israel Lands Council on the lands allocated to agricultural settlers (primarily to *kibbutzim* and *moshavim*).[33] Potentially, the judgment heralds the commencement of an era in which judicial review examines the more general distributive effects of land policies.[34] The decisions dealt by the court in this matter granted the settlers rights in their leased lands in excess of their previous contractual entitlements. More specifically, the decisions allowed the settlers to develop land originally leased for agricultural purposes for non-agricultural uses as well. And, where settlers were required to return lands to the state due to rezoning and new planning of the area for urban uses, the compensation offered them would be based on (a certain percentage of) the new value of the lands after rezoning.[35]

The central petition against these decisions was filed by the Mizrachi Democratic Rainbow, an association of intellectuals and descendants of Jewish immigrants from Arab (Mizrachi) countries, who claimed to represent the relatively indigent sectors of the Israeli (Jewish) population. The Mizrachi Democratic Rainbow regarded the decisions as a perpetuation of the injustice caused by the original allocation of lands, in which most of the immigrants from Arab countries did not participate. Legally speaking, it argued that these decisions exceeded the powers of the Council, because they included substantive ('primary') arrangements which should have been established by legislation, and that they were also unreasonable, principally because of the discrimination in favour of the agricultural sector and the disregard of social, economic, and ecological considerations. Another petition was filed by the Society for the Protection of Nature, emphasizing the preservation of open areas.

The Supreme Court annulled these decisions, which it deemed unreasonable because of their disregard for 'distributive justice'. The judgment in this matter signified an important transition from the narrowly-based consideration of personal equality to broader considerations of distributive justice. It is interesting to note that after the petitions were filed, an inter-office committee was set up to examine the decisions and their ramifications (the Milgrom Committee).[36] The Committee held that the decisions were unreasonable, and ought to be replaced by decisions that would significantly reduce the benefits to the agricultural sector. In light of these conclusions, the position adopted by the State was that the original decisions could not stand and new decisions should be adopted. Against this background, it is not surprising that the petitions were accepted. Therefore, the primary importance of the judgment was not in the actual invalidation of the decisions, but rather in the normative guidelines proposed by the court for future decisions regarding Israel lands.[37]

The court expressed dissatisfaction with the fact that under current legislation the primary principles which guide land policy are decided by administrative bodies (rather than by the legislature), but refrained from invalidating the decisions for this reason.[38] The main thrust of the judgment was that allocation of lands must comport with the principle of distributive justice. According to Justice Or:

> Distributive justice is a paramount value, warranting appropriate emphasis in any decision of an administrative authority regarding allocation of public resources. This is particularly true in the case before us. The Israel Lands Administration is the body charged with responsibility for Israel lands in their entirety, and it is impossible to overstate the importance of this asset and the importance attaching to its distribution and allocation in a just and appropriate manner. The decisions in the petitions before us have critical implications for the allocation of this limited, and particularly valuable resource. There is an essential public interest that resources of this kind be allocated by the State, or authorities acting on its behalf, in a manner that is fair, just and reasonable.[39]

The judgment emphasized the scarcity of land resources in Israel and the need for land reserves. While it did not discount the possibility of considering the historical claim raised by the settlers, which emphasized their contribution to the Zionist enterprise, the court made it clear that this consideration would have to be factored in with other social interests.[40]

The novelty of the attitude expressed in the *Rainbow* judgment regarding the principle of distributive justice is particularly striking when compared with a previous judgment given by Justice Or regarding prior decisions that preferred agricultural settlers,[41] in *Mehadrin v. Government of Israel*.[42] In that case, the petitioners argued against decisions which distinguished between the rates of compensation awarded to lessees belonging to the cooperative settlements sector and those awarded to private farmers (although in both cases the lands had to be returned due to rezoning). Justice Or refrained from deciding the question of this alleged discrimination after accepting the petitioners' preliminary claim regarding the conflict of interests of those Council members belonging to the cooperative settlements sector who had participated in the decision-making process. Explaining the nature of their conflict of interests, Justice Or stated that these Council members were expected 'to decide on the minimal, suitable rate of compensation that would ensure the goal of timely construction on lands zoned for agricultural purposes',[43] as opposed to the interest of their sector in the maximization of compensation. This argumentation implied that the Israel Lands Council was supposed to aspire to decisions that were optimally efficient (and thrifty) from an economic perspective. By implication, these concepts were rejected by the *Rainbow* judgment, in its endorsement of distributive justice as a guiding principle in the administration of Israel Lands.

The decisions discussed by the *Rainbow* judgment were not invalidated because they were not efficiency-based, but rather because they failed to address the needs and considerations pertaining to other groups, external to the agricultural sector. Regarding the decision awarding compensation to the agricultural lessees based on the future value of their land when planned for urban development purposes,[44] the court held that besides ensuring quick availability of lands for development (by giving the lessees incentives to cooperate with the new plans), it was necessary to consider additional factors, including: the planning aspect (preservation of open areas, and the focus on urban development in the metropolitan regions of Israel); social considerations (the social tensions liable to result from high compensation awarded to a limited, defined group); the availability of alternative methods for changing the use of land leased in the past for agricultural purposes (requiring lessees to return land not used for agricultural purposes); and the possibility of making distinctions between various regions of the country (center or periphery) in accordance with the demand for land.

The judgment also criticized the rate of compensation and the mechanism for calculating compensation (based on the future value of the land) because in effect it created a partnership between the lessee and the state, even though the alleged purpose was only to create an incentive for vacating the land. The percentage-based formula adopted by the decisions engendered uncertainty regarding the scale of the benefit and contributed to discrimination between lessees in different parts of the country (unacceptable in general, and especially in view of the historical claim raised by the agricultural settlers concerning reward for their past efforts and their investments).[45] The court added that the degree of disparity between the compensation calculated on the basis of past investments (the contractual criterion) and the compensation actually decided upon, was indicative per se of the decision's unreasonableness.[46] Another decision which was discussed in the judgement had paved the way for extensive 'enlargements' of *moshavim* by authorizing the building of new residential houses on agricultural land.[47] This decision was deemed problematic because it contradicted existing planning policy (by drawing the stronger populations out of the cities and increasing traffic congestion). Despite the fact that this decision was justified by the need to strengthen the population of agricultural settlements, the court held that the decision went too far, by significantly reducing the lease fees (and thus also creating an incentive for speculative investment). Notably, here too the ruling differs considerably from the *Beerotaim* case.[48] The third decision discussed by the court and deemed unreasonable concerned the development of industrial zones in an agricultural area.[49] The court once again recognized the need to locate additional sources of employment in the agricultural settlements, but here too it ruled that there was no justification for the significant reduction in the lease fees for land used for industrial purposes.

DISTRIBUTIVE JUSTICE: ISSUES OF SUBSTANCE

The importance of the *Rainbow* judgment lies first and foremost in the recognition it conferred on the value of distributive justice, which became part of the legal discourse in the context of Israeli public law. However, numerous questions remain regarding the practical application of this principle. How does one realize distributive justice? What are the judgment's implications or dictates with respect to other cases, such as the distribution of lands in the Arab sector?[50]

Indeed, the concept of distributive justice is considered amorphous, and serious disputes will probably arise regarding the scope and manner of its application. Conceivably, the court's decision could have benefited from a greater effort to clarify its practical implications and applications. Even so, the principle, as such, is not an empty slogan. Firstly, it clearly extends beyond the requirements of individual equality as expressed in the *Poraz* precedent, which mandated that, all things being equal, the allocation of land should be effected through a competitive format. Secondly, it requires that the Israel Lands Council—and the Israel Lands Administration in its wake—would refrain from consistently disregarding the needs of any segment or group in Israel, and obligates it to consider actively the needs of the diverse segments of the population. Thirdly, it necessitates considering the needs of future generations of Israelis (by securing unexploited land reserves available for them). In other words, distributive justice is not just intra-generational, but also inter-generational.[51] Interestingly enough, despite their opposition to the *Rainbow* judgment, even the arguments of the agricultural settlers were based on the idea of distributive justice in its broad sense, albeit with a different result in mind. The settlers' claims regarding the consideration of their historical rights and their contribution to the state and the defence of its borders exceeded the ambit of their rights as individuals, and attempted to confer on them benefits based on their group affiliation.

The emerging dialogue concerning the duty to administer Israel Lands in accordance with the principle of distributive justice may draw inspiration from writings dealing with questions of just planning. Even in countries in which the lands are privately owned, administrative authorities influence the uses of the land and the degree of benefit derived from it using their statutory powers in the area of planning. Decisions adopted by the authorities necessarily affect residential standards and access to communal services and employment opportunities. As such, they have clear distributive significance. The lessons of the attendant theoretical discussion in the area of planning can serve as a source of inspiration for the application of the principle of distributive justice in the context of land allocation.

In his book *Social Justice and the City*, political geographer David Harvey presented a theory of regional distributive justice based on the following central criteria: need, contribution to the common good, and compensation for difficulties. The 'need' criterion mandates consideration for the basic needs of those sectors of the population affected by the planning, addressing a number of aspects, such as housing, employment, communal services and leisure culture. The criterion of 'contribution to the common good' considers the influence of resource allocation on other places or groups (including negative externalizations, such as pollution, etc.). The consideration of 'compensation for difficulties' essentially expresses the concept of affirmative action and mandates consideration for the difficulties occasioned by residence in zones with adverse basic conditions whether geographic (floods, earthquakes, etc.) or social (crime).[52] In his later writings, Harvey broadened his analysis to include environmental justice and implications for future generations.[53]

DISTRIBUTIVE JUSTICE: ISSUES OF PROCESS

In addition to developing a substantive concept of distributive justice, emphasis should also be given to the administrative decision-making process, in order to maximize the chances that proper consideration will be given to the largest possible spectrum of relevant interests. In order to achieve this goal, it is important to guarantee public access to the process in order to achieve a more comprehensive participation of diverse sectors of the population in it.

One important procedural safeguard should be to guarantee public access to information about the administrative procedures while they still take place. Decisions pertaining to the uses of Israel Lands are more vulnerable to the improper influences of organized interest groups when they are taken covertly, remote from the public eye and knowledge. Due to such potential influences, proposals under consideration must be publicized. Generally, until now, decisions pertaining to Israel Lands had a low public profile at the time of their adoption. Nor was the public aware of significant deliberations taking place, or of other proposals under consideration. On the other hand, 'those who were supposed to know' knew. The 1995 Amendment of the Israel Lands Administration Law led to a slight improvement, but regretfully of limited benefit. Today, the Law requires publication of decisions adopted by the Israel Lands Council.[54] However the Law explicitly provides that a breach of this duty will not impugn the validity of the decision. According to the concluding passage of section 4M of the Law, 'the effective date [of the decision] shall not be contingent upon publication, unless provided otherwise in the decision'. And most importantly, the statutory duty to publicize only relates to the final decisions and therefore deprives the public of the requisite tools for influencing the formative moments of the decision-making process whereas the advance publication of decision proposals is important primarily when there are well-organized interest groups who have better access to the administrators.[55] The Law must create conditions that promote public awareness of proposed decisions prior to the termination of the administrative process.

From the perspective of public awareness of the decisions pertaining to Israel lands, there were democratic advantages to legislative initiatives in this area—the Public Housing Law Bill, 1998,[56] for which the legislative proceedings were completed,[57] and the Entrenchment and Registration of Farmers' Rights in Land Bill, 1996,[58] which did not get to legislation. While these initiatives were considered controversial, they were preferable to the decisions of the Israel Lands Council in the sense that they were presented for public debate. In other words, the administrative decisions on Israel Lands, adopted under conditions of no publicity and without due acknowledgment of their political character, have been inferior even to legislation promoted by interest groups. In the latter, there is no attempt to camouflage the political disputes. The legislative bills in this area were initiated by politicians whose political motives and agendas are usually of public knowledge, thus increasing the chance of their being deliberated by the general public. In fact, the administration of Israel Lands was heavily handicapped in comparison to both professional and political decision-making processes: it was not based on purely professional considerations, nor was it conducted under conditions of public review and criticism. Of course, access to the process and openness may be achieved also in the framework of administrative decision-making, and not only in the Knesset.[59] Notably, the Milgrom Committee, which reviewed the decisions on the agricultural lands, published notifications requesting all those interested to present their positions to the Committee.

A second procedural concern relates to the active participation of various groups in the processes leading to distributive decisions. Distributive decisions reflecting social preferences should not be accepted solely on the basis of 'expert' knowledge. In other words, in this context, the administrative process need not necessarily aspire to a 'correct' result, but rather to a result that reflects the desires of the equitable owner—the public. The question is how to attain public input into administrative decision-making when direct democracy is no longer practicable (and certainly not with respect to the ongoing administration of assets) and when the legislator too is unable to provide specific responses to all the questions which arise. Should the solution be based on a more representative composition of the Israel Lands Council as opposed to the partial format of public representation, reflected in the existing statutory arrangement? Presumably, this kind of reform would promote democratic values in the administrative decision-making process. The appointment of Arab representatives to the Israel Lands Council signified a first step in this direction.[60] On the other hand, one cannot dismiss the fear that here, too, well-organized interest groups will be more successful in effectively utilizing this system. The 1995 Amendment of the Law endorsed the representation-based approach, but included only very general guidelines, once again exposing itself to interest-based exploitation. As stated, the Amendment recognized the possibility of appointing 'public representatives' as members of the Israel Lands Council (in limited numbers), but it lacks provisions regarding the method for appointing them.

In addition, the question arises as to how to differentiate between legitimate representation and illegitimate bias. As noted in the *Mehadrin* case[61] the Supreme Court invalidated decisions adopted by the Council in relation to compensation for agricultural lessees, because some of the participants in the proceedings were members of *kibbutzim* and *moshavim* and, as such, stood to benefit from the decision. According to further judgments, members with pecuniary interests in agricultural lands were disqualified from serving on a sub-committee connected to the rezoning of their land, even when it only had advisory powers.[62]

These judgments expose the inherent paradox ingrained in the implementation of representative statutory schemes. It is precisely when the representation principle fulfils its goals that the blight of bias kicks in.[63] The question that arises is whether to apply a softer version of the law of conflict of interests with respect to bodies defined as political, as opposed to authorities whose decisions are supposed to be essentially professional, subject to the condition that they also be required to operate in accordance with equality-based criteria. The dilemma is far from simple. At any rate, with regard to the Israel Lands Council, it would seem that the main problem lies elsewhere: Endorsing the principle of representative appointments in this context can be expected to further empower the organized interest groups, and thus perpetuate the inaccessibility of the decision-making process to weaker groups which suffer from under-representation in the Israeli public administration. Moreover, it would be at the expense of 'the silent majority'—those citizens who are not defined to a degree that warrants their recognition as a defined interest group, but who in fact constitute the backbone of Israeli society.

For these reasons, it would seem appropriate to consider alternative methods for the realization of the democratic-representative ideal in fundamental decisions relating to benefits gained from public property. For example, since it is unlikely that the appointments to the Israel Lands Council will fully reflect the entire complex of interests deserving of representation, it may be preferable to waive altogether the principle of representative appointments to the Council, and replace it by a system of professional appointments in the areas relevant to the Administration's activity and simultaneously to open the Council proceedings to the representatives of the different groups, thus enabling them to present their positions to the Council. It must be stressed that participation in the Administration's decision-making process is of tremendous importance and has the potential to significantly influence the decisions adopted, as indicated by the comparison of decisions adopted with the participation of bodies external to the Administration with decisions adopted in forums closed to them.[64]

Another option may be to consider transferring the main policy decisions of the Israel Lands Council to the political arena, where the debates are more accessible to the public and covered by the media. A solution in this vein, not involving an upheaval of the entire system, would be to add a requirement of governmental approval to such decisions.[65] Admittedly, the government has no advantage over the Israel Lands Council from a professional perspective, but it is a more representative body and its decisions are subject to an ongoing public debate. Submitting the main decisions on land policy for official approval by the government would make the government directly responsible for the distributive implications of the land policy, and would guarantee public deliberation in these matters.

While these proposals for procedural reforms are important, it should be remembered that a fair process does not always guarantee the quality of the decisions adopted or the ability to reach a consensus. Nor can it eliminate the structural biases resulting from the composition of the deciding body or from effective activities of certain pressure groups. The aftermath of the *Rainbow* judgment serves as an example of the limitations of procedural reforms. The *Rainbow* judgment instructed the Israeli Lands Council to issue transitional provisions, which would apply to the transactions concluded pursuant to the decisions invalidated by the court. To that end, the Council appointed a committee headed by Moshe Nissim, formerly a senior minister in the Israeli government, and then decided to adopt transitional provisions that were essentially consistent with the Committee's recommendations.

This decision prompted renewed petitions to the High Court by the Mizrachi Democratic Rainbow and other social organizations. They contested the transitional provisions, claiming that in essence they divested the *Rainbow* judgment of any practical significance. Interestingly, although the Nissim Committee heard both the parties with interests in the lands, and their counterparts, it did not generate social consensus regarding the appropriate policy. Following the petition, the attorney general gave notice that he would not be able to defend the transitional provisions decided upon by the Israel Lands Council, and his position triggered a new decision that curtailed their scope, so that they would apply only to a smaller number of transactions which had reached a relatively advanced stage.[66] This in turn prompted a number of additional petitions by lessees who did not fall within the purview of the new transitional provisions. Ultimately, the court dismissed all the petitions in this matter—both those submitted by the protesting social organizations and those of the lessees who claimed that they were aggrieved by the second decision.[67]

Arguably, in the matter of transitional provisions, the appropriate administrative process did not engender social consensus. This result does not indicate, however, that an emphasis upon the importance of process is futile. In the circumstances of the case, the magnitude of the burden assumed by the Council made disagreement almost inevitable. On the one hand, the transition provisions were required to amend previous decisions pertaining to agricultural lands, in accordance with the principle of distributive justice. On the other hand, they had to consider issues of individual justice (with regard to those who had planned transactions and even begun realizing them on the basis of previous decisions). Reconciling these conflicting positions was a particularly difficult task. Furthermore, the transition provisions were debated against the background of prior animosity between the rival parties and a previous history of a flawed process, and in the absence of any significant changes in the composition of the Israel Lands Council. One may hope that a fair process—open and accessible—will succeed in producing more successful results at least in relation to new policy decisions.

ISRAEL LANDS AND THE FUTURE OF LAND LAW IN ISRAEL

The developing judicial review of decisions regarding the administration of Israel Lands has made it clear that these decisions should be based on principles of individual equality (as implemented by the court since the beginning of the 1990s) and distributive group-oriented equality (as made clear by the *Rainbow* judgment). It remains to be seen whether these principles will be integrated into the everyday decision-making processes of the Administration, or whether they will remain only obscure principles guiding judicial review.

Another question relates to the possibility of more fundamental legal reforms regarding Israel lands. A potentially important reform, which has to be considered would aim to amend the Israel Lands Administration Law by adding to it provisions on the objectives and principles that should guide the operations of the Land Administration.[68] Indeed, statutory provisions of this kind would be necessarily broad and would not impose substantial restrictions on the exercise of the Administration's discretionary powers. Still, they would confer some limitations and guidelines.

A more radical reform, occasionally proposed, is to abandon the tradition of public ownership of lands and progress towards a private ownership-based land regime. It is doubtful whether proposals of this kind have any significant chance of passing, taking into consideration that the public ownership of land in Israel has been traditionally justified also by security considerations related to the Arab–Israeli conflict. At any rate, it is important to remember that any decision to privatize Israel lands would necessarily face significant distributive questions, similar to those discussed so far in the context of administering them. In fact, current land administration in Israel leads to de-facto privatization, given the long periods of leasing and the limited impact of the Land Administration on the use of land. These questions will become even more critical in the context of full privatization in which the distribution is, by definition, a final distribution by the state.

NOTES

1. The basic constitutional norm that preserves public ownership of land is established in section 1 of the Basic Law: Israel Lands, which provides that 'The ownership of Israel lands . . . shall not be transferred either by sale or in any other manner'. This arrangement was influenced by the format for land acquisition prior to the establishment of the state, the collectivist world view prevalent in Israeli society at that time and, obviously, by national considerations relating to the Israel–Arab conflict. See further J. Weisman 'Israel's State-Owned Land', *Mishpatim*, Vol. 21 (1991), p. 79 (Hebrew).
2. See M. Mautner (ed.), *Distributive Justice in Israel*, Tel Aviv, 2001 (Hebrew).
3. Hereinafter: 'Israel Lands Administration Law' or 'the Law'.
4. Professor Zamir notes that the powers granted to the Israel Lands Administration serve a classic example of the legislative practice of conferring an administrative body with 'sweeping authority', and warns that a law of this kind (occasionally referred to as a 'framework law'), is not consistent with the concept of the rule of law. See I. Zamir, *Administrative Power*, Jerusalem, 1996, Vol. 1, pp. 236–237 (Hebrew).
5. Israel Lands Administration Law (Amendment), 1995 (hereinafter, the 1995 Amendment) added a number of provisions regarding these matters, but they include restrictions of a particularly limited nature.

6. Compare H.C. 840/79, *The Union of Israeli Constructors and Builders v. Government of Israel*, 34 (3) P.D. 729.
7. See section 197 of the Municipal Corporations Ordinance [New Version].
8. For example, according to Decision 1 of the Israel Lands Council, 'The transfer of urban lands, with the exception of land zoned for public purposes, shall be effected by way of a public tender'. In the context of this provision it was determined that 'In accordance with the decision of the director of the Israel Lands Administration, the Council is entitled to exempt the Administration from its obligation to transfer land by way of a public tender'.
9. An exceptional example of a judicial review of a deviation from the directives of the Israel Lands Administration is H.C. 143/64, *Adato v. Amidar*, 18 (3) P.D. 51.
10. H.C. 5023/91, *Poraz v. Ministry of Housing and Construction*, 46(2) P.D. 793 (hereinafter, *Poraz*).
11. Ibid., p. 801.
12. H.C. 6176/93, *Elyakim 1986—Cooperative Agricultural Settlement Association Ltd v. Israel Lands Administration*, 48(2) P.D. 158 (hereinafter, *Elyakim*).
13. Ibid., p. 165.
14. *Poraz*, p. 801.
15. Ibid., p. 801.
16. *Elyakim*, p. 165
17. P.C.A. 5817/95 *Rosenberg v. Ministry of Housing and Construction*, 50(1) P.D. 221 (hereinafter, *Rosenberg*).
18. C.A. 2962/97, *Beerotaim, Workers Moshav for Cooperative Agricultural Settlement v. Arad*, 52(4) P.D. 614 (hereinafter, *Beerotiam*).
19. P.C.A. 10623/02 *Kefar Hittim—Cooperative Moshav for Agricultural Settlement Ltd v. Bein*, 57(2) P.D. 943.
20. Ibid., p. 947.
21. Hereinafter, Mandatory Tenders Law.
22. Section 2 of the Mandatory Tenders Law.
23. Section 4(b) of the Mandatory Tenders Law.
24. Sections 25–26 of the Mandatory Tenders Regulations, 1993 (hereinafter, Mandatory Tenders Regulations).
25. Section 42 of the Mandatory Tenders Regulations.
26. Section 25(20) of the Mandatory Tenders Regulations.
27. C.A 1444/95 *Eilat Municipality v. Israel Lands Administration*, 49 (3) P.D. 749 (hereinafter, *Eilat Municipality*).
28. *Eilat Municipality*, pp. 762–763.
29. *Rosenberg*, p. 227.
30. See H.C. 6532/94, *Abu-kaf v. Minister of Agriculture*, 50 (4) P.D. 391.
31. Ibid., p. 394.
32. H.C. 6698/95 *Kada'an v. Israel Lands Administration*, 54 (1) P.D. 258, 279. The court noted this fact in its examination of the possibility of closing the settlement to Arabs, based on the claim of 'separate but equal'. In the absence of allocation of lands for Arab settlements, this claim is bound to be rejected on the factual plane alone, even before addressing the normative problems it raises.
33. The *kibbutz*, *moshav* (singular form) and *kibbutzim*, *moshavim* (plural form) are two Israeli frameworks of communal living, distinguished from each other by their particular economic structures
34. H.C. 244/00 *Association for New Dialogue for Democratic Dialogue v. Minister of National Infrastructures*, 56(6) P.D. 25 (hereinafter, *Rainbow*).
35. The details of these decisions were as follows: compensation for the agricultural settlers in cases of rezoning on a percentage basis of between 27 and 29 percent of the value of the land after the rezoning (Decision 727 which replaced previous decisions in the same spirit: Decisions 533, 611 and 666); development of industrial zones on lands previously leased as agricultural lands under conditions that included a significant reduction in lease payments, an exemption from tender, and possible cooperation of external developers (Decision 717 which replaced Decision 441); and rezoning for the purpose of expanding the *moshavim* while offering a reduction in lease payments and an exemption from tender (Decision 737, which replaced Decision 612). These decisions directly benefited the two sectors which worked for

their promotion—the settlers themselves and the land developers who sought to capitalize on the new opportunities for building, and in doing so demonstrated one of the weaknesses of the administrative process: its vulnerability to being biased in favour of the specific entities which the administrative authority is supposed to supervise. This tendency was discussed in the literature, in which it was referred to as the 'capture' problem (the dynamic of administrative agencies becoming 'captured' by the very same economic factors and players over which they are supposed to supervise). See S.P. Huntington, 'The Marasmus of the ICC: The Commission, Railroads, and the Public Interest', *Yale L.J.*, Vol. 61 (1952) 467; L.L. Jaffe 'The Effective Limits of the Administrative Process: A Reevaluation', *Harv. L. Rev.*, Vol. 67 (1954), pp. 1105, 1107.

36. The Committee Submitted a detailed report – *Report of the Interoffice Team for Examination of Aspects Regarding Rezoning of Agricultural Land*, 2001.
37. Justice Or delivered the main opinion, which was concurred with by the other justices on the panel—Justices Barak, Matsa, Shtrasberg-Cohen, Dorner, Beinish, and Procaccia.
38. *Rainbow*, p. 83. In the context of American constitutional law, the concern regarding delegation of legislative powers to the executive branch shaped the 'non-delegation doctrine'.
39. Ibid., pp. 65–66.
40. Ibid., pp. 64.
41. Decisions 666 and 667.
42. H.C. 5575/94, *Mehadrin Ltd. v. Government of Israel*, 49(3) P.D. 133 (hereinafter, *Mehadrin*).
43. Ibid., p.148.
44. Decision 727.
45. Actually, when history is taken into account, agricultural settlers should be compensated in correlation to their investments in the land and the duration of their settlement. From this perspective, the current value of the land is of less relevance especially when compensation correlated with this value awards bigger sums to settlers whose history is not necessarily long or significant. Furthermore, the historical consideration gives additional weight to the argument that those living in the periphery of the country, who had survived difficult periods in the defence of the state borders, should receive higher compensation, not only in percentages, but also in absolute figures, despite the low economic value of their lands.
46. *Rainbow*, p. 74.
47. Decision 737.
48. *Beerotaim*, p. 18.
49. Decision 717.
50. The Or Commission Report, which addressed the problem of discrimination against Arabs in Israel, mentioned also the discrimination against the Arab sector in the area of lands. See *Report of the National Commission of Inquiry for the Examination of the Confrontation between Israeli Citizens and the Security Forces in October 2000*, Vol. 1 (2003), p. 43.
51. For additional discussion of the obligations on the Israel Lands Administration to operate in accordance with the principle of sustainable development, see D. Barak-Erez and O. Perez 'Planning in Israel Lands: Toward Sustainable Development', *Mishpat U'mimshal*, Vol. 7 (2004), p. 865 (Hebrew).
52. David Harvey, *Social Justice and the* City, London, 1973, pp. 101–108. For a criticism of Israeli planning bodies for their tendency to prefer profit maximizing considerations over considerations of social justice, see Y. Blank 'The Location of the Local: Local Government Law, Decentralization and Territorial Inequality in Israel', *Mishpatim*, Vol. 34 (2004), pp. 197, 265–281 (Hebrew). For example, municipalities tended to prefer commercial building which produced higher payments of municipal taxes, and opposed the construction of small apartments, whose purchasers were generally characterized as being poor.
53. D. Harvey, 'Social Injustice, Postmodernism and the City', 16 *International Journal of Urban and Regional Research*, Vol. 16 (1992), p. 588; D. Harvey, *Justice, Nature and the Geography of Difference*, Cambridge, MA, 1996.
54. Section 4M, Israel Lands Administration Law.
55. Compare: P.C.A. 3577/94, *Phoenix Israeli Insurance Company Ltd v. Moreano*, 48(4) P.D. 70.
56. Public Housing Bill, 1998, H.H. 306 (hereinafter, Public Housing Bill).
57. Public Housing (Purchasing Rights) Law, 1999.
58. Entrenchment and Registration of Farmer' Land Rights Bill, 1996, H.H. 656.

59. Justice Zamir expressed the idea of partnership and participation in administrative decisions in his famous judgment in H.C. 164/97 *Contram Ltd. v. Ministry of Finance, Duties and V.A.T Department*, 52(1) P.D. 289, 342. See also D. Barak-Erez, 'The Democratic Challenge of Administrative Law', *Tel-Aviv U.L. Rev.*, Vol. 24 (2000), p. 369 (Hebrew).
60. H.C. 6924/98, *Association for Civil Rights in Israel v. Government of Israel*, 55(5) P.D. 15.
61. *Mehadrin*, p. 42.
62. H.C. 5734/98, *Azriel v. Subcommittee of the Israel Lands Council*, 53 (2) P.D. 8.
63. An additional question discussed in the case law regarding representative appointments was to which extent is a representative of a particular body, or group, obliged to act in accordance with the dictates and guidelines that he receives. See H.C. 5848/99, *Paritzky v. District Committee for Planning and Construction in Jerusalem*, 54(3) P.D. 5.
64. For example, the decision on the 'Build Your House' plan in Eilat (discussed in *Eilat Municipality*), which did not give priority to the local residents, was adopted without coordination with the Municipality. Justice Cheshin criticized the Lands Administration for that, adding: 'in terms of proper administrative proceedings, it is inconceivable that the Israel Lands Administration should be the only instance determining how lands are to be allocated for building within the boundaries of Eilat, and be forced to unquestioningly accept the decision made in Jerusalem'. The same applies to the issue of Tel Aviv and in other subjects involving the Israel Lands Administration. Ibid., p. 769. In contrast, the decision regarding the 'Build Your House' project in Ramat HaSharon (discussed in the *Rosenberg* case), which granted priority to the local residents, was coordinated with the Municipality. A comparison between the two cases indicates that cooperation at the decision-making stage has a potential for significantly influencing the process.
65. It should be clarified that decision-making in the government is also subject to the rules of administrative law, including the prohibition on conflict of interests.
66. Decision 972 of the Israel Lands Council, of 2 September 2003. The transitional provisions were premised on two main parameters: 'Reliance' and 'Planning', and accordingly led to the validation of transactions which had moved forward either from a contractual perspective or from a planning perspective.
67. H.C. 10934/02, *Kibbutz Kfar Azza Association for Cooperative Agricultural Settlement v. Israel Lands Administration* 58(5) P.D. 144. The court was satisfied that the second decision provided appropriate protection to the reliance interests of the parties to the transactions.
68. It is worthwhile to mention that in another famous judgment which dealt with administrative policy with distributive implications, the non-drafting of Yeshiva students to military service, the court held that the issue of group exemption from service should be legislated, rather than based only upon administrative decisions. See H.C., 3267/97 *Rubinstein v. Minister of Defence*, 52(5) P.D. 481.

The Case for Judicial Review over Social Rights: Israeli Perspectives

YORAM RABIN AND YUVAL SHANY

Despite voluminous judicial and political rhetoric adopted by jurists and politicians from around the world, proclaiming the importance of social rights and their indivisibility from civil and political rights, social rights remain the unprivileged child of the human rights movement. Some view social rights as utopian or counter-productive;[1] others view them as inferior to civil and political rights or as non-rights.[2] Even those who accept their importance often regard them as non-justiciable—i.e., not amenable to meaningful judicial supervision—citing both practical and legitimacy concerns.[3] Furthermore, when viewed from a positive law prism, social rights are often under-protected and under-enforced. Indeed, the constitutions of many Western states do not explicitly protect social rights as constitutional rights; and international treaties introduce only a weak obligation to protect social rights (obligations of a progressive or programmatic nature).[4]

Taken together, these obstacles in the path of the realization of social rights indicate deep scepticism over the ability of legal systems in general, and courts in particular, to promote the redistributive agendas and policies underlying social rights through constitutional means.

However, a number of voices in the legal profession and others walks of life have become increasingly critical of this sceptical approach and its opposition to the constitutionalization of social rights.[5] In particular, critics have exposed the hidden biases and political agendas underlying the positions of many objectors to the incorporation of social rights into constitutional law.[6] Some of the aforementioned scepticism might not really be directed against the intrinsic shortcomings of social rights, but rather against their specific distributional policy implications.

This article seeks to introduce an Israeli perspective into the debate over the appropriate constitutional status of social rights. Specifically, it addresses the question of the desirability and feasibility of judicial review on the basis of constitutionally protected social rights, which is a major source of contention in contemporary Israeli constitutional discourse. Indeed, the question of the constitutionalization of social rights in Israel and the ensuing bestowal of judicial review powers upon courts has two practical projects in sight—explicit incorporation of social rights into the future constitution (or Basic Laws) or reinterpretation of existing constitutional rights in a manner consistent with the protection of social rights. Consequently, the article describes the main contours of the Israeli debate over constitutional judicial review, as applied to social rights, and reviews both potential incorporation projects; though it ultimately focuses on the pros and cons of a policy of explicit incorporation of judicially enforceable social rights in a manner comparable to the way in which civil and political rights enjoy constitutional protection.

Although many of the questions raised here are universal and common to many societies, we feel that the Israeli example is particularly instructive for several reasons. First, a constitution writing project is currently underway in Israel and various alternative modes of reference to social rights are being considered. Furthermore, the expansive nature of some constitutional interpretation doctrines adopted by the Israeli Supreme Court raises the possibility that existing constitutional protections will be extended in the foreseeable future to several social rights, by way of judicial interpretation. Hence, in the Israeli context, the theoretical questions raised in this article might have immediate practical application. Second, the contrast between Israel's socialist heritage[7] and extensive social legislation,[8] on the one hand, and the reluctance of constitution drafters and judges to fully constitutionalize social rights, on the other, provides convenient background conditions for discussing the constitutional status of social rights. Arguably, it is harder to discuss modalities of the constitutionalization of social rights in societies where there is strong resistance to the very existence of these rights (either as ordinary or constitutional rights). Third, the Israeli debate over the constitutional status of social rights is conducted in the shadow of a wider debate over judicial activism, especially in the field of constitutional law.[9] This too helps to focus the debate on the question of the desirability and feasibility of authorizing courts to exercise judicial review over legislation which might compromise social rights.

Following these introductory remarks, this article will briefly survey the main developments since the early 1990s in the Israeli project of constitutionalizing human rights. It will also assess the status of social rights in the project. The second part will explore the main alternative strategies for constitutionalizing social rights—declarative incorporation in the constitution, partial or full incorporation and reinterpretation of existing constitutional provisions. We contend, in this context, that it is more likely than not that the drafters of the constitution would incorporate within it some reference to social rights (even a symbolic reaffirmation thereof), and that courts are expected, in all events, to continue their policy of extending some constitutional protections towards social rights. The third section, which is the main part of this article, critically examines the central arguments against the grant of powers of constitutional judicial review to courts over social rights (in contrast to judicial review over civil and political rights), focusing mainly on the possible grant of such powers through a future constitution. We then demonstrate several possible modalities for such review—corresponding to distinct elements comprising social rights. We conclude by arguing that a host of policy considerations and theoretical arguments generally support, in the Israeli context, the full incorporation of social rights in the nascent Israeli constitution, and a concomitant effective, yet cautious, exercise of judicial review by the judiciary.

Before embarking on a discussion of the constitutional status of social rights in Israel, it could be useful to propose a working definition of the term 'social rights'. Numerous writers have made different proposals to that effect, alluding sometimes to the positive nature of social rights (i.e. requiring positive governmental action or expenditure), to their distributive attributes (i.e. transfer of resources from the 'haves' to the 'have nots')[10] or to their welfare characteristics (i.e. providing public services which might otherwise be inaccessible to large parts of the population). In previous publications we offered a flexible definition of social rights,[11] which cumulatively incorporate three principal elements: a) dominant positive characteristics—social rights typically introduce considerable positive obligations of conduct upon governments and entail significant costs; b) non-affluent constituency—the principal beneficiaries of social rights are less-well-off individuals who would not have been able to obtain these services in the free market; and c) historical context—social rights were mostly developed within the context of the welfare state project from the late nineteenth century onwards. The rights contained in the International Covenant on Economic, Social and Cultural Rights (ICESCR) meet as a rule most, if not all, of the three proposed elements. Hence, they serve as convenient indicia for the scope of coverage of the term social rights.

It should be noted, however, that social rights, as commonly understood nowadays, encompass a panoply of obligations and relationships: negative obligations (the right of parents to choose educational facilities for their children); direct positive obligations upon the government (the duty to provide health services); obligations incumbent upon private parties (the duty of employers to pay decent wages); core obligations (the right to be free from hunger) and penumbral obligations (the right to university education). Hence, discussion of the appropriate constitutional status of social rights must be sensitive to the complex and diverse nature of these rights: as the various social rights aspects differ in their definitiveness, relativity and costs. Clearly, judicial review might be more apposite with regard to some right components than others.

THE ISRAELI PROJECT OF CONSTITUTIONALIZING HUMAN RIGHTS

After the failure of the constitutional assembly and the first Knesset to adopt a comprehensive constitution in the formative years following Israel's independence, Israeli constitutional law developed along two parallel avenues. Pursuant to the terms of the 1950 Harari Resolution,[12] the Knesset adopted between 1958 and 1992 nine basic laws, which laid out the organizational structure of the State's political and legal system and demarcated the powers of its principal institutions.[13] These basic laws did not however contain specific human rights protections (with the exception of the right to vote and be elected). At the same time, the Supreme Court moved to identify several human rights as 'fundamental principles of the Israeli legal system',[14] which derive from the democratic nature of the state, its 'national spirit' and the prevalent 'social consensus'. These rights included, inter alia, the right to personal liberty;[15] freedom of occupation;[16] freedom of speech;[17] freedom of religion and conscience;[18] the right to equality;[19] and certain procedural due process rights (normally referred to in Israeli jurisprudence as 'rules of natural justice').[20] Notably, only a few social rights were recognized through this methodology: the right to education (pronounced by the Supreme Court as a fundamental right only in 2002)[21] and some social dimensions of the right to equality.[22] In all events, the limits of this constitutionalization methodology ought to be acknowledged: judicially pronounced human rights can never lead to the revocation of primary legislation, but may only influence their interpretation.[23]

This state of affairs underwent a fundamental transformation in the 1990s. In 1992, the Knesset adopted two new basic laws designed to protect human rights: Basic Law: Human Dignity and Liberty[24] and Basic Law: Freedom of Occupation.[25] These two laws established for the first time in Israel's constitutional history the normative supremacy of a range of important human rights: the right to life, the right to bodily integrity, the right to human dignity, the right to property, the right to personal liberty, the right to leave the country and the right of citizens to re-enter it, the right to privacy and the freedom of occupation.[26] From 1992 onwards, subsequent legislation[27] infringing upon protected constitutional rights had to meet the terms of a limitation clause in order to retain their validity. In particular, infringing legislation must be compatible with Israel's basic values as a Jewish and democratic state; it should promote a worthy purpose and it cannot introduce excessive restrictions upon constitutionally protected rights.[28]

The introduction of limitation clauses in the two 1992 basic laws changed the basic constitutional configuration of the Israeli legal system from a British-type system based on the notion of parliamentary supremacy (epitomized by the maxim that 'Parliament cannot bind itself or future parliaments') to a legal system governed by a supreme constitutional instrument, protecting human rights, which the judiciary is empowered to enforce. Indeed, prominent Israeli jurists referred to the 1992 basic laws as the harbinger of a 'constitutional revolution'.[29] This theoretical proposition was soon to become official policy: despite certain reservations offered by some judges,[30] the Supreme Court, under the leadership of President Barak, asserted its powers of judicial review over legislation,[31] and repealed in the following years five 'unconstitutional' statutory provisions.[32]

However, the 'constitutional revolution' of 1992 was incomplete. Three additional government-sponsored draft basic law bills which were submitted to the Knesset in the early 1990s have not been adopted until now[33]—Draft Basic Law: Social Rights being among these abandoned bills.[34] Still, the failure of the constitution drafters to constitutionalize many fundamental human rights, such as the right to equality, freedom of expression and the right of access to court, seem to have been partly remedied throughout the years by way of expansive interpretation of the rights enumerated in the 1992 Basic Laws. So, for example, the right to human dignity (article 2 of Basic Law: Human Dignity and Liberty) was construed in the case law in a way that encompasses the prohibition against discrimination,[35] freedom of speech,[36] freedom of religion,[37] (including freedom from religion),[38] and freedom of contracts.[39] Two caveats should be noted, however. First, no law was ever nullified on the basis of these non-enumerated human rights; hence, their constitutional status has so far been supported only by *obiter dicta*.[40] Second, and more relevant to our topic, social rights have been largely excluded from this 'judicial constitutionalization' project—the exception being the right to minimal conditions of subsistence[41] and the free choice of employment,[42] which the Supreme Court proclaimed in a few early twenty-first century cases to be part of the constitutional right to human dignity (and, in one case, part of the right to bodily integrity).[43]

In sum, the major constitutional transformation which Israel underwent from the 1990s has resulted in the direct and indirect constitutionalizion of numerous human rights. However, social rights were, by and large, left out of the process: They were not explicitly incorporated into the new Basic Laws; and the Supreme Court showed until recently limited interest[44] in promoting their full constitutionalization through interpretation of the existing basic laws or by way of recognizing them as 'fundamental principles of the legal system'. This has led, in turn, to the emergence of a constitutional imbalance—some human rights (civil and political rights) have become more protected than others (social rights). Such imbalance has given rise to speculation that in future conflicts between rights belonging to the two distinct categories, protected rights might trump unprotected rights (the right to property of the factory owner might trump the right to adequate work conditions of the workers).[45]

The unsatisfactory record of the Knesset and Supreme Court in constitutionalizing social rights, at a time in which economic developments in Israel have resulted in deteriorating economic and social conditions, has spurred a barrage of academic criticism.[46] There have also been numerous political initiatives to augment the constitutional status of social rights through the introduction of several draft basic laws on social rights and numerous court petitions. At present, the main focus of these efforts seems to revolve around attempts to integrate social rights within a comprehensive constitutional text currently drafted by the Knesset Constitution, Legislation and Law Committee—a project supported by several NGO initiatives. The next part maps out the various policy alternatives available to the constitution drafters in relation to the incorporation of social rights in the draft constitution, whereas the final part discusses key policy arguments relating to the choice between these alternatives. Although the discussion focuses on constitution drafting, analogous considerations would govern the desirability of extending existing constitutional protection to social rights by way of judicial interpretation.

ALTERNATIVE STRATEGIES FOR CONSTITUTIONALIZING SOCIAL RIGHTS

Recent initiatives to promote the Israeli constitution writing project with a view to finalizing a comprehensive constitution present the constitution drafters with a choice between three principal alternative strategies for addressing social rights within the future constitution. These alternatives generally conform to the three principal models of constitutionalizing social rights accepted around the world:

a) Exclusion of social rights from the constitution—this is the model applied in the United States[47] and in the more recent Canadian Charter of Rights and Freedoms.
b) Declarative commitment to social rights, not entailing, as a rule, judicial review over legislation—this is the model presented in various degrees of explicitness in the Irish[48] and German Constitutions,[49] and in the text of the Indian Constitution[50] (though not necessarily in the practice of the Indian courts).[51]
c) Incorporation of some or all social rights in the constitution in a manner entailing judicial review—this is the model introduced, for instance, in the recent South African[52] and Finish Constitutions.[53]

In actuality, the choice seems however to be narrower, as selection of the first alternative is highly unlikely in the Israeli context. The historical configuration of Israel as a socialist state whose laws and government were designed to promote social welfare[54] seems to undercut the relevance of the North American model, which was shaped by a different historical experience and a particular political theory of the role of government in society. Moreover, the tendency of many of the new constitutions adopted or reformed in the late twentieth and early twenty-first century to embrace some or all social rights as constitutional rights[55] is perhaps indicative of the outmoded nature of the exclusionary model.

Indeed, exclusion of social rights from a contemporaneously drafted Israeli constitution seems politically and legally untenable, in the light of the growing awareness of the importance of social rights in Israel (demonstrated, inter alia, through a number of recent successful public campaigns for the expansion of social benefits).[56] In the words of Yoram Aridor (a former Minister of Finance, and a member of the Steering Board of the Israel Democracy Institute 'Constitution by Consensus' campaign): 'In this day and age in Israel, no constitution would be adopted without social rights.'[57]

Aridor's view on the non-viability of the first alternative is largely confirmed by an examination of the main positions taken in various Israeli think-tank discussions over the constitutionalization of social rights, parliamentary deliberations and academic writing and conferences. The record of these discussions seems to establish a general consensus that social rights *should* be included in the future Israeli constitution. The increasing willingness of the Supreme Court to partly constitutionalize some social rights also demonstrates growing acceptance in Israel of the need to protect such rights through constitutional means. Hence, the question seems to be no longer whether social rights should be constitutionalized in Israel but rather how, or to what degree, they should be constitutionalized—i.e., in accordance with the declarative or fully incorporative model.

Indeed, all versions of the draft constitution currently pending before the Knesset refer to social rights as constitutional rights. However, the various alternatives proposed by the Knesset Committee on Constitutional, Legislative and Legal Affairs differ significantly in their approach to the 'bindingness' of constitutional social rights. Whereas some alternative versions use strict right formulations, parallel to those used in relation to civil and political rights, some other alternatives use declarative 'non-right' formulations, which generally require the state to promote social rights and shield their implementation from judicial scrutiny.[58]

The uncertainty over the constitutional status of social rights is also reflected in the 'Constitution by Consensus' campaign organized by a politically influential NGO—the Israel Democracy Institute (IDI). A thorough comparative research paper, written by two prominent IDI experts, originally leaned towards the declarative model and concluded that: 'the preponderance of arguments leans in favour of selecting an option, according to which the constitution shall include a declaration on social-economic rights, without judicial review over primary legislation in the field of budgetary resource allocations'.[59]

However, the latest IDI draft constitution takes a more nuanced approach: article 39, the general limitation clause, which entails judicial review, encompasses both civil and political and social rights.[60] Still, articles 33–36 which enumerate the right to social security, health, education and work-related rights, and article 32, which governs the application of these social rights, are drafted in loose language,[61] which stands in contrast to the language used in the draft constitution for civil and political rights (and two 'singled out' social rights—the right to strike and children's social rights).[62] So, while article 39 subjects the enforcement of social rights to judicial review, the diluted content of these rights might render such review rather meaningless.[63]

A radically different position to that of the IDI was taken by a number of prominent academics and politicians,[64] who have advocated the full incorporation of social rights—formulated in strong 'rights language'—in any future Israeli constitution. Such incorporation should, in particular, authorize courts to review the constitutional lawfulness of legislation in ways comparable to those exercised by the courts under the two 1992 basic laws. A number of non-government-initiated draft bills, embracing this justiciable model, have been submitted in the Knesset in recent years.[65]

Finally, one should perhaps note a third, interim, approach advocated in Israel mainly by Gavison. She suggests that social rights should be protected in a comparable manner to civil and political rights (embracing the 'equal importance' and 'indivisibility' rhetoric of the proponents of the incorporative model), but that courts should not review legislation infringing both sets of rights (adopting the positions of advocates of the declarative model on the non-justiciability of social rights).[66]

So, at the end of the day, one is left with a choice between a constitution including or excluding the power of judicial review over legislation conflicting with protected social rights. The policy considerations underlying that choice are addressed in the final part of this article.

SHOULD THE COURT REVIEW LEGISLATION INFRINGING UPON CONSTITUIONALLY PROTECTED SOCIAL RIGHTS?

Two principal arguments have been directed against the empowerment of courts in a way that would enable them to uphold social rights and strike down infringing legislation (or even incompatible government programmes), in a manner comparable to their powers in relation to civil and political rights. This section reviews these arguments and presents counter-arguments, which we believe ultimately tilt the balance in favour of the full constitutionalization of social rights. Arguments by Nozick and others, which challenge the very justification for recognizing social rights per se,[67] are not addressed here, as they exceed the scope of the present article, and run contrary to our assessments that non-incorporation of social rights no longer presents a viable option in the Israeli context. In the same vein, Gavison's arguments which challenge the general justifications for constitutional judicial review (with respect to all human rights),[68] will not be discussed here either, since constitutional judicial review in Israel is by now a fait accompli.

The Anti-majoritarian Argument

The distributional implications of social rights call for two principal policy choices: a) substantive choice—*how* should societal resources be allocated among diverse needs; b) procedural choice—*who* should decide upon the manner of allocation. The question before us on the propriety of judicial review over constitutional social rights goes to the identity of the decision-makers: whether or not the legislator and the executive should enjoy exclusive decision-making power with relation to the implementation of social rights. While such questions are relevant in all constitutional review cases, it may be alleged that decisions over resource distribution relating to social rights represent particularly sensitive areas of policy-making, entailing a series of value choices, which courts are ill-placed to make.

Those who argue against the full incorporation of social rights in the constitution often believe that the ideological nature of the substantive choices implicit in the implementation of social rights (whether to spend available resources on health or education) requires that elected politicians, representing the popular will, should take the necessary decisions—i.e. that anti-majoritarian objections to constitutionalization apply with greater force to social rights.[69]

A related argument is that the exclusion of social rights from the constitution shields the courts from the political fray. By contrast, expecting courts to embrace or reject certain distributive policies would transform them into political actors (in a more pronounced fashion than in cases relating to civil and political rights, which have fewer across-the-board societal implications). Arguably, the constitution, and courts acting pursuant thereof, ought not to promote any particular social policy.[70] Instead, they should rather maintain a considerable degree of neutrality, and leave appropriate room for the political process to select between competing substantive policies.

An even more forceful argument against constitutional review of social rights advocates a democratic process-oriented vision of constitutionally protected human rights. According to this vision, developed in Israel by writers such as Yoav Dotan,[71] constitutional judicial review should mainly focus upon the proper functioning of the democratic process through their powers of constitutional review. Hence, only the constitutional protection of human rights associated with the political process is justified: the right to vote and be elected, freedom of speech, freedom of association and freedom of movement. Such rights ensure the application of neutral 'rules of the game', which facilitate a legitimate political process. However, social rights are fundamentally different: their full incorporation in the constitution would limit the majority's freedom of determining substantive distributional outcomes. In other words, whereas political rights are a prerequisite for adopting a fair decision-making methodology within a given society, social rights pertain to the actual decisions adopted at the end of that process. Dotan thus posits that the constitutionalization of social rights (beyond an indispensable core) is undesirable and inefficient.[72] Questions relating to social rights should not be excluded from the ordinary political process through entrenching social rights as constitutional rights; rather they should remain part and parcel of the political process.

Despite the elegance of the distinction between process-oriented and substantive human rights, we believe that Dotan's position is misguided as it represents an excessively narrow conception of the role of a constitution in a liberal democracy. First, even according to Dotan, some social rights support the democratic process no less than their civil and political counterparts. For example, it is hard to envision meaningful participation in the democratic process of the hungry, homeless or uneducated.[73] Hence, even democratic process-oriented arguments should support the protection of core social rights.[74]

More importantly, the democratic process-oriented stance proposes an instrumentalist reduction of human rights to tools for guaranteeing majority rule in societal decision-making. This position ignores the potential minority-protection attributes of social rights, which are designed to serve as a counterbalance to majority rule and to protect the minority from the 'tyranny of the majority' in relation to distribution-related decisions. Indeed, the human rights movement seeks to subject *all* societal policies, including policies couched in democratically taken decisions, to substantive, pre-political human rights standards.[75]

So, if we were to accept the proposition that social rights protect important and recognizable interests of the weaker strata in society, which merit legal protection, then the lawfulness of societal decisions affecting those rights should be subject to some form of checks and balances. In particular, it is unclear why majority decisions over resource allocation which affect the economically or socially disempowered deserve less scrutiny than other majority decisions which affect the politically disenfranchised—prison conditions, rights of aliens or minority groups. Viewed from this majority–minority perspective, the non-representative nature of the judiciary constitutes an *advantage*, since it balances the majoritarian trends of the political system against the pre-political values enshrined in the constitution (or international human rights law instruments). This basic observation seems to hold true for social rights, as much as it holds true for civil and political rights.

Furthermore, we believe that the democratic process-oriented approach to human rights has been implicitly rejected in Israel (and in many other jurisdictions), as the domestic legal system recognizes human rights, such as the right to privacy,[76] the right to property,[77] the prohibition against torture,[78] whose relevance to the democratic process is limited or non-extant. Instead, another rationale—human dignity—underlies the constitutionalization of these human rights.[79] Significantly, the same human dignity rationale has also been cited in favour of constitutionalizing many social rights.[80] It would therefore be, in our minds, inconsistent to reject the constitutionalization of social rights on the basis of instrumentalist arguments, while at the same time retain the constitutionality of non-instrumental civil and political rights.

Indeed, empowering courts to review legislation necessarily entails a certain degree of politicization of the judiciary—i.e. the power to take essentially political decisions—and thus warrants judicial prudence.[81] Still the decision *not* to empower the courts might be equally political, as it could tilt the societal equilibrium of power in favour of the majority, at the expense of disenfranchised segments of society. It thus enables powerful interest groups to exert considerable influence over the political process, without introducing necessary checks and balances against such an exercise of power.[82] In other words, the decision whether or not to invest courts with powers of constitutional judicial review in cases involving social rights necessarily affects the distribution of political power between the majority and minority, and is therefore inevitably political in nature.

Finally, it may be noted that the decision to exclude social rights from the scope of constitutional judicial review might lead to under-enforcement of social rights (especially when limitations of social rights are justified by reference to constitutionally protected civil and political rights, such as the right to property). This might, in turn, bring into question the state's compliance with its international obligation to give full effect to those social rights it is materially capable of providing.[83]

The Professional Expertise Argument

Another line of argument, directed against the exercise of judicial review over legislation affecting social rights, highlights the institutional constraints of courts as decision-makers. Unlike the aforementioned anti-majoritarian arguments, the professional expertise argument does not question the need for implementing constitutional social rights, but challenges the methodology of their implementation.[84]

Arguably, courts lack professional expertise for undertaking decisions having significant long term distributional implications, as such decisions often require sophisticated practical expertise and might have unforeseeable spill-over effects, which might compromise other distributional agendas (e.g. a decision to increase welfare spending might require cuts in health benefits). These concerns also derive from the nature of the judicial decision-making methodology: courts take decisions on a case-by-case basis and lack a broader perspective on social issues.[85] This form of decision-making is also inauspicious to political compromises or 'package deals', which could represent a pragmatic way of promoting social agendas and balancing between conflicting social needs.

These criticisms against judicial decision-making, which apply to many judicial decisions that have distributional implications, apply with greater force to social rights given their vague nature (e.g., the right to an adequate standard of living) and significant effects in terms of government spending. In other words, courts might lack the capacity to efficiently manage the distribution of society's resources (and, as suggested above, they might also lack legitimacy to undertake the value choices implicit in these decisions). Consequently, it might be imprudent to authorize Israeli courts to oversee the constitutionality of legislation providing or depriving of material resources needed for the full implementation of social rights. Instead, such decisions arguably should be taken by the state bureaucracy, which is better placed to evaluate across-the-board and over time the implications of implementing social rights.

Once again we question the accuracy of these sweeping assertions. First, the distinction between 'positive' social rights and 'negative' civil and political rights is being increasingly viewed both inside and outside Israel as anachronistic.[86] Instead, a competing vision of human rights, comprising of a combination of positive and negative features, seems to be gaining ground with relation to both groups of rights.[87] Differences between social rights and civil and political rights may thus be quantitative, not qualitative. So, if one is ready to acknowledge the expediency of constitutional judicial review over the distributional implications of civil and political rights (e.g. affirmative action or land redistribution), considerations of coherency support comparable powers of review over social rights.

In the same vein, the argument that social rights are inherently uncertain loses much of its persuasive force when these rights are juxtaposed against the no-less-vague civil and political rights such as the right to privacy or access to court (or commonly used vague legal standards such as reasonableness or good faith), which invite a comparable degree of concretization by way of judicial interpretation. These remarks apply with particular force in relation to *positive* civil and political rights, such as the right to life or due process (which may entail obligations to maintain law and order and provide legal aid) that seem to be as uncertain as any social right. At the same time, there seems to be an uncontroversial core of social rights, such as the right to elementary education or to emergency medical treatment, which could be readily applied by courts.[88] In fact, it may be argued that reluctance to authorize courts to apply social rights perpetuates their uncertainness, as it debars courts from developing judicial practice which could elucidate their content. The differences between social and civil and political rights thus seem overblown and hardly call for radically different configurations of judicial supervision (unless one disputes the proposition that both groups of rights protect equally important human rights).

How Should Israeli Courts Oversee the Constitutional Protection of Social Rights?

We are by no means oblivious to the problems associated with judicial supervision over legislation affecting constitutionally protected social rights. While the aforementioned democratic legitimacy and professional expertise concerns are not prohibitive in our minds, they should certainly be accorded due consideration. Consequently, the model for judicial supervision we propose seeks to take care of some of these concerns, yet preserve a core essence of judicial supervision.

The first and foremost aspect that should be acknowledged when discussing the desirable scope of judicial review is the multi-faceted nature of social rights. They comprise negative and positive obligations (i.e. duties not to interfere and duties to act); direct and indirect obligations (i.e. obligations directly incumbent on the state and obligations on the state to regulate relations between private individuals); and hard-core and penumbral obligations. These distinct elements entail varying costs, and are characterized by different degrees of relativity and normative ambiguity. Thus, we believe that the intensity and methodology of judicial supervision over these distinct aspects should vary accordingly.

We submit that intensive judicial supervision is fully justified with relation to three right components:

a) *Negative obligations*—many social rights include important negative features which forbid excessive governmental interference in their application. These may include the right to establish private schools (not funded by the state), the right not to be excluded from medical treatment, the right not to be barred from certain professions, the right not be arbitrarily disconnected from utility infrastructures (e.g. water, electricity, etc.). In our view, there is no reason why courts should not be able to constitutionally oversee the protection of these negative rights from infringing legislation, as they do not generally have major distributional implications.[89] In fact, the Israeli legal system has demonstrated in the past its willingness to afford legal protection, including sometimes constitutional protection, to some negative aspects of social rights.[90]

b) *Private obligations*—there is growing support for the proposition that human rights require states to regulate relations between individuals in a manner compatible with their protection.[91] Hence, social rights might require states to prevent abusive employment practices, oversee educational standards in private schools and prohibit discrimination by landlords.[92] Here, too, the societal distributional implications of the constitutional review are minor or indirect; again, comparable non-constitutional powers of review already exist in Israel.[93] So, if one accepts the proposition that constitutional social rights include a private obligation component, it makes little sense not to authorize courts to review the constitutionality of legislation defining and regulating these private obligations (e.g. working hours or private health care legislation).

c) *Hard-core social rights*—an increasingly influential theory identifies a hard-core of social rights, which underpin minimal conditions for dignified human subsistence, such as the right not to be hungry, the right to emergency medical treatment, minimal shelter and clothes. The distinction between hard-core and penumbral social rights has been applied by international bodies,[94] and was adopted by President Barak in a number of court decisions.[95] Arguably, the preponderant importance of hard-core elements of social rights, and the social consensus surrounding the need to allocate the resources needed to fulfil them, supports judicial review over legislation compromising this hard-core. The willingness of the Israeli Supreme Court to construe the right to human dignity as encompassing a hard-core of social rights is indicative of the compatibility of judicial powers of review over legislation impinging upon hard-core elements of social rights with existing theories and practices of judicial review in Israel.[96]

Thus, we maintain that judicial review over the constitutionality of legislation affecting some elements of social rights is supportable by virtue of the limited distributional implications of such review, the social consensus surrounding these elements and their sheer importance. Both the democratic legitimacy and professional expertise arguments do not support, in our view, the exclusion of Israeli courts from engaging in constitutional review of these elements, especially in light of their power to exercise no less consequential powers in relation to civil and political rights.

As for the remaining social right elements—positive obligations, directly imposed upon the state and covering more controversial penumbral components (i.e. situated outside the hard-core of social rights)—we propose that the general benefits of judicial review—mainly the effective protection of important minority interests from the tyranny of the majority—generally outweigh, as a matter of desirable policy, the negation of any form of judicial review. Still, such judicial review should proceed carefully by reason of the judiciary's democratic deficit and relative lack of expertise in undertaking major distributional decisions.[97]

First, the state should be granted by the courts a wide margin of appreciation in devising policies relating to positive social rights, and courts should apply considerable judicial restraint.[98] Intervention in legislation should be resorted to only in extreme situations of manifest unconstitutionality, and not in borderline cases. Second, in cases relating to administrative decisions, courts should focus more on the executive's decision-making procedures than on their substantive outcomes—whether data had been collected or proper consultation had been resorted to by the relevant administrative agencies.[99] Of course, in evaluating the propriety of the procedure no expertise gap exists. Third, courts should develop a host of non-intrusive remedies in cases where violation of constitutionally protected social rights had been identified, in order to minimize inter-governmental–branch conflicts. These may include inter alia the adoption of 'second-look' doctrines,[100] redirecting questions pertaining to the implementation of social rights to the legislator or executive;[101] suspended remedies, providing the state with lavish adjustment periods,[102] and declarative remedies.[103]

In addition, if courts were accorded powers of judicial review over legislation and executive acts affecting social rights, they would have to expound appropriate decision-making methodologies to overcome their relative lack of expertise—i.e. develop a suitable constitutional 'tool box'. Such methodologies may include, inter alia, the invitation of inter-disciplinary expert opinions (as in the 'Brandeis brief'), admission of *amicus curia* briefs[104] and insisting that the state elaborates social goals and benchmarks—determine what constitutes constitutionally protected standards of health, housing or education.[105]

CONCLUSIONS

The role of social rights in the Israeli constitutional project will probably be determined in the coming years. It seems that contemporary political and intellectual trends lean towards supporting the inclusion of social rights in any future constitutional instrument, albeit in a weak form, without substantive judicial review. We have made the argument in this article that this position merits reconsideration.

We submit that despite the difficulties associated with the judiciary's non-representative composition and its limited capacity to undertake decisions with major long term distributional implications, the importance of social rights, their minority protection purpose, and, most significantly, the existence of analogous judicial decision-making powers with relation to civil and political rights, support judicial review over legislation and administrative acts incompatible with protected social rights. However, such review must be exercised carefully, especially in relation to positive social rights, which impose a direct obligation on the state to protect the penumbral, and less certain, elements of social rights. Hence, the difficulties associated with constitutionalizing social rights should not lead to an abdication of the court's role in enforcing such rights, but rather to a policy of judicial restraint in exercising constitutional supervision.

NOTES

1. See Linda M. Keller, 'The American Rejection of Economic Rights as Human Rights and the Declaration of Independence: Does the Pursuit of Happiness Require Basic Economic Rights?', *N.Y.L. Sch. J. Hum. Rts.*, Vol. 19 (2003), pp. 557, 561.
2. See Maurice Cranston, 'Human Rights, Real and Supposed', in D.D. Rapheal (ed.), *Political Theory and the Rights of Man*, London, 1967, pp. 43, 49.
3. See Michael J. Dennis and Dennis P. Stewart, 'Justiciability of Economic, Social, and Cultural Rights: Should There be an International Complaints Mechanism to Adjudicate the Rights to Food, Water, Housing, and Health?', *Am. J. Int'l. L.*, Vol. 98 (2004), pp. 462, 472.
4. See International Covenant on Economic, Social and Cultural Rights, 16 December 1966, art. 2(1), 993 U.N.T.S. 3 (hereinafter, ICESCR).
5. Louis Henkin, 'Revolutions and Constitutions', *La. L. Rev.*, Vol. 49 (1989), pp. 1023, 1054–1055; Herman Schwartz, 'Do Economic and Social Rights Belong in a Constitution?', *Am. U.J. Int'l L. & Pol'y*, Vol. 10 (1995), p. 1233.
6. Andrei Marmor, 'Bikoret Shiputit Be-Yisrael' (Judicial Review in Israel), *Mishpat U-Mimshal*, Vol. 4 (1997–1998), p. 133; Ali Zaltzberger and Alexander Kedar, 'Ha-Ma'hapecha Hashketa—Od Al Bikoret Shiputit Lefi Hukei Hayesod Hahadashim' (The Silent Revolution—More on Judicial Review under the New Basic Laws), *Mishpat U-Mimshal*, Vol. 4 (1997–1998), pp. 489, 504.
7. Ran Hirschl, 'Israel's Constitutional Revolution: The Legal Interpretation of Entrenched Civil Liberties in an Emerging Neo-Liberal Economic Order', *Am. J. Comp. L.*, Vol. 46 (1998), pp. 427, 432.
8. See National Insurance Law (Consolidated Version), 1995; Compulsory Education Law, 1949; National Health Insurance Law, 1994; Work and Leisure Hours Law, 1951; Annual Leave Law, 1951. One should note in this regard that Israel ratified in 1991 the ICESCR and that some notable Supreme Court decisions reaffirmed the importance of social rights. See e.g. H.C.J. 164/97, *Contram Ltd. v. Ministry of Finance—Custom and VAT Department*, 52(1) P.D. 289; H.C.J. 4905/98, *Gamzu v. Yeshayau*, 55(3) P.D. 360; H.C.J. 2599/00, *YATED—Association for Parents of Downs Syndrome Children v. Minister of Education*, 56(5) P.D. (2002) 843; H.C.J. 6973/03, *Marciano v. Minister of Finance*, 58(2) P.D. 270.
9. Ruth Gavison, Mordechai Kremnitzer and Yoav Dotan, *Activism Shiputi—Be'ad Ve-Neged* (Judicial Activism—For and Against), Jerusalem, 2000.
10. Yoav Dotan, 'Beit Hamishpat Ha-Elyon Ke-Magen Zchuyot Hevratiot' (The Supreme Court as the Protector of Social Rights), in Yoram Rabin and Yuval Shany (eds.), *Zchuyot Kalkalyot, Hevratiot Ve-Tarbutiot Be-Yisrael* (Economic, Social and Cultural Rights in Israel), Tel Aviv, 2004, pp. 69, 72–73 (hereinafter *Rights in Israel*).
11. Yoram Rabin and Yuval Shany, 'The Israeli Unfinished Constitutional Revolution: Has the Time Come for Protecting Economic and Social Rights?', *Is. L.R.*, Vol. 38 (2005), p. 299; Yoram Rabin and Yuval Shany, 'Zchuyot Hevratiot—Ra'ayon She-higia Zmano' (Social Rights—An Idea Whose Time has Come), in Rabin and Shany, *Rights in Israel*, pp. 11, 18.
12. 5 DK 1743 (1950).

13. Basic Law: The Knesset, 12 LSI 85 (1958); Basic Law: The Government, 22 LSI 257 (1969); Basic Law: The President of the State, 18 LSI 111 (1964); Basic Law: The Judicature, 38 LSI 101 (1984); Basic Law: The State Comptroller, SH 1988, No. 1237, p. 30 (1988); Basic Law: Israeli Land, 14 LSI 48 (1960); Basic Law: State Economy, 29 LSI 273 (1975); Basic Law: The Armed Forces, 30 LSI 150 (1976); Basic Law: Jerusalem, the Capital of Israel, 34 LSI 209 (1980).
14. See H.C.J. 292/83, *Mount Temple Faithful Association v. Chief of the Jerusalem District Police*, 38(2) P.D. 449, 454; H.C.J. 680/88, *Shnitzer v. Chief Military Censor*, 42(4) P.D. 617, 627.
15. See H.C.J. 7/48, *Al-Karbutli v. Minister of Defence*, 2 P.D. 5.
16. See H.C.J. 1/49, *Bejerano v. Minister of Police*, 2 P.D. 80.
17. See H.C.J. 73/53, *Kol Ha'am v. Minister of Interior*, 7 P.D. 871. For an English version, see *Selected Judgments of the State of Israel*, Vol. 1 (1953), p. 90.
18. See H.C.J. 262/62, *Peretz v. Local Council of Kfar Shmaryahu*, 16 P.D. 2101. For an English version, see *Selected Judgments of the State of Israel*, Vol. 4 (1962), p. 191.
19. See H.C.J. 509/80, *Younes v. Director General of the Office of the Prime Minister*, 35(3) P.D. 589; H.C.J. 953/87, *Poraz v. Mayor of Tel Aviv-Yaffo*, 42(2) P.D. 309, 332–333.
20. See H.C.J. 3/58, *Berman v. Minister of the Interior*, 12 P.D. 1493. For an English version, see *Selected Judgments of the State of Israel*, Vol. 3 (1958), p. 29. Judge-made rights have sometimes been also referred to as the Israeli 'judicial bill of rights'. See H.C.J. 112/77, *Fogel v. Israel Broadcasting Authority*, 31(3) P.D. 657, 664.
21. H.C.J. 2599/00, *YATED*.
22. See H.C.J. 6488/02, *National Committee of Heads of Arab Municipalities in Israel v. Committee of Ministry Directors for Specific Action in Municipalities* (not yet published); H.C.J. 2814/97, *Supreme Supervisory Council for Arab Education in Israel v. Ministry of Education, Culture and Sport*, 54(3) P.D. 233; H.C.J. 727/00, *National Committee of Heads of Arab Municipalities in Israel v. Minister of Construction and Housing*, 56(2) P.D. 79. One could also claim that the court's affirmative jurisprudence contributes to the closing of social gaps. See e.g. H.C.J. 2671/98, *Israeli Woman's Network v. Minister of Labour and Welfare*, 52(3) P.D. 630; H.C.J. 6924/98, *Association for Civil Rights in Israel v. Government of Israel*, 55(5) P.D. 15. For a theoretical discussion of the right to economic equality, see Andrei Marmor, 'The Intrinsic Value of Economic Equality', in Lukas H. Meyer, Stanley L. Paulson and Thomas W. Pogge (eds.), *Rights, Culture and the Law—Themes from the Legal and Political Philosophy*, Oxford, 2003, p. 127.
23. See C.A. 6871/99, Rinat v. Rom, 56(4) P.D. 72, 92; 482; V.C.P 4459/94, *Salmonov v. Sharbani*, 49 P.D. 479, 482; C.A. 524/88, *Pri Ha'Emek—Agricultural Cooperative Association Inc. v. Sde Ya'akov—Workers Cooperative Village*, 48(4) P.D. 529, 561; H.C.J. 693/91, *Efrat v. Population Registry Supervisor, Ministry of the Interior*, 47(1) P.D. 749, 763; Yoram Rabin, *Hazchut Lehinuch* (The Right to Education), Jerusalem, 2003, p. 339.
24. Basic Law: Human Dignity and Liberty, 1992, S.H. 150, translated in *Is. L.R.*, Vol. 31 (1997), p. 21.
25. Basic Law: Freedom of Occupation, 1992, S.H. 114, translated in *Is. L.R.*, Vol. 31 (1997), pp. 21–25.
26. A prior example of a constitutional supremacy arrangement may be found in article 4 of the Basic Law: The Knesset, which pronounces, among other things, the right to equality in voting to the Knesset. This article contains a so-called 'entrenchment clause' providing that its provisions shall not be amended except by a special majority vote in the Knesset. In 1969, the Supreme Court invalidated legislation conflicting with the entrenchment provision since it was not adopted by the requisite majority. See H.C.J. 98/69, *Bergman v. Minister of Finance*, 23 P.D. 639, translated and abridged in *Isr L.R.*, Vol. 4 (1969), p. 577.
27. Basic Law: Freedom of Occupation even subjected antecedent legislation to its provisions. Basic Law: Freedom of Occupation, art. 8.
28. Basic Law: Human Dignity, article 8; Basic Law: Freedom of Occupation, article 4. Basic Law: Freedom of Occupation also contains in article 7 a 'procedural entrenchment clause', which requires an absolute majority in the Knesset in order to amend the Basic Law.
29. The term 'constitutional revolution' had been coined by Professor Aharon Barak—then a Justice of the Israeli Supreme Court and subsequently the President of the Supreme Court—in an article published in 1992. Aharon Barak, 'Ha-Ma'hapecha Ha-Hukatit: Zchuyot Adam

Muganot' (The Constitutional Revolution: Protecting Human Rights), *Mishpat U-Mimshal*, Vol. 1 (1992), p. 9. See also Aharon Barak, 'The Constitutionalization of the Israeli Legal System as Result of the Basic Laws and its Effect on Procedural and Substantive Criminal Law', *Is L.R.*, Vol. 31 (1997), p. 3. But see Ruth Gavison, 'A Constitutional Revolution?', in Antonio Gambaro and Mordechai Rabello (eds.), *Towards a New European Ius Commune*, Jerusalem, 1999, p. 517.

30. See CA 6821/93 *Bank Hamizrachi Hameuhad Ltd. v. Migdal Cooperative Village*, 49(4) P.D. 221, 567 (Heshin, J., dissenting).
31. ibid., pp. 352–355.
32. H.C.J. 1715/97, *Israeli Investment Managers Bureau v. Minister of Finance*, 51(5) P.D. 367; H.C.J. 6055/95, *Tsemach v. Minister of Defence*, 53(5) P.D. 241; H.C.J. 1030/99, *Oron v. Chairman of Knesset*, 56(3) P.D. 640; *Gaza Beach Regional Council v. Knesset of Israel*, 59(2) P.D. 481; H.C.J. 8276/05 *Adalah—Legal Centre for Arab Minority Rights v. Minister of Defence*, judgment of 12 December 2006.
33. This could be attributed to the opposition of powerful Jewish religious parties in the Knesset to the competence of post-'constitutional revolution' courts to strike down legislation protecting religious interests. See Lili Galili, 'Benizri: Nitnaged Gam Le-Aseret Ha-Dibrot Ke-Hok Yesod' (Benizri: We Will Also Oppose the Ten Commandments as a Basic Law), *Ha'aretz Online*, (available at www.haaretz.co.il), 3 July 1997.
34. Draft Basic Law: Social Rights, 1994, S.H. 326.
35. H.C.J. 453/94, *Israel Women's Network v. Government of Israel*, 48(5) P.D. 501 (per Maza, J.); H.C.J. 4541/94, *Miller v. the Minister of Security*, 49(4) P.D. 94 (per Dorner, J.).
36. H.C.J. 2481/93, *Dayan v. Vilk*, 48(2) P.D. 456.
37. H.C.J. 5016/96 *Horev v. Minister of Transportation*, 51(4) P.D. 1; H.C.J. 4298/93, *Jabbarin v. Minister of Education*, 48(5) P.D. 199; H.C.J. 3261/93, *Menning v. Minister of Justice*, 47(3) P.D. 282.
38. C.A. 6024/97, *Shavit v. Hevra Kadisha GHSA Rishon Le Zion*, 53(3) P.D. 600, 649; H.C.J. 6111/94, *Committee of Tradition Protectors v. Israel Supreme Rabbinical Council*, 49(5) P.D. 95, 106.
39. C.A. 239/92, *Egged—Israel Transportation Cooperative Union Ltd. v. Mashiah*, 48(2) P.D. 66, 72; Gabriela Shalev, *Dinei Hozim* (*The Law of Contracts*), 2nd edition, Jerusalem, 1995, p. 25.
40. See e.g. Hillel Sommer, 'Mi-Yaldut Le-Bagrut: Sugiot Ptuchot Be-Yisuma Shel Ha-Ma'hapecha Ha-Hukatit' (From Childhood to Adulthood: Open Questions in the Application of the Constitutional Revolution), *Mishpat Ve-Asakim*, Vol. 1 (2004), pp. 59, 66.
41. See H.C.J. 4905/98, Gamzu; H.C.J. 4128/02 *Adam, Teva Va-Din v. Prime Minister of Israel*, 58(3) P.D. 503; H.C.J. 1384/04, *B'tsedek—American–Israel Centre for Promotion of Justice in Israel v. Minister of the Interior*, at para. 14 (not yet published); H.C.J. 5578/02 *Manor v. Minister of Finance*, 59(1) P.D. 729; H.C.J. 494/03, *Physicians for Human Rights v. Minister of Finances*, 59(3) P.D. 322; H.C.J. 366/03, *Association for Commitment to Peace and Social Justice v. Minister of Finance* (not yet published).
42. H.C.J. 4542/02, *Hotline for Workers v. Government of Israel* (not yet published). Note that the free choice of employment may also be covered by Basic Law: Freedom of Occupation.
43. H.C.J. 494/03, *Physicians for Human Rights*, at para. 18.
44. We have discussed elsewhere some possible explanations for the court's relative lack of interest in promoting social rights. Rabin and Shany, 'The Israeli Unfinished Constitutional Revolution'.
45. However, there is little evidence in practice that the Supreme Court has been reluctant until now to limit civil and political rights in order to further social interests. See H.C.J. 450/97, *Tnuffa Manpower and Maintenance Services Ltd. v. Minister of Labour and Social Affairs*, 52(2) P.D. 433. See also Dotan, 'Supreme Court as Protector', pp. 113–119.
46. See Ruth Ben-Israel, 'Dinei Avoda' (Labour Laws), *Israel Yearbook of Law* (1992–1993), p. 433; Aeyal Gross, 'Ha-Huka Ha-Yisraelit: Kli Le'Tzedek Halukati o Kli Negdi?' (The Israeli Constitution: A Tool for Distributive Justice, or A Tool Which Prevents It?), in Menachem Mautner (ed.), *Tsedek Halukati Be-Yisrael* (Distributive Justice in Israel), Tel Aviv, 2000, pp. 79–96.
47. See Frank E.L. Deale, 'The Unhappy History of Economic Rights in the United States and Prospects for their Creation and Renewal', *How. L.J.*, Vol. 43 (2000), p. 281; Cass

R. Sunstein 'Why Does the American Constitution Lack Social and Economic Guarantees?', *Chicago Public Law and Legal Theory Working Paper* (2003), p. 36, available at www.law.uchicago.edu/academics/publiclaw/resources/36.crs.constitution.pdf.

48. Constitution of Ireland, article 45.
49. German Basic Law, article 20(1) ('The Federal Republic of Germany is a democratic and social federal state'). For discussion of the status of social rights under the German Basic Law, see Peter E. Quint, 'The Constitutional Guarantees of Social Welfare in the Process of German Unification', *Am. J. Comp. L*, Vol. 47 (1999), p. 303.
50. Indian Constitution, art. 36–51.
51. Jamie Cassels, 'Judicial Activism and Public Interest Litigation in India: Attempting the Impossible?', *Am. J. Comp. L.*, Vol. 37 (1989), p. 495; Guy Seidman, 'Zchuyot Hevratiot: Mabat Hashva-ati Le-Hodu Ve-Le-Drom Africa' (Social Rights: A Comparative Look at India and South Africa), in Rabin and Shany, *Rights in Israel*, pp. 347, 356–374.
52. Constitution of the Republic of South Africa, article 23–30. See discussion in Pierre De Vos, 'Pious Wishes or Directly Enforceable Human Rights? Social and Economic Rights in South Africa's 1996 Constitution', *South Africa Journal of Human Rights*, Vol. 13 (1997), p. 67; Albie Sachs, 'The Creation of South Africa's Constitution', *N.Y.L. Sch. L. Rev.*, Vol. 41 (1997), p. 669.
53. Constitution of Finland, art. 16–20.
54. Declaration on the Establishment of the State of Israel ('The State shall maintain complete equality in *social* and political rights to all of its citizens, without distinction . . . It shall ensure freedom of religion, conscience, language, education and culture') (emphasis added).
55. In addition to the South African and Finnish Constitutions, one may note, for example the following instruments: Charter of Basic Rights and Fundamental Freedoms (Czech Republic), art. 26–35; Constitution of Poland, art. 64–78; Interim Iraqi Constitution, art. 14; Constitution of the Democratic Republic of East Timor, ss. 50–61.
56. See Judy Siegel, 'Health Basket Expanded by NIS 150m, but Won't get Automatic Yearly Update', *Jerusalem Post*, 22 March 2005.
57. Israel Democracy Institute, *Sugiyat Ha-Igun Shel Zchuyot Hevratiot Ba-Huka: Hakinus Ha-Tshiy'i* (The Question of Incorporation of Social Rights in the Constitution: Proceedings of the 9th Session of the Public Council), Jerusalem, 2003, 76.
58. See Committee on Constitutional, Legislative and Legal Affairs, *Huka Be-Haskama Rehava* (Constitution by Wide Consensus), Jerusalem, 2006, art. 17–20, available through www.knesset.gov.il/huka/.
59. Avi Ben-Bassat and Momi Dahan, *Zchuyut Hevratiot Ba-Huka Ve-Mediniyut Kalkalit* (Social Rights in the Constitution and Economic Policy), Jerusalem, 2004, p. 102. It should be noted however that Ben-Bassat and Dahan are of the view that there is no direct link between constitutionalization of social rights and government spending on social programmes. Gerald N. Rosenberg, *The Hollow Hope: Can Courts Bring about Social Change?*, Chicago, 1991, p. 336.
60. Israel Democracy Institute, *Hatza'a Le-Huka Be-Haskama* (Proposal for a Constitution by Consensus), (2005), Chapter Two: Fundamental Human Rights, http://www.e-q-m.com/clients/Huka/huka_01.html (hereinafter IDI Draft Constitution). The full article provides: 'Rights protected by the Constitution shall not be impaired, but through legislation compatible with the values of the State of Israel, designed for a worthy purpose, and not excessive, or through by-laws specifically authorized by such legislation, which preserves, to the largest possible degree, the essence of the right' (unofficial translation).
61. IDI Draft Constitution, chapter 2, art. 32 provides that: '(a) The State of Israel shall endeavour to promote the personal and economic welfare of its citizens and residents out of recognition of human dignity. b) The scope of the social rights enumerated in articles 33–36 shall be specified in legislation or secondary legislation.' Article 33 provides that 'The State of Israel shall act to promote social security'; article 34 provides that: 'The State of Israel shall ensure public health and shall guarantee the provision of health service'; article 35 provides that: '(a) The State of Israel shall diligently advance education out of recognition of its value and importance to the development of human spirit and talent and to ensure equal opportunities to all of its residents; (b) ensure thirteen years of free education, the first eleven being compulsory'; article 36 provides: 'The State of Israel shall act to maintain decent conditions of work out of recognition of the value of work.'

62. IDI Draft Constitution, chapter 2, art. 15(a) ('everyone has the right to life, body integrity and dignity'). See also chapter 2, art. 31 (the right to strike); chapter 2, art. 37(a) (children's right to basic subsistence and development).
63. Significantly, the position of the IDI echoes a 1998 government-sponsored draft Basic Law: Social Rights, which also included mere hortatory reference to the need to protect social interests. Draft Basic Law: Social Rights, article 3, in Ministry of Justice, Basic Laws Memorandum, 25 January 1998 (copy with authors) ('The State of Israel shall diligently promote and develop the conditions necessary to ensure its residents' subsistence in human dignity, including in the fields of labour, education, health, social welfare and environmental protection. All as determined in law, or according to law or governmental decisions').
64. See Guy Mundlak, 'Zchuyot Hevratiot-Kalkaliot Ba-Siah Hachukati Ha-Hadash: Mi-Zchuyot Hevratiot La-Meimad Ha-Hevrati Shel Zchuyot Ha-Adam' (Socio-Economic Rights in the New Constitutional Discourse: From Social Rights to the Social Dimension of Human Rights), *Shnaton Mishpat Ha-Avoda*, Vol. 7 (1999), p. 65; Ruth Ben-Israel, 'Hashlachot Hukei Ha-Yesod Al Hukei Ha-Avoda' (The Impact of the Basic Laws on Labour Law), *Shnaton Mishpat Ha-Avoda*, Vol. 4 (1994), pp. 27, 31; Gross, 'The Israeli Constitution: A Tool for Distributive Justice'; Michael Atlan, 'Zchuyot Ha-Adam Ve-Haezrach Be-Yisrael—Mikra'a' (Human and Civil Rights in Israel—A Text Book), *Mishpatim*, Vol. 22 (1993), p. 251; Anat Maor, 'Hor Paur Be-Sefer Hahukim: Hatza'at Hok Yesod Zchuyot Hevratiot: Chronika Shel Kishlon Ha-Hakika' (A Gaping Hole in the Law Gazette: Draft Basic Law: Social Rights—Chronicle of a Legislative Failure), in Rabin and Shany, *Rights in Israel*, p. 195; IDI, *Question of Incorporation*, pp. 67–68, 70–72, 78–79, 99–100, 105–106.
65. See Draft Basic Law: Social Rights (P1634) (submitted 1 December 2003); Draft Basic Law: Social Rights (P2581) (submitted 5 March 2001).
66. Ruth Gavison, 'Al Ha-Yahasim Bein Zchuyot Ezrahiot-Mediniot U-Bein Zchuyot Kalkaliot-Hevratiot' (On the Relations between Civil-Political Rights and Socio-Economic Rights), in Rabin and Shany, *Rights in Israel*, pp. 25, 66. For similar positions, see Jeremy Waldron, *Law and Disagreement*, Oxford, 1999, pp. 255–312; Mark Tushent, *Taking the Constitution Away from the Courts*, Princeton, NJ, 1999, pp. 129–176.
67. See Robert Nozick, *Anarchy, State and Utopia*, New York, 1974. According to Nozick, taxation could be justified only if it is designed to sustain the state's function as a 'night watchman'; taxation designed to serve re-distributional agendas violates fundamental human rights—because it compels taxed individuals to labour for the welfare of others, it constitutes a form of slavery. For support, see Samuel Scheffler, 'Natural Rights, Equality and the Minimal State', in Paul Jeffrey (ed.), *Reading Nozick: Essays on Anarchy, State and Utopia*, Oxford, 1981, p. 148; Chandran Kukathas and Philip Petit, *Rawls—A Theory of Justice and its Critics*, Stanford, CA, 1990, p. 76. Naturally, the Nozikian model has also attracted considerable criticism. G.A. Cohen, *Self-Ownership Freedom and Equality*, Cambridge, 1995, pp. 19–37. In addition, it had been argued that the provision of public services and the empowerment of weak groups, facilitated by taxation, could promote the general welfare, including that of the taxpayers (it might be more efficient to fight crime through welfare programmes than through policing). See also John Rawls, *A Theory of Justice*, Cambridge, 1971, p. 303 (the 'maximin' moral principle supports a policy of assisting society's least favoured segments); Ronald Dworkin, *Taking Rights Seriously*, London, 1977, p. 227 (Liberal thought should protect some notion of equality).
68. Gavison, 'On the Relations Between Rights'. See also Waldron, *Law and Disagreement*; Tushent, *Taking the Constitution Away*.
69. Tim Murphy, 'Economic Inequality and the Constitution', in Tim Murphy and Patrick Twomey (eds.), *Ireland's Evolving Constitution*, Oxford, 1988, pp. 163, 169 ('The main reason ... why the Constitution should not Confer [such rights] is that these are essentially political matters which, in a democracy, it should be the responsibility of the elected representatives of the people to address and determine. It would be a distortion of democracy to transfer decisions on major issues of policy ... from the government ... elected to represent the people and do their will, to an unelected judiciary').
70. Aharon Barak, 'Ha-Huka Hakalkalit Shel Medinat Yisrael' (The Israeli Economic Constitution), *Mishpat U-Mimshal*, Vol. 4 (1998), p. 357 ('The Constitution is not a political manifesto ... Market economy or centralized economy may find living space within

it ... From this perspective, one may refer to the neutrality of our Constitution') (unofficial translation); Committee on Economic, Social and Cultural Rights, General Comment 3, The nature of States parties' obligations, (Fifth session, 1990), U.N. Doc. E/1991/23, annex III at 86 (1991), at para. 8 ('the [ICESCR] is neutral and its principles cannot accurately be described as being predicated exclusively upon the need for, or the desirability of a socialist or a capitalist system, or a mixed, centrally planned, or laisser-faire economy, or upon any other particular approach').

71. John H. Ely, *Democracy and Distrust: A Theory of Judicial Review*, Cambridge, MA, 1980, p. 103.
72. Dotan, 'Supreme Court as Protector', pp. 85–87.
73. ibid., p. 84.
74. ibid., p. 84
75. Gavison, 'On the Relations Between Rights', p. 29.
76. Basic Law: Human Dignity and Liberty, art. 7.
77. Basic Law: Human Dignity and Liberty, art. 3.
78. H.C.J. 5100/94 *Public Committee against Torture v. Government of Israel*, 53(4) P.D. 817.
79. See Aharon Barak, 'A Judge on Judging: The Role of a Supreme Court in a Democracy', *Harv. L. Rev.*, Vol. 116 (2002), pp. 16, 44–45 ('Most central of all human rights is the right to dignity. It is the source from which all other human rights are derived. Dignity unites the other human rights into a whole'); Margaret J. Radin, *Reinterpreting Property*, Chicago, 1993.
80. John Rawls, 'Distributive Justice: Some Addenda', in Samuel Freedman (ed.), *Collected Papers*, London, 1999, pp. 154, 166.
81. Mundlak, 'Socio-Economic Rights in the New Constitutional Discourse', p. 100.
82. See Daphne Barak-Erez, 'Dunam Po Ve-Dunam Sham: Minhal Mekarke'ei Yisrael Be-Zvat Ha-Interesim' (A Dunam Here and a Dunam There: Israel's Land Administration Caught between Interests), *Iyunei Mishpat*, Vol. 21 (1998), pp. 613, 617–620; Barak Medina, 'Hovata Shel Hamdina Lesapek Zrahim Bsisi'yim: Mi-Siah Shel Zchuyot Le-Teoria Shel Mimun Ziburi' (The State's Duties to Provide Basic Needs: From a 'Discourse of Rights' to a 'Public Finance Theory'), in Rabin and Shany, *Rights in Israel*, pp. 131, 144–146. However, it has been argued that conflicts between competing interest groups may introduce sufficient checks and balances. Einer R. Elhauge, 'Does Interest Group Theory Justify More Intrusive Judicial Review?' *Yale L. Rev.* Vol. 101 (1991), p. 31.
83. ICESCR, art. 2(1) ('Each State Party to the present Covenant undertakes to take steps, individually and through international assistance and co-operation, especially economic and technical, to the maximum of its available resources, with a view to achieving progressively the full realization of the rights recognized in the present Covenant by all appropriate means, including particularly the adoption of legislative measures'); Committee on Economic, Social and Cultural Rights, General Comment 9, The domestic application of the Covenant, (Nineteenth session, 1998), U.N. Doc. E/C.12/1998/24 (1998), at para. 10.
84. Mundlak, 'Socio-Economic Rights in the New Constitutional Discourse', p. 91 ff.
85. H.C.J. 240/98, *Adalah—The Legal Centre for the Rights of the Arab Minority in Israel v. Minister of Religious Affairs*, 52(5) P.D. 167, 190 (per Cheshin, J.) ('[N]ullifying budgetary legislation and ordering the redistribution of the budget total—and this is the petition of the petitioners—might lead to a kaleidoscope-like activity: the shifting of one sand-stone results in the automatic shifting of other sand-stones and to a radical change of the total picture...') (unofficial translation). See also H.C.J. 3472/92, *Brand v. Minister of Communication*, 47(3) P.D. 143, 153.
86. See Waldron, *Law and Disagreement*, p. 233; Michael MacMillan, 'Social Versus Political Rights', *Canadian Journal of Political Science*, Vol. 19 (1986), pp. 283, 303; Mathew C.R. Craven, *The International Covenant on Economic, Social and Cultural Rights: A Perspective on its Development*, Oxford, 1995, p. 15. See also Rabin, *The Right to Education*, pp. 60–64; Yuval Shany, 'Beiti Eino Mivzari: Alimut Ba-Mishpaha Ke-Sug Shel Inuy Asur Al-Pi Hamishpat Ha-BeinLeumi' (My Home is Not My Castle: Domestic Violence as a Form of Torture under International Law), *Hamishpat*, Vol. 7 (2002), pp. 151, 165–167. For a survey of Israeli case law on positive aspects of civil and political rights, see Mundlak, 'Socio-Economic Rights in the New Constitutional Discourse', pp. 94–96.

87. Jeremy Waldron, 'Liberal Rights—Two Sides of the Coin', in Jeremy Waldron, *Liberal Rights— Collected Papers*, Cambridge, 1993, pp. 339, 343 ('Reflection on the rights of the citizen also undermines the other claim about individualism—the claim that first generation rights call only for inaction, rather than collective intervention, by the state. In fact, rights to democratic participation require much more than mere omissions by the state. They require officials to approach their task in a certain spirit, and they require the establishment of political structures to provide a place for popular participation and to give effect to people's wishes, expressed by voting and other forms of pressure ... Even with regard to those first generation rights which are not participatory, it is seldom merely *inaction* that is called for. As I argued ... we set governments up according to traditional liberal theory, not only to *respect* our rights (what would be the point of that?), but to protect, uphold, and vindicate them. That involves positive collective action, action which makes use of scarce manpower and resources. It involves the operation of police force, law courts, and so on, which are certainly not inconsiderable expenditures on the part of the state and of society collectively'). See also ibid., p. 344.
88. Mundlak, 'Socio-Economic Rights in the New Constitutional Discourse', p. 99.
89. Medina, 'The State's Duties to Provide Basic Needs', p. 133.
90. See e.g., Basic Law: Freedom of Occupation; H.C.J. 4363/00 *Upper Puria Committee v. Minister of Education*, 56(4) P.D. 203.
91. Shany, 'My Home is Not My Castle'.
92. Committee on Economic, Social and Cultural Rights, General Comment 14, The right to the highest attainable standard of health (22nd session, 2000), U.N. Doc. E/C.12/2000/4 (2000), at para. 35.
93. Equal Opportunities in Employment Law, 1988; Prohibition of Discrimination in Products, Services and Entry to Entertainment and Public Places, 2000.
94. Committee on Economic, Social and Cultural Rights, General Comment 3, The nature of States parties' obligations (Fifth session, 1990), U.N. Doc. E/1991/23, annex III at 86 (1991), at para. 10 (establishing a 'minimum core' which states must comply with, in almost all circumstances).
95. H.C.J. 4905/98, *Gamzu*; H.C.J. 4128/02, *Adam, Teva Va-Din*; H.C.J. 366/03, *Association for Commitment to Peace*.
96. Aharon Barak, 'Hakdama' (Introduction), in Rabin and Shany, *Rights in Israel*, pp. 5, 8.
97. See Medina, 'The State's Duties to Provide Basic Needs', pp. 154–157.
98. C.A. 6281/93 *Bank Hamizrachi Hameuhad Ltd. v. Migdal Cooperative Village*, 49(4) P.D. 221, 331 (per Shamgar, C.J.) ('the court does not nullify economic or other legislation because it deems it unwise or if its contours seem to entail in the eyes of the court undesirable economic implications. The court examines the constitutional aspect, i.e., the human rights aspect... I support the position of the German Constitution interpreters, according to which no intervention is warranted unless the approach taken is clearly and obviously erroneous, so that it may not be considered a reasonable basis for legislative action'); H.C.J. 389/80 *Dapei Zahav Ltd. v. Israel Broadcasting Authority*, 35(1) P.D. 425, 443; *Handyside v. UK*, 1976 Eur. Ct. H.R. (Ser. A), No. 24.
99. H.C.J. 987/94, *Euronet Golden Line (1992) Ltd. v. Minister of Communication*, 48(5) P.D. 412; 5042/96, *Cohen v. Israel Land Administration*, 53(1) P.D. 743. See also Yoav Dotan, 'Shnei Musagim Shel Svirut' (Two Reasonableness Concepts), *Sefer Shamgar: Ma'amarim (Liber Amicorum Shamgar: Articles)*, Vol. 1, Tel Aviv, 2003, p. 417. It remains to be seen whether in the future courts would assert their authority to also supervise the legislative decision-making process, e.g. whether the Knesset accorded due consideration to legislation compromising constitutionally protected social rights. Cf. H.C.J. 3106/04, *Association for Civil Rights in Israel v. The Knesset* (not yet published) (identifying serious deficiencies in budgetary legislation, though refusing to nullify the legislation).
100. Dan T. Coenen, 'A Constitution of Collaboration: Protecting Fundamental Values with Second-Look Rules of Interbranch Dialogue', *Wm. and Mary L. Rev.*, Vol. 42 (2001). 1575.
101. Cf. H.C.J. 3267/97, *Rubinstein v. Minister of Defence*, 52(5) P.D. 481 (court referred to the Knesset the decision on the legality of the exemption given to ultra-orthodox youth from military service). In H.C.J. 161/94, *Attari v. State of Israel*, 94(1) *Takdin-Supreme* 1283, the court recommends that the Minister of Health regulate by way of regulations or the introduction of legislation legal limits on trade in body organs.

102. H.C.J. 3239/02, *Mar'ab v. IDF Judea and Samaria Commander*, 57(2) P.D. 349 (published) (delaying for six months the entry into force of a decision annulling a military ordinance). Cf. *Baker v. Vermont*, 774 A.2d 864, 889.
103. See declarations of incompatibility under Human Rights Act, 1998.
104. The original 'Brandeis Brief' was submitted in 1908 to the US Supreme Court and surveyed the social implications of minimum-hours legislation governing women's work. *Muller v. Oregon*, 208 U.S. 412 (1908). For discussion, see e.g. Mundlak, 'Socio-Economic Rights in the New Constitutional Discourse', pp. 100–101.
105. H.C.J. 366/03, *Association for Commitment to Peace and Social Justice v. Minister of Finance*, interim decision of 5 January 2004 (not yet published) (ordering the state to specify dignified subsistence standards). The interim order was revoked on 16 March 2004 and replaced by a general order instructing the state to provide a detailed response to the petition against welfare benefit cuts.

Judicial Behaviour: A Socio-Cultural Strategic Approach—Conceptual Framework and Analysis of Case Studies in Israel

ASSAF MEYDANI

This article will analyze two controversial decisions made by the Israeli Supreme Court. The first case is known as the 'Torture decision, 1999';[1] the second case is the 'Land decision, 2002'.[2] This study highlights the variables explaining those decisions. The role of cultural factors and values in explaining judicial activism in Israel has been studied by various researchers. However, current studies tend to overlook the strategic calculations of various social groups turning to the court, as well as the role of socio-cultural explanations and the ways in which social players act as agents of political and institutional change.[3]

The study will present a twofold analysis: a strategic analysis and a cultural-political participation analysis. This analysis will examine individual and structural factors in explaining the empirical cases and the court's judicial behaviour. The argument stated in this study reflects a positive approach based on public choice rationalization. This approach is less emphasized in the law and society in Israel literature. Such an approach is needed, especially at times when most studies determine that Israel faced a values crisis during the 1990s.[4] Such value disorientation has an effect on the determination and stability of the policy-making process.[5] The methodology used in this article is based on a literature analysis of the decisions made by the court and on secondary literature emphasizing the social and cultural aspects of Israeli society.[6]

This study will analyze two main events in Israel's conflicting values debate. The first case is a petition against the interrogation methods of the General Security Service: *The Public Committee against Torture in Israel v. the State of Israel*.[7] The court declared that Israeli law prohibits physical methods of interrogation. This decision marked a policy change in Israel since the former policy, known as the *Landau Commission Report* (1987)

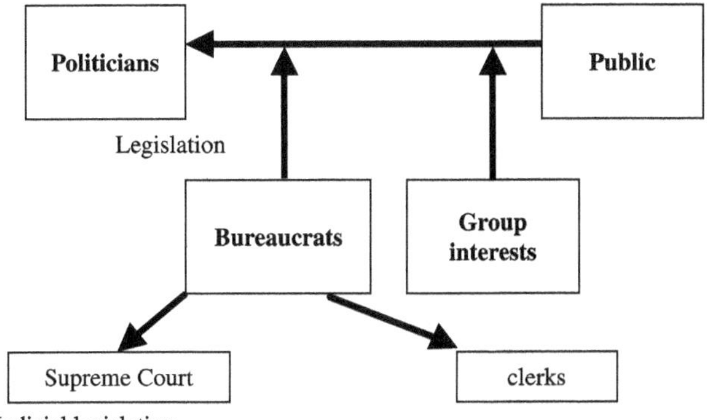

Judicial legislation

- Public trust: maximization of legitimacy;
- Community viewpoint;
- Ideological view;
- Maximization of power.[8]

FIGURE 1
THE STRATEGIC VIEW

enabled the use of both psychological pressure and 'a moderate degree of physical pressure'.[9]

The second case examined here is a petition submitted to the court in 2000 by the Mizrahi Democratic Rainbow—a New Discourse movement demanding the cancellation of certain decisions (no. 727, 737 and 727) made by Israel Lands Administration (ILA), which enabled the agricultural sector, Kibbutzim and Moshavim, to implement numerous programmes which aimed to change land designations from agricultural to non-agricultural. On 28 August 2002, the Israeli Supreme Court ruled in favour of the appeal and against the Israel Lands Administration decision on account of it being unreasonable. The court believed that the ILA decisions gave unfair benefits to certain sectors (particularly the agricultural sector). Because of their extreme un-reasonability and the fact that they constitute an infringement of the principles of justice they were found to be null and void. The court decision led to a public debate on the issue of land policy in Israel.

This study identifies two variables which explain those decisions:

1. Non-governability of the political system.[10]
2. Israeli political participation characterized by instrumental democratic values, which attempt to create alternative policy decisions.

These two variables will serve as the structural factors creating the framework for the actions of several players in the political-judicial sphere.

In that sense the decision of the Supreme Court is explained as an outcome of the actions of four players: politicians, the public, interest groups and bureaucrats. The Supreme Court is perceived here as a unique institution. This study emphasizes the maximization of legitimacy; the ideological view of Supreme Court judges, the legal community viewpoint and the power of the Supreme Court in all issues regarding justice.[11]

In this article a court decision is perceived as a socio-political equilibrium in a given set of players who are acting according to certain premises and to a pre-given set of structural conditions that serve as a framework for their actions. The more a society tends to be characterized by non-governability and by instrumental political participation, the more we can expect players to use short-term instrumental views as a guide for behaviour. This kind of behaviour can be explained by public choice rationalization theory.

EXISTING LITERATURE

Since the 1980s, and mainly since the 1990s, studies in politics and law have adopted an economic attitude when explaining judicial behaviour. This tradition, which began with the studies of Herman,[12] and Murphy,[13] continued with other studies. Those studies emphasized an individual aspect that was less obvious in the work of scholars dealing with socio-politics and traditional legal issues.[14] These individual aspects perceived the behaviour of judges as a key factor in a given socio-political structure. When we take these aspects into consideration, law becomes a long-term public good based on short-term strategies. The judicial work is a complex procedure consisting of legal doctrines, expectations from professionals, cooperation with other judges and the social political atmosphere. Thus, the Supreme Court can only bring slow and incremental changes.[15]

While there are various explanations for judicial activism in Israel, there are very few studies which focus on the behaviour of judges from a strategic individualistic point of view. Most studies emphasize cultural factors and values in explaining judicial activism in Israel. For example, Menachem Mautner argues that the court took a stand in cultural, social and political debates in order to defend liberal values from significant groups that tried to challenge these values, while counting on the support of sympathetic sectors in Israeli society.[16] This process, of increasing judicial activism and the growing hegemonic position of the court, could be explained, according to Gad Barzilai, by two parallel processes/factors: the growing impact of liberal values on the political culture, combined with the lack of a written constitution in a highly divided, polarized, and fragmented setting.[17]

Few studies examine the relationship between the Supreme Court and politicians in Israel from a strategic point of view. For example, Stefan Voight and Eli Salzberger claim that an independent judicial system can serve politicians who are unable to govern. Thereby, politicians can maximize their interest whenever the political costs derived from delegating power to the judicial system are smaller than the benefit derived from it.[18] Yet these studies do not tend to emphasize the affect that Israeli public political participation has on judicial behaviour, as well as on the strategic calculations of the Supreme Court.[19]

Current literature regards cultural and structural conditions as a key factor in explaining judicial behaviour. It divides into two branches with regard to the United States Supreme Court: the 'strategic school'[20] and the 'attitudinal approach'.[21] Both claim that there is a structural conflict between politicians and judges. However, the 'attitudinal approach' suggests that justices vote for the positions most consistent with their policy preferences, given that the institutional structures facing the court allow sincere voting. On the other hand, the 'strategic school' views high court justices as players who act strategically to advance their preferences. In order to minimize the possibility of congressional override, justices often adjust the court's doctrinal positions and do not vote according to their sincere preferences.

Another approach for explaining judicial behaviour is 'judicial behaviouralism'. These studies focus on judges' background: their education, religion, political orientation etc.[22] This study will present an analytic framework in an attempt to explain judicial behaviour based on the preliminary institutional setting and the political culture dominant in the society.

THE TORTURE DECISION, 1999

In September 1999, the court declared that Israeli law prohibits physical methods of interrogation. This decision marked a policy change since the former policy, known as the *Landau Commission Report* (1987), enabled both the use of psychological pressure and 'a moderate degree of physical pressure'.[23]

The explanation given by the court raises a paradox regarding the relationship between law and politics. The court stated:

> we have not decided up till now since we did not have the opportunity to hear arguments that will enable us to see the whole normative picture. Now we heard such arguments and we thank both sides for presenting them. Although part of the appeal is not actual, nevertheless we decided that it is essential to rule in such a complex issue.[24]

The court's explanation is a formalistic one. This explanation is a paradoxical one since the court has the ability to develop the law, as it did on several occasions. A good example of such action is the Yardor case from 1965 where judges Agranat and Zusman, in a majority, ruled that the law of voting was inappropriate, since Israel was a Jewish state.[25] The outcome was that the Arab-Israeli movement El-Ard was not allowed to participate in the elections for the Israeli parliament, the Knesset. Similarly, Judge Landoy in the Bergman Decision, 1969, expanded the principle of equality stated in section 4 of the Basic Law: the Knesset, towards the right to be elected, deciding that the law of finance contradicts the principles of equality and ought to be cancelled.[26]

Therefore, the explanation should go beyond the formal legal disciplinary approach. The framework employed in this article is similar to the rhetorical approach[27] in explaining judicial behaviour.[28] These studies conclude that judges are political players operating in a powerful political sphere, trying to maintain their autonomy and legitimacy.[29]

The framework elaborated here is different from the one in the normative studies.[30] It tries to combine factors stated in current literature such as the relationship with the prosecution[31] and the role of the petitioners as interest groups.[32]

THE LAND DECISION, 2002

On 28 August 2002, the Israeli Supreme Court ruled in favour of the Keshet movement and against the Israeli Land Administration decision, on account of it being unreasonable. The court decided that the decisions which were the object of the appeal (no. 727, 737 and 727) awarded unjust benefits to certain sectors (the agricultural sector). Because of their impingement of the principles of justice, they were found to be null and void. The court's decision was considered a precedent and it started a public debate about land policy in Israel.

The court claimed that the law of the Israeli Land Administration was a 'lazy law', since the ability to determine fundamental arrangements was in the jurisdiction of the land council instead of the parliament. Thus, the court chose to adopt the existing system instead of cancelling the law as it used to do in the past. However, using a reasonable approach, the court finally decided to intervene. This created a paradox, since the Israeli Land Administration has accepted the argument of the Keshet movement at its initial stage, and declared that the decisions would be cancelled. At that point there was no conflict to be solved by court. However, the court decided to adopt this case in order to declare a fundamental value. There was no formal explanation; in order to understand the court's behaviour one must adopt an interdisciplinary approach.

PUBLIC CHOICE THEORY AS A FRAMEWORK FOR ANALYZING PUBLIC POLICY REGARDING COURT DECISIONS: A BOUNDED RATIONALITY APPROACH

In this section a process model for analyzing public policy regarding court decisions will be developed. The process model maintains that public policy is the product of interactions between four main players: politicians, interest groups, bureaucrats and the general public. These players interact according to certain premises rooted deep in Public Choice Theory. Yet, due to the disadvantages of the rational explanation we shall use another socio-cultural explanation called 'alternative political participation', rooted in Israeli society. Such forms of participation coupled with non-governability serve as structural factors explaining the interactions between the above four players and also explaining judicial behaviour. In this sense, public choice theory integrates structural and individual aspects so that social reality is determined by the acts of individuals acting rationally under the influence of structural factors (bounded rationality).[33]

Non-governability and Political Participation as Explanatory Variables

The Supreme Court of Israel, with respect to justiciability, authority and standing of the petitions filed in fields concerning human rights, becomes an active player in the determination of human rights public policy.[34] The explanation of judicial behaviour focuses on two key processes that have taken place in Israeli society (i.e. structural changes in the political system, as well as social and cultural processes affecting the relative power of the various players).

From the mid-1970s, two significant changes took place in Israeli society. First, the Labour Party lost its dominance of the political system, creating a two-bloc system. In the 1980s, this situation gave power to sectoral parties, such as the religious parties; finally, in the 1990s, with the introduction of the direct election of the prime minister, there was a further rise in sectoral politics in the Knesset. These changes led to the weakening of legislative authority in comparison to judicial authority.[35] Second, key features in Israeli political culture, which were repressed in the 1950s and 1960s, came to the fore and largely shaped the role of the law and the Supreme Court in Israeli society.

Historically, before the establishment of Israel in 1948, the political, social and economic institutions developed through channels which were either semi-legal or totally illegal. This development took place through the creation of facts on the ground and by forcing a certain reality on the British mandatory authorities. Later on, after the foundation of the state, in the 1950s and 1960s, the political, economic and administrative system became extremely centralized.[36] The combination of extremely centralized systems with a tradition of influence through semi-legal channels or, as I call them here, 'alternative patterns of behaviour', had a significant impact on Israeli political culture.

This extreme centralization prevented the development of alternative power bases such as interest groups, and greatly slowed down the development of a civil society with liberal features. Furthermore, due to the problem of collective action, no public pressure arose to change the situation, until it reached catastrophic proportions. Such a catastrophe did indeed occur in the 1973 Yom Kippur War, which exposed the public's deep dissatisfaction with the policy of the Labour party in many respects. In order to change the government and influence policies, the public used mainly democratic, legal tools such as elections, demonstrations, strikes and the media. By the late 1960s, however, illegal courses of action had also become noticeable, creating a new reality by establishing facts on the ground. The illegal settlements were at the forefront of this process, forcing a certain reality on the government. Over the years, the public gradually despaired of its ability to wield influence in democratic, legal ways. This modus operandi has also spread into other areas of life. Consequently, during the 1980s, the black market economy flourished, as did privately paid supplements to state education, private payments to physicians in public service, and the pirate cable industry.

In terms of public choice theory, this conduct may be termed as an alternative political pattern of participation. In other words, when people are dissatisfied with a particular policy or the level of supply of a public good, they do not make use of the accepted ways of protest, nor do they totally leave society, but they adopt one of two courses of action. The first takes the form of an internal and passive departure, when citizens simply cut themselves off, on an intellectual level, from events on the political and social level, focusing instead on their own personal lives. The second, a proactive course of action, is the alternative supply of a public good.[37] As a consequence the public creates a threat to the government monopoly on the public product, compelling the politicians to change the policy in accordance with the new demands they make. Thus, in many cases, politicians react to pressures of this kind by formalizing the non-formal institutions created by parts of the public. This was indeed the reaction of the political system with respect to the settlements, pirate cable operators, black market economy, private payments to public physicians and privately paid supplements to state education.

A similar analysis may be applied to the development of the place of the Supreme Court in Israeli society. As explained before, in the 1970s and 1980s the public made intensive use of democratic, legal means of influence, such as elections, demonstrations and strikes. Yet these means did not bring about any real change in public policy. Among the Israeli public, there was a growing sense of the total inability to exert any influence over the political system. The best expression of this came in the form of National Unity governments which ruled from 1984 to 1990—a system which increased the sense of deadlock.

The fact that the means of influence available to the public were totally ineffective gave rise to demands to change the election system and attempts to find an alternative which would achieve the desired public policy. The alternative identified was the Supreme Court, mainly since it lacks a clear definition of its political role. Consequently, using an ever-increasing number of legal petitions, the public attempted to create a new reality by establishing facts on the ground. Similar to alternative behaviour in other areas, in the legal field this behaviour was also intended to threaten politicians,[38] compelling them to institutionalize a new reality—be it by accepting the new constitutional arrangement that arose or by limiting and redefining the power of the Supreme Court.

It follows, then, that the deep rifts within Israeli society, together with the institutional structure created a situation whereby the political system has been unable to deal with problems which require the shaping of public policy. In light of this inability, Israeli society has adopted the alternative behaviour of filing an ever-increasing number of petitions to the Supreme Court, with a twofold purpose: to bring about policy decisions, and to put pressure on politicians to change the institutional structure, in one way or another.

Moving towards an Individualistic Approach

The above explanation is a structural one, creating the framework for an institutional design or for a public policy design, whereas an individualistic approach serves as a positive explanation. In that sense, public policy manifested in court decisions is composed of a collection of decisions made by competent authorities related to the regulation and management of various areas of life. This insight is based on the premise that law is a social product and in order to explain it one must consider its surrounding environment.[39]

Every court decision is called a policy decision, and the proposed theoretical basis could help explain such policy decisions. For example, the land case and the torture case are both court decisions manifested in the form of a judicial decision, but in order to explain them we need to consider the interactions between certain players in the realm of these decisions. Both of the above decisions are perceived by the Israeli public as a precedent in the broad realm of human rights.

However, the courts are not the sole player. In fact, though courts are unique bureaucrats, in a democratic arena the body which makes the final decision at the end of the process is composed of politicians. Therefore, the final stage of the process which needs to be explained is the interaction in the decision-making body amongst the politicians themselves. However, sometimes non-governability along with a certain political participation creates an additional 'alternative governor'. These two variables, among others, explain why the Supreme Court became such a crucial player in Israeli politics.[40] In order to understand the conduct of politicians, we need to take a few steps back and examine the basic interests and motivations driving them.

Citizen–Politician Relations

The model proposed by public choice theory is based on the assumption that any policy decision made by a politician, including the Torture and the Land cases, is related to human rights. This assumption is underpinned by the reciprocal relations between the politician and the electorate, based on the demand and supply mechanism.[41] In other words, the public makes demands for certain human rights policies, such as a demand for more just land distribution to be included in its economic-social rights; or a demand for the policy on various methods of interrogation, used by the General Security Service, to be contained within the country's civil rights, and the politicians will respond positively solely to those demands which increase their chances of being re-elected. This is how we may explain, for example, the decision of the Israeli government to set up a National Commission of Inquiry in 1987 to examine the methods of interrogation used by the General Security Service (the Landau Commission) and its decision to adopt the *Landau Report*. It might also be the explanation for the establishment of the Milgrom Committee with regard to the amount of compensation given to the Kibbutzim and Moshavim in Israel.

The basic model assumes that the main interest (and, occasionally, the only interest) of politicians is to maximize their chances of being re-elected. That is why no matter which policy decisions they might take, they will be striving to find the alternative which represents the position of the median voter.[42] If they consistently represent voters' positions in various policy areas, they are likely to maximize their chances of being re-elected. The rationale behind this model is that politicians are dependent on public support through the mechanism of elections (in democracies) or due to the need to achieve the minimum cooperation of the public (in non-democratic regimes).

Yet this article aims to emphasize the bounded rationality in the sense that it is not so clear that politicians always act in ways that maximize their ability to be re-elected. Though this might often be the case, here it will be claimed that such a motivation is bounded or enhanced by the formal or informal rules of the game. The claim is that in Israel, non-governability along with alternative political participation serve as enhancing instrumental factors. In that sense one can view the behaviour of politicians from the point of view of public choice theory.

Consequently, politicians need information concerning the division of public preferences regarding the various policy alternatives in any given case, as well as information regarding credible measures which will bring them into line with the position of the median voter. It follows that the main goal of politicians is not to maximize economic efficiency, but to maximize his/her chance of being re-elected. As a consequence, from the outset, we cannot expect human rights public policy to be optimal in terms of social welfare. Furthermore, politicians will always prefer the status quo, as long as no public demands are being made on them. This may serve as a partial explanation as to why, in many cases, human rights public policy is not formulated before the situation reaches catastrophic proportions. This rationale may be applied to explain the shaped policy with respect to the various methods of interrogation used by the General Security Service (GSS) after the persistent pattern of perjury by its interrogators was exposed. This explanation also serves as a main variable in explaining the three decisions (no. 727, 737 and 727) made by the Israeli Land Administration after a major crisis in most Kibbutzim and Moshavim in Israel. These decisions enabled the Kibbutzim and Moshavim sectors to implement numerous programmes that changed land designations from agricultural to non-agricultural.

The need for state intervention, by means of public policy, usually emerges when there is a shortage in a 'public good'. A public good is defined as a product whose use, from the very moment it had been created, cannot be prevented, and as a consequence, it is not possible to collect the real payment due for its supply.[43] A public good may be defined as such since there are no regulations regarding the product which restrict its use (air, water) or since, according to a political-social decision, the real price for the public's use of the product is not collected (subsidies in education, health and security). In reality, the decision regarding interrogation methods used by the GSS and the decision regarding the distribution of land are applied to all citizens including those who are not directly involved in it.

The argument posed by public choice theory is that when it comes to public goods, most of the public does not tend to be involved with the supply of the product, but will consume as much as possible.[44] The result is a shortage, on the one hand, and a lack of interest in creating public pressure calling for a change in the situation (collective action), on the other. Applying this rationale to the sphere of human rights public policy, it can be said that the fact that human rights are a public good from which anyone can benefit without being involved in its production creates the motivation to become a free rider. As a consequence, the players do not get involved with each other in efforts to advance and promote human rights. The result is a shortage in human rights policy, on the one hand, and a lack of interest in creating public pressure in order to change the situation, on the other. In the absence of demand by the general public, the power of those groups which manage to overcome the problem of collective action in order to form interest groups substantially increases. The latter, exerting significant influence over human rights public policy, are the non-governmental organizations which act to advance and promote human rights.[45]

Non-Governmental Organizations as Interest Groups over Human Rights

The actions and influence of interest groups in the field of public policy have been studied intensively by researchers of political economy.[46] The literature on the subject emphasizes the reciprocal relationship in which the interest groups supply financial or electoral support to the politicians, and, in return, the latter supply preferential policy (privileges) to the interest groups (rules of regulation, such as price control, monopoly control, etc.). Politicians attempt to shape policy which will be consistent with the position of the median voter. For this purpose, they need to be well-acquainted with the distribution of preferences in society.[47]

Others maintain that, under certain conditions, competition between interest groups enables maximum economic efficiency, in other words, contributions to social welfare.[48] However, evidence shows that politicians are seeking to maximize their chances of being re-elected and interest groups are seeking to maximize the preferential regulation services which they receive.[49] As a consequence, the politicians act most favourably towards those interest groups that make the greatest possible contribution towards their chances of being re-elected. In return, the politicians supply these groups with maximum regulation services.

This article draws a bridge between those two insights by emphasizing the aspect of structural conditions that affect the behaviour of both politicians and interest groups. The more the political system is characterized by governability and fundamental (as opposed to instrumental) political participation, the more the relationships between politicians and interest groups will be based on a more fundamental view since those structural conditions impose long term calculations on the political players.

The role of non-governmental organizations acting to advance and promote human rights is very important in explaining the policy reflected in the court's decisions. These groups, such as the Israeli Civil Rights Association (ACRI), the B'Tselem Organization and the Mizrahi Democratic Rainbow, have managed to overcome the general public problem of collective action in order to present demands concerning human rights policy. The systematic activity, for example, of the Public Commission Against Torture in Israel throughout the 1990s, with recurrent petitions to the High Court of Justice, which enjoyed the support of ACRI and B'tselem, led to a change in human rights policy regarding the interrogation methods used by the GSS (High Court of Justice, The Public Commission Against Torture in Israel, 1999). On the other hand, the activities of non-governmental organizations acting to advance human rights have come up against the activities of interest groups seeking, for their own interests, to limit the scope of human rights. The absence of counter-pressure by the human rights organizations created a situation whereby the politicians identified a violation of freedom of speech as a policy which would be instrumental in their being elected. However, this view is not so clear in societies controlled by non-governability and alternative political participation. These rules motivate politicians not to take a decision, but instead to pass the ability to govern to another institution.[50] This institution is the one identified by the public as one of its interest groups.[51]

The Involvement of Bureaucrats in Human Rights Policy

Evidence shows that even after politicians formulate their position, they still face obstacles which could totally sway their preferred policy. The main obstacle is bureaucrats, who are motivated by interests different to those of politicians.[52] In the context of this article, the focus will be on two types of bureaucrats. One is the standard bureaucrat, a member of the administration who, by virtue of his position, allocates budgets to various activities and thus determines, in practice, whether certain activities take place. This type of bureaucrat works vis-à-vis the politicians and affects the determination of specific policy. With regard to the discussed cases we may see the role of the Israel Land Administration as controlled by the agenda designed by the Kibbutzim and Moshavim[53] and by the GSS, which have interests identical to those of the Israeli prosecutors.[54] Another type of bureaucrat is the Supreme Court, which plays a significant role in the determination of public policy on human rights.

Researchers assume that bureaucrats are driven, first and foremost, by the desire to maximize the budget of their ministries, since that is how they augment their power and, indirectly, also maximize the material remuneration which they receive.[55] However, the situation is slightly more complex, since politicians can adopt different strategies in order to control the bureaucrats.[56]

Assuming that bureaucrats' interests are achieved, we face a certain inconsistency: on the one hand, the maximization of ministry budgets is not in keeping with maximum economic efficiency. On the other hand, when the politicians' interests are satisfied, by weakening bureaucrats, the policy becomes totally subordinate to political considerations without any essential checks and balances. This may harm social welfare.

The process described here illustrates the power of bureaucratic players to undermine initiatives put forward by politicians, in addition to the changing of political objectives as a function of political interests. In effect, with the aid of the above model, we are able to point out a circle which is hard to break. In centralized economic and political systems, human rights policy would be expected to reduce the powers of the bureaucratic entities. In these systems, however, the power of bureaucrats is huge, as compared to that of politicians, and therefore the bureaucrats will strive to undermine the application of human rights policy, and will indeed succeed in their efforts. One way to create fundamental, long-lasting, change is to focus on the decentralization of the bureaucratic, political and economic systems as a means of achieving human rights, instead of concentrating on the issue itself.

The Involvement of the Supreme Court in Human Rights Policy

By examining the place of the Supreme Court in the policy determination process described so far, it would appear that its influence is particularly strong at the decision stage rather than at the stage of understanding the problem or at the stage of formulating a position. The Justices of the Supreme Court cannot initiate a hearing, but are dependent on petitions lodged with the court. Since they are not elected to their position by the general public, but are appointed by a political entity, we may consider the Supreme Court to be a bureaucratic player which is striving to maximize its powers and authority over politicians, who act within executive and legislative authority. The method of appointment and the appointing entity will affect the degree of Supreme Court politicization. However, from the moment they are appointed, the Justices of the Supreme Court may act, according to public choice theory, in order to maximize their power and influence, within the limits of the rules of the game. However, notwithstanding its definition as a bureaucratic player, the power balance between the Supreme Court and the politicians in the executive and legislative authority differs in models analyzing public administration. Public choice theory, therefore, proposes a separate discussion of these reciprocal relations according to a separation-of-powers model.[57]

According to this model, while the Supreme Court has the ability and power to interpret the decisions of the legislative authority, and thus to change the decision to a certain extent, the legislative authority has the ability and power to revoke that interpretation by legislating new laws. It follows that there is a built-in conflict in these reciprocal relationships, similar to the relationships between politicians and their subordinate bureaucrats. The difference is that not all political means of control over the bureaucrats, such as political appointments, are available to the politicians in their relationship with the Supreme Court.

The pattern of conduct described above has also been adopted by the non-governmental organizations seeking to promote human rights. The main channel of activity for advancing human rights public policy is through the legal system, as is evident in the public and legal struggle of the Association for Civil Rights in Israel, the B'Tselem Organization, the Mizrahi Democratic Rainbow, and the Public Commission Against Torture in Israel.

The strategy described above, however, is likely to endanger the chances of establishing democratic and liberal norms in Israeli society, in two ways. First, by having almost exclusive recourse to the legal channel and preferring to pursue it instead of pressuring the executive and legislative authority, non-governmental organizations are undermining the separation of powers principle as one of the fundamental elements of a democratic liberal society. In actual fact, these organizations permit, and even demand, the Supreme Court to act as a policy-shaper, even though there are no defined rules imparting it the power to act as one. Such conduct could be interpreted by various players as the lack of respect of these non-governmental organizations towards defined rules of the game and, consequently, as a seal of approval granted to the non-observance of the law. Second, by concentrating most of the efforts on judicial authority and preferring it to activities involving the other authorities, in particular activities involving the general public, the non-governmental organizations may be creating the belief among the public that human rights are indeed a matter of interest belonging to a narrow, usually elitist, group, with extremely well-defined social features. In all likelihood, a process of this nature will significantly slow down the establishment of democratic norms, and harm the ability of these organizations to provide a basis for civil society in Israel.

Analyzing the decisions of the Supreme Court regarding the Land case and the Torture case, we may discern several factors which serve as a source of legitimacy and support to the conduct of the Supreme Court along with the involvement of ideology and the maximization of political power.

The Maximization of Legitimacy

When the law is clear and explicit the courts are required to implement it. In these cases the problem of outside judicial analysis does not arise. However, when the law is silent, the court needs to adopt certain strategies in order to cope with the existent reality. Such a case is the torture case where the court stated: 'Is there an instruction of law which authorizes the GSS investigators to conduct investigations as mentioned before? Such special instruction, dealing with the inquiry by people of the GSS did not exist' (HCJ ruling, the torture case, paragraph 16). As mentioned above, the outcome of this kind of intervention in the determination of political values is that the Supreme Court is advancing its power at least according to the existing rules of the game.[58]

The timing of the decision bears certain importance, as 1999 was characterized by a relatively quiet security reality. In a period that had an absence of terrorist attacks, the actions of the GSS investigators in using severe methods are very noticeable, and the Supreme Court adopted the following view: 'In fact those physical methods of torture are being adopted even in cases which do not constitute "ticking bombs". In these last cases, the use of such force is illegal.'[59]

The Supreme Court strategically turned its decisions towards certain communities—the public, the legal community and human rights NGOs—in an attempt to acquire approval and legitimacy for its precedent ruling.[60]

With regard to public opinion one might think the Supreme Court is using surveys in order to examine public beliefs. But the example of physical torture proves that the court does not ignore the situation of war and the fact that certain methods of interrogation are needed in order to fight terrorism. Nevertheless, the court declared that at certain points in time a different attitude is needed to preserve democracy: the liberal attitude. In this author's view, in order to understand the paradox of public opinion, we need to distinguish between beliefs and preferences. The Israeli public is still torn between two beliefs: Israel as a human rights beacon and Israel as a beacon of security. However, with regard to the role of the GSS the Israeli public has a clear preference: public opinion does not allow the GSS as an executive security branch to impose power over other branches in the political arena.[61] The Supreme Court emphasizes these preferences.

The Legal Community Viewpoint

Similarly, we may see that the Supreme Court is aiming towards the local and international human rights community: 'This conclusion matches the principles of international contractual law—confirmed by Israel—prohibiting the use of torture as well as cruel or inhuman treatment or degrading treatment. Such prohibitions are absolute.'[62]

Another community is the local and international legal community, especially the American one.[63] For example, right after the decision, the court administration translated the decision and distributed it abroad. Furthermore, the Supreme Court consistently quotes local and international scholars, i.e. in the Torture case the court quoted Mordechai Kremnitzer's view in favour of judicial review in matters concerning human rights violations of security prisoners. This notion is supported also by Ruth Gavison, Alan Dershovitz and others.[64] The Supreme Court also quoted Itzchak Zamir and Baruch Bracha regarding the principle of legal administration and Judge Yaakov Kedmi regarding the nature of interrogation.

In the Land case several communities can also be identified: the new discourse movement, a social non-governmental movement, mostly consisting of social activists and academic scholars, environmental social activists, and petitioners from the agricultural sector, all supported this petition. As noted before, the Supreme Court quoted local and international scholars such as Daphne Barak-Erez and S.R. Simpson. Moreover, it emphasized the consistency of the present decisions with the earlier ones, regarding the importance of land in Israel as a national resource.

The Power of the Supreme Court

The literature is divided by the question of whether the Supreme Court is motivated to maximize its power or rather to establish an ideological view. However, there is no doubt that judicial activism, as seen in the Torture case and the Land case, places the Supreme Court in a unique position.

The result of this behaviour, in a given set of rules, is that the Israeli Supreme Court became, mostly during the 1990s, a unique governing institution dealing with the allocation of values in security.

Regarding the Torture case, in 2002 the Israeli parliament legislated the GSS law, but did not legalize the power used in its interrogation,[65] thus leaving the decision to the Supreme Court as the last legal source of appeal on that issue. This behaviour emphasized the Knesset's inability to govern in crucial cases, as well as its decision not to decide but instead to pass the issue over to the Supreme Court. Another important aspect is the implementation side which will not be dealt with in this article.[66]

CONCLUSIONS

This article focused on two controversial cases: the Torture case and the Land case. Both cases reflect the central place of the Supreme Court as an alternative policy maker. In both cases the Supreme Court interfered with the actions of governmental authorities: the GSS and the Israeli Lands Administration. This study identified several variables which explain the reasons for its intervention.

Non-governability of the political system and the unique Israeli political participation characterized by instrumental democratic values attempted to create an alternative supply of policy decisions. These two variables serve as structural factors creating the framework for the actions of several players in the political judicial sphere. In this sense the decision of the Supreme Court should be explained as an outcome of the interactions between four players: politicians, the public, interest groups and bureaucrats, in a given social and cultural environment. The Supreme Court was analyzed as a unique bureaucrat. Regarding judicial behaviour, the study emphasized the maximization of legitimacy, the ideological view of the Supreme Court judges, the legal community viewpoint and the power of the Supreme Court.

This positive analysis can also contribute to normative discussions and the question of whether we need this activist court. It follows, then, that Israeli society with its formal and non-formal rules creates the situation whereby the political system is unable to deal with problems which require the shaping of public policy.

In light of this inability, Israeli society has adopted alternative behaviour, by filing an ever-increasing number of petitions with the Supreme Court, with a twofold purpose: to cause policy decisions to be made, and to apply pressure on politicians to change the institutional structure, in one way or another. We may point out that the choices Israeli society has made reflects hidden preferences which, together with the existence of strong security aspects, create a demand for liberal values on certain issues. Can we draw a generalization that Israeli society is advancing a liberal direction? The answer is not clear. It is without doubt a matter of equilibrium between certain structural and cultural conditions, as well as individual motivations, both of which could be flexible.

NOTES

1. HCJ case 5100/94: *Public Committee against Torture in Israel v. The State of Israel*, PD 54(4) 817
2. HCJ case 244/00: *New Discourse movement et al. v. Minister of National Infrastructure et al.*, PD 56(6) 25
3. Menachem Mautner, 'Law and Culture in Israel: The 1950s and the 1980s', in Ron Harris, Alexander Kedar, Pnina Lahav and Assaf Likhovski (eds.), *The History of Law in a Multi-Cultural Society: Israel 1917–1967*, London, 2002, pp. 175–217; Martin Edelman, *Courts, Politics, and Culture in Israel*, Charlottesville, 1994; Martin Edelman, 'The Judicialization of Politics in Israel', *International Political Science Review*, Vol. 15 (1994), pp. 177–186; Yoav Dotan and Menachem Hofnung, 'Interest Groups in the Israeli High Court of Justice: Measuring Success in Litigation and In-Out-Of Court Settlements', *Law and Policy*, Vol. 23 (2001), pp. 1–27; Barzilai Gad and Itai Sened, 'How do Courts Accumulate Power and Why they Lose it: An Institutional Perspective', unpublished paper, presented in APSA, Boston, 1997; Stefan Voight and Eli M. Salzberger 'Choosing Not to Choose: When Politicians Choose to Delegate Powers', *Kyklos*, Vol. 55 (2002), pp. 289–310.
4. Baruch Kimerling, *Immigrants, Settlers, Natives*, Tel Aviv, 2004; Mautner, 'Law and Culture in Israel'.
5. Asher Arian, The *Second Republic: Politics in Israel*, Princeton, NJ, 1998; Joel S. Migdal, *Through the Lens of Israel: Explorations in State and Society*, Albany, NY, 2001; Yael Yishai, *Interest Groups in Israel*, Tel Aviv, 1987.
6. See, for example, Gal Dor and Menachem Hofnung, 'Litigation as Political Participation', *Israel Studies*, Vol. 11, No. 2 (2006), pp. 131–157.
7. HCJ case 5100/94: *Public Committee against Torture in Israel v. The State of Israel*, PD 54(4) 817.
8. For the purpose of this article a distinction can be draw between motivations of power that govern judges' behaviour and the result of being active with respect to the power of other policy makers. In accordance with the literature dealing with maximization of power I shall refer in this article to the later distinction.
9. Suzie Navot, 'More of the Same: Judicial Activism in Israel', *European Public Law*, Vol. 7 (2001), pp. 335–348; Daphne Barak-Erez, *Milestone Judgments of the Israeli Supreme Court*, Tel Aviv, 2003 p. 27.
10. Non-governability is a general term indicating that in a given society there are certain, formal and informal, rules of the game, (i.e. deep rifts and polarization within Israeli society as well as certain institutional structure) as well as the factors that create the situation whereby the political system is unable to deal with problems, which require the shaping of public policy.
11. Kevin T. McGuire and James A. Stimson, 'The Least Dangerous Branch Revisited: New Evidence on Supreme Court Responsiveness to Public Preferences', *Journal of Politics*, Vol. 66 (2004), pp. 1018–1035; Kevin T. McGuire and Barbara Palmer, 'Issues, Agendas, and Decision Making on the Supreme Court', *American Political Science Review*, Vol. 90 (1996), pp. 853–865.
12. Pritchett C. Herman, *The Roosevelt Court: A Study in Judicial Politics and Values, 1937–1947*, New York, 1948.
13. Walter M. Murphy, *Elements of Judicial Strategy*, Chicago, 1964.
14. Talcott Parsons, 'The Law and Social Control', in William M. Evan (ed.), *Law and Sociology*, New York, 1962, pp. 56–72; Philippe Nonet, 'For Jurisprudential Sociology', *Law and Society Review*, Vol. 10 (1976), pp. 525–545; Glendon A. Schubert, *Political Culture and Judicial Behavior*, Lanham, MD, 1985; Thomas A. Cowan, 'Group Interests', *Virginia Law Review*, Vol. 44 (1958), pp. 331–345.
15. Bradley C. Canon and Charles A. Johnson, *Judicial Policies: Implementation and Impact*, 2nd edition, Washington, DC, 1998; Michael McCann, *Rights at Work: Pay Equity Reform and*

the Politics of Legal Mobilization, Chicago, 1994; Gerald Rosenberg, *The Hollow Hope: Can Courts Bring about Social Change?*, Chicago, 1991; C. Neal Tate and Torbjorn Vallinder (eds.) *The Global Expansion of Judicial Power*, New York, 1995.

16. Edelman, 'The Judicialization of Politics in Israel'; Ran Hirschl, 'The Political Origins of Judicial Empowerment through Constitutionalization: Lessons from Israel's Constitutional Revolution', *Comparative Politics*, Vol. 32 (2001), pp. 315–336; Gad Barzilai, 'The Supreme Court in Israeli Legal Culture", *International Social Science Journal*, Vol. 152 (1997), pp. 193–208; Gershon Shafir and Yoav Peled, *Being Israeli: The Dynamics of Multiple Citizenship*, Cambridge, 2002; Dan Avnon, 'The Israeli Basic Laws: (Potentially) Fatal Flaw', *Israel Law Review*, Vol. 32 (1998), pp. 535–566; Dotan and Hofnung, 'Interest Groups in the Israeli High Court of Justice'; Menachem Mautner, *The Decline of Formalism and the Rise of Values in Israeli Law*, Tel Aviv, 1993 [Hebrew].
17. Gad Barzilai, 'Courts as Hegemonic Institutions: The Israeli Supreme Court in a Comparative Perspective', *Israel Affairs*, Vol. 5 (1999), pp. 15–33 see also Ronen Shamir, '"Landmark Cases" and the Reproduction of Legitimacy: The Case of Israel's High Court of Justice', *Law and Society Review*, Vol. 24 (1990), p. 781.
18. Voight and Salzberger, 'Choosing Not to Choose'; see also Omri Yadlin, 'Shikol Daat Shipoti Veactivism Shipoti Lemischak Astrategi' (Judicial Discretion and Judicial Activism as a Strategic Game), *Bar-Ilan Law Studies*, Vol. 19 (2003), pp. 665–721 (Hebrew).
19. For litigation as political participation see Gal Dor and Menachem Hofnung, 'Litigation as Political Participation', *Israel Studies*, Vol. 11, No. 2 (2006), pp. 131–157.
20. Marks A. Brian, 'A Model of Judicial Influence on Congressional Policymaking: Grove City College v. Bell', *Working Papers in Political Science*, The Hoover Institution, Stanford, CA, 1988, pp. 88–97; Gely and Spiller, 'A Rational Choice Theory'; Pablo T. Spiller and Rafael Gely, 'Congressional Control or Judicial Independence: The Determinants of U.S. Supreme Court Labor-Relations Decisions, 1949–1988', *Rand Journal of Economics*, Vol. 23 (Winter 1992), pp. 463–492; Lee Epstein and Thomas G. Walker, 'The Role of the Supreme Court in American Society: Playing the Reconstruction Game', in L. Epstein (ed.), *Contemplating Courts*, Washington, DC, 1995.
21. Glendon Schubert, *The Judicial Mind: The Attitudes and Ideologies of Supreme Court Justices, 1946–1963*, Evanston, 1965; Jeffrey A. Segal and Albert D. Cover, 'Ideological Values and the Votes of U.S. Supreme Court Justices', *American Political Science Review*, Vol. 83 (June, 1989), pp. 557–565; Segal and Spaeth, *The Supreme Court and The Attitudinal Model*; Jeffrey A. Segal, Lee Epstein, Charles M. Cameron and Harold J. Spaeth, 'Ideological Values and the Votes of U.S. Supreme Court Justices Revisited', *Journal of Politics*, Vol. 57 (August, 1995), pp. 812–823; Jeffrey A. Segal, 'Separation-of-Powers Games in the Positive Theory of Congress and Courts', *American Political Science Review*, Vol. 91 (1997), pp. 28–44.
22. See, for example, Lee Epstein and Jack Knight, *The Choices Justices Make*, Washington, DC, 1998.
23. Navot, 'More of the Same: Judicial Activism in Israel', pp. 335–348.
24. Paragraph 16.
25. EA (Elections Appeal) 1/65 *Yardor v. Chairman of the Central Elections Committee for the Sixth Knesset*, 19(3) P.D. 365, 386 (Hebrew).
26. H.C. 98/69 *Bergman v. Minister of Finance* 27 (2) P.D. 785.
27. Yoav Dotan, 'Do the Haves Still Come Out Ahead ? Resource Inequalities in Ideological Courts: The Case of the Israeli High Court of Justice', *Law and Society Review*, Vol. 33 (1999), pp. 1059–1080.
28. Roger Cotterell, *Law's Community: Legal Theory in Sociological Perspective*, Oxford, 1995; M. McCann, 'Reform Litigation on Trial', *Law and Social Inquiry*, Vol. 17, No. 4 (1993), pp. 715–744; Arye Naor, 'The Security Argument in the Territorial Debate in Israel: Rhetoric and Policy', *Israel Studies*, Vol. 4 (1999), pp. 150–177.
29. Barzilai, 'Courts as Hegemonic Institutions', pp. 15–33.
30. Mordechai Kremnitzer, 'The Landau Commission Report—Was Subordinated to the Law or the Law to the Needs of the Security Service the Security Service', *Israel Law Review*, Vol. 23 (1989), pp. 216, 244–247
31. David Scharia, 'Al Hadrei Hakirot VeKirot Acostim' (On Torture Chambers and Acoustic Walls), *Politika*, Vol. 10 (2003), pp. 1061–1087 (Hebrew)

32. Navot, 'More of the Same: Judicial Activism in Israel', pp. 335–348
33. Dennis C. Mueller, *Public Choice II*, Cambridge, 1989; Michael Taylor, *The Possibility of Cooperation*, Cambridge, 1987.
34. Ruth Gavison, Mordechai Kremnitzer and Yoav Dotan, *Activism Shipoti: Bead VeNeged* (Judicial Activism: For and Against), Jerusalem, 2000 (Hebrew)
35. Barzilai, *Wars, Internal Conflicts and Political Order*; Menachem Hofnung, 'Israeli Constitutional Politics: The Fragility of Impartiality', *Israel Affairs*, Vol. 5 (1999), pp. 34–54; Ronen Shamir, 'Landmark Cases and the Reproduction of Legitimacy: The Case of Israel's High Court of Justice', *Law and Society Review*, Vol. 24 (1990), pp. 781–805; Ronen Shamir, 'Litigation as Consummatory Action: The Instrumental Paradigm Reconsidered', *Studies in Law, Politics and Society*, Vol. 11 (1991), pp. 41–67; Dan Horowitz and Moshe Lissak, *Tsarot BaOtopia* (Trouble in Utopia), Albany, NY, 1990.
36. Horowitz and Lissak, *Tsarot BaOtopia*.
37. Sam N. Lehman-Wilzig, 'Loyalty, Voice and Quasi-Exit", *Comparative Politics*, Vol. 24 (1991), pp. 97–108.; S.N. Lehman-Wilzig, *Wildfire: Grassroots Revolts in Israel in the Post-Socialist Era*, Albany, NY, 1992; Shlomo Mizrahi and Assaf Meydani, 'Political Participation via the Judicial System: Exit, Voice and Quasi-Exit in Israeli Society', *Israel Studies*, Vol. 8, No. 2 (2003), pp. 118–138.
38. See also Gal Dor and Menachem Hofnung, 'Litigation as Political Participation', *Israel Studies*, Vol. 11 (2), (2006), pp. 131–157.
39. Gad Barzilai, *Communities and Law: Politics and Cultures of Legal Identities*, Ann Arbor, 2003, pp. 147–208.
40. Yoav Dotan and Menachem Hofnung, 'Interest Groups in the Israeli High Court of Justice'; Barzilai, *Communities and Law*, pp. 147–208; Mizrahi and Meydani, 'Political Participation via the Judicial System'.
41. Anthony Downs, *Inside Bureaucracy*, Boston, 1967.
42. Ibid.; David L. Weimer and Aidan R. Vining, *Policy Analysis*, Upper Saddle River, NJ, 1999.
43. Weimer and Vining, *Policy Analysis*.
44. Michael Taylor, *The Possibility of Cooperation*, chapter 1; Robert Axelrod, *The Evolution of Cooperation*, New York, 1984.
45. Eyal Benvenisti, 'Exit and Voice in the Age of Globalization', *Michigan Law Review*, Vol. 98 (1990), pp. 167–212.
46. Mancur Olson, *The Logic of Collective Action*, Cambridge, 1965; William Mitchell and Michael Munger, 'Economic Models of Interest Groups: An Introductory Survey', *American Journal of Political Science*, Vol. 35 (1991), pp. 512–546.
47. David Austen-Smith, 'Allocating Access for Information and Contributions', *Journal of Law Economics and Organization*, Vol. 14 (1998), pp. 277–303; Scott Ainsworth and Itai Sened, 'The Role of Lobbyists: Entrepreneurs with Two Audiences', *American Journal of Political Science*, Vol. 37 (1993), pp. 834–866; Susanne Lohmann, 'A Signaling Model of Information and Manipulative Political Action', *American Political Science Review*, Vol. 87 (1993), pp. 319–333; Susanne Lohmann, 'Information, Access, and Contributions: A Signaling Model of Lobbying', *Public Choice*, Vol. 85 (1995), pp. 267–284.
48. George J. Stigler and Claire Friedland, 'What Can Regulators Regulate? The Case of Electricity', *Journal of Law and Economics*, Vol. 5 (1962), pp. 1–16; S. Peltzman, 'Toward a More General Theory of Regulation', *Journal of Law and Economics*, Vol. 19 (1976), pp. 211–240; Richard A. Posner, 'Taxation by Regulation', *Bell Journal of Economics and Management Science*, Vol. 2 (1971), pp. 22–50.
49. James R. Buchanan, Robert Tollison and Gordon Tullock (eds.), *Towards a Theory of Rent-Seeking Society*, College Station, Texas, 1980.
50. Voight and Salzberger, 'Choosing Not to Choose'.
51. Barzilai, Gad Efraim Yuchtman-Yaar, and Zeev Segal, *The Israeli Supreme Court and the Israeli Public*, Tel Aviv, 1994.
52. David Dery, 'Birocratia VeDemocratia BeIsrael' (Bureaucracy and Democracy in Israel), in Rafi Cohen-Almagor (ed.), *Fundamental Issues in Israel's Democracy*, Tel Aviv, 1999; Jonathan Bendor, 'Formal Models of Bureaucracy: A Review', in N.B. Lynn and Aron Wildavsky (eds.), *Public Administration: The State of the Discipline*, Chatham, NJ, 1990.

53. Dafne Barak-Erez, 'Land in Israel between Public Management and Privatization: Distribution of Justice in the Administrative Procedure', in Menachem Mautner (ed.), *Distributive Justice in Israel*, Tel Aviv, 2000 (Hebrew).
54. Yoav Dotan, 'Judicial Rhetoric, Government Lawyers, and Human Rights: The Case of the Israeli High Court of Justice during the Intifada', *Law and Society Review*, Vol. 33 (1999), pp. 319–358
55. William A. Niskanen, *Bureaucracy and Representative Government*, New York, 1971.
56. Gary Miller, and Terry Moe, 'Bureaucrats, Legislators, and the Size of Government', *American Political Science Review*, Vol. 77 (1983), pp. 297–322; Jonathan Bendor, Serge Taylor and Roland van Gaalen, 'Politicians, Bureaucrats, and Asymmetric Information', *American Journal of Political Science*, Vol. 31 (1987), pp. 796–828.
57. Jeffrey A. Segal, 'Separation-of-Powers Games in the Positive Theory of Congress and Courts', *American Political Science Review*, Vol. 91 (1997), pp. 28–44
58. We refer here to the notion that politicians have the power to allocate rules as being chosen by the people for more see David Easton, *The Political System*, New York, 1953.
59. The Torture case, paragraph 14.
60. Orna Ben-Naftali and Sean S. Gleichgevitch, 'Missing in Legal Action: Lebanese Hostages in Israel', *Harvard International Law Journal*, Vol. 41 (2000), pp. 185–252.
61. Barzilai, Gad Efraim Yuchtman-Yaar, and Zeev Segal, *The Israeli Supreme Court and the Israeli Public.*
62. The Torture case, paragraph 21.
63. Moutner, *Law and Culture in Israel*; Pnina Lahav, *Israel Ba-Mishpat: Simhon Agrenat VeHaMeha HaZionit* (Israel in Law, revised and expanded version of Judgment in Jerusalem), Tel Aviv, 1999.
64. The Association for Civil Rights In Israel, *Human Rights and Civil Liberties in Israel, A Reader*, Tel Aviv, 1991.
65. The General Security Service Act, paragraph 7.
66. See, for example, Angela Browne and Aaron Wildavsky, 'Implementation as Exploration', in Jeffrey L. Pressman and Aaron Wildavsky (eds.), *Implementation*, 3rd edition, CA, 1983, pp. 232–256; Richard Elmore, 'Backward Mapping: Implementation Research and Policy Decisions', *Political Science Quarterly*, Vol. 94, No. 4 (Winter 1979), pp. 601–616; Malcolm L. Goggin, Ann O.M. Bowman, James P. Lester, and Laurence J. O'Toole Jr., *Implementation Theory and Practice: Toward a Third Generation*, Glenview, IL, 1990.

Index

Page numbers in **Bold** represent figures.

For Product Safety Concerns and Information please contact our EU
representative GPSR@taylorandfrancis.com
Taylor & Francis Verlag GmbH, Kaufingerstraße 24, 80331 München, Germany

www.ingramcontent.com/pod-product-compliance
Lightning Source LLC
Chambersburg PA
CBHW050521280326
41932CB00014B/2406

* 9 7 8 1 1 3 8 9 7 9 4 9 9 *